Edward B. Segel

Nonconformity in Modern British Politics

Dr John Clifford and David Lloyd George
Detail from a cartoon in 'The Westminster Gazette', 5 December 1902

Nonconformity in Modern British Politics

STEPHEN KOSS
Professor of History, Columbia University

B. T. BATSFORD

London & Sydney

For Bob Webb, my teacher

First published 1975
© Stephen Koss 1975
ISBN 0 7134 2981 x

Printed in Great Britain by
Bristol Typesetting Co. Ltd, Bristol
for the Publishers
B. T. Batsford Ltd
4 Fitzhardinge Street, London, WC1 0AH &
23 Cross Street. PO Box 586, Brookvale, NSW 2100, Australia

Contents

Acknowledgments

In the course of research and writing, I received warm encourage-ment, sage advice, and helpful criticism from friends and colleagues on both sides of the Atlantic. I was immensely stimulated by their suggestions, including the occasional ones that, for one reason or another, I felt myself unable to heed. First and foremost, I should like to thank those who read this book in typescript: Professor Bernard Barber, Dr P. F. Clarke, Professor Robert McCaughey, and the late Ivan Yates. To Professor Robert K. Webb, who took time from his own sabbatical year to help sharpen my ideas and polish my prose, I owe a further debt that can be more easily acknowledged than repaid.

Elsewhere in this volume, I have enumerated those individuals who permitted me access to family papers, who facilitated my use of documents in their keeping, and who generously shared bibliographical information. Those who gave me permission to quote unpublished material to which they hold copyright have received my private thanks. Special mention must be made, however, of Mr John Grigg and Mr Graham Watson, who gave expert guidance.

Chapter Nine is a revised version of an article that I contributed to the *English Historical Review*, lxxxix (1974), and appears here by arrangement with the editor of that journal. I have also borrowed from my essay in *Edwardian Radicalism* (1974), edited by Mr A. J. A. Morris, and from another article in the *Historical Journal*, xviii (1975).

A year's intensive research was made possible by a fellowship from the John Simon Guggenheim Memorial Foundation for which I am honoured and grateful. Supplementary grants were received from the American Philosophical Society, the Barnard College faculty research fund, and the Dunning Fund of the Columbia University history department. As an academic visitor (1972–73) at the London School of Economics, I enjoyed many kindnesses and privileges.

Not least, I should like to record my abiding gratitude to my wife, who assisted at every stage with her customary patience, humour, and expertise.

Introduction

In the early hours of 21 June 1972, the House of Commons debated the provisions of the United Reform Church Bill, a measure promulgated to effect a property settlement between the merging Congregational and English Presbyterian churches.[1] Despite the time of night and the nonpartisan nature of the proposed legislation, the chamber was crowded, and the proceedings were followed more attentively than one might have expected. One after another, and without reference to party affiliation, M.P.s rose to applaud this preliminary step towards Christian unity. In most cases, they took the occasion to acknowledge their own indebtedness to a religious tradition that had played so prominent a part in the nation's political history.

The Bill was moved by Alexander W. Lyon, Labour member for York and a practising Methodist, and it received enthusiastic endorsement from Michael Clark Hutchison, a Conservative who spoke ' as a member of the Church of Scotland and as the grandson of a Moderator and son-in-law of the Clerk to Presbytery in Aberdeen '.

David Steel, the single Liberal to be heard, identified himself as the product of a union between a Scottish Presbyterian divine and a Congregationalist woman. From the Labour side, speakers included Anthony Wedgwood Benn ('Three generations of Congregationalists went to make me '), Eddie Griffiths, another Congregationalist, Ron Lewis, and Eric Ogden, both Methodists, and John Roper, ' the son, grandson and great grandson of Congregational ministers ' who, to his further distinction, was baptised by a Presbyterian. Among Conservative spokesmen were Marcus Worsley, an Anglican with strong Unitarian connections on his mother's side, and, more anomalously, Norman St John Stevas, a Roman Catholic. Had the House heard from all its members with similar credentials, debate would have continued long past 1.26 a.m., when the Bill was successfully brought to a vote.

In political as distinct from ecclesiastical terms, the incident was significant not so much for the widespread parliamentary interest it evoked as for the unmistakable indication it provided of the extent to which denominationalism had ceased to be a vital factor in determining relationships within and between parties. In the early years of the century, and indeed well into the interwar period, any bill that related to particular religious interests was unlikely to receive dispassionate, non-partisan consideration. In the Edwardian period, for example, disestablishment remained a live issue, battles over education were waged along strict sectarian lines, and even proposals to modify the anti-Papist sentiments of the coronation oath threatened to unleash fierce controversy. Until relatively recent times, one did not find Free Churchmen so widely dispersed throughout the House. Nor, in previous generations, would Nonconformists have expected to enlist oratorical assistance from a prominent Roman Catholic on the Tory side.

Without necessarily sacrificing their beliefs, although this has increasingly been the case, British electors and their representatives have generally come to distinguish between their political and religious convictions. Among other things, this separation of interests has reflected a series of social and theological adjustments, as well as the fact of an accelerating decline in church membership since 1910. More demonstrably, however, it has testified to a general realignment of political forces in Parliament and the country, as evidenced in the debate on the United Reform Church Bill by the relatively modest contribution from the minuscule Liberal Party, which had once flourished as the accredited agency of a militant Nonconformity.

As late as the early decades of this century, religious influence imparted a significant measure of character and impetus to each of the parties; today, to the extent that such influences survive, they cut across the normal divisions of party conflict. A Conservative Free Churchman is no longer a contradiction in terms, either in the constituencies or in the House. The gravitation of massive numbers of Nonconformists to the Labour Party has highlighted the shift from sectarian (in the classical sense) to secular enthusiasms. And the Liberals, while retaining considerable loyalty among Nonconformists of particular persuasions in isolated areas, have recently undertaken to cultivate antithetical interests in an effort to exert a more popular appeal.

Over the course of decades, Nonconformists, like other traditional elements in British society, have revised their priorities, and have adopted new, often competing strategies. Preserving their formal institutions, including their interdenominational councils and committees, they would now be embarrassed to employ them for the specifically political purposes for which many of them were originally conceived. Without pretence either to social exclusiveness or political unity, both properties with which they had entered the century, they have been ultimately forced to acknowledge their inability to set moral standards even for the majority of those whom they claim as members. Meeting at Bristol in 1974, the Methodist Conference went so far as to abandon its traditional policy of total abstinence, voting to leave to the dictates of personal conscience the once fundamental question of drink.[2]

This reorientation on the part of Nonconformists was doubtless inevitable, given their depleted resources and the increasing complexities, social as well as political, that confronted them. But at least in the first instance, it was dictated by their abject failure to achieve their primary objectives, which in any event tended to lose relevance with the passing years. At once subtle and profound, the process was reciprocal: on the one hand, Free Church leaders retreated from partisan combat when they belatedly came to realise that they were more likely to compromise their positions than to obtain the redress of their grievances; on the other, party chiefs could afford to discount Nonconformist demands when it became evident that the churches could no longer deliver electoral support.

The effects of this withdrawal on the structure of twentieth-century British politics were far-reaching, if often indirect. The diminution of Nonconformity's political dynamic contributed materially to a weakening of those institutions which, to one degree or another, Nonconformity had previously helped to buttress. The most notable case in point, at least for the purposes of the present study, is the historic Liberal Party, whose precipitous decline has usually been ascribed to conflicts of personality (Asquith v. Lloyd George) or policy (*laissez-faire* v. state control), but which was surely not unrelated to the wholesale defection – in a real sense the disappearance – of those interest groups from which it had customarily drawn its support.

There was an underlying affinity between the Nonconformist and Liberal experiences, each of which owed something to the other. With remarkably few exceptions, Nonconformists at the turn of the century had voted for Liberal candidates as an article of faith; their children and grandchildren, however, including those who chose to remain within the Liberal fold, voted with scant reference to their religious heritage. The estrangement between Nonconformity and Liberalism, as much the symptom as the cause of a lessened impact on both sides, anticipated the First World War and the consequent fissure in party ranks. As early as 1910, there was a steady drift of Free Churchmen into the Labour and Conservative camps, where their influence was dissipated and their denominational commitments were transcended. As a rule, clergymen were slower to break with tradition than were members of their congregations. Similarly, the respective denominations, reflecting acute differences in perspective and social status, joined the exodus from Liberalism at different stages. By the outbreak of the Second World War, the process was virtually complete.

The disintegration of the Liberal Party and its supersession by Labour, perhaps the crucial fact of twentieth-century politics, left Nonconformists confused in theory and divided in action. Yet, to an extent they themselves usually failed to appreciate, they were the among the agents of the changes that overtook them. Their automatic adherence to the Liberal cause, which worked to the party's distinct advantage in the 1906 General Election, soon thereafter proved restrictive and mutually debilitating. Coincidentally, as the Free Churches withdrew from collective intervention in political controversy, their followers were encouraged to affiliate elsewhere in individual capacities. The transfer of various Nonconformist allegiances to Labour, galvanised by wartime and postwar developments, was instrumental in shaping Labour attitudes during a formative period, in infusing that fledgling party with a generous measure of its evangelical fervour, and in assuring the evolution of Socialist doctrines that were not incompatible with fundamental Christian tenets.

Incurably optimistic, Nonconformist leaders, lay and ministerial, clung to the hope of an eventual Nonconformist revival which, like that of Edwardian times, would take a political as well as a spiritual form. Their expectations, although hopelessly mistaken, are more easily credited than those of the politicians, Lloyd George preeminent among them, who assiduously enlisted Free Church dignitaries as confederates. Periodic attempts were made to reactivate Nonconformity as a political vehicle and to bring its waning influence to bear in domestic and international affairs. The last and most spectacular of these efforts was the Council of Action campaign, launched in 1935, which revealed beyond any doubt that Radical Nonconformity, once a force to be reckoned with in national life, was not dormant but dead. Like other features of the age to which it properly belonged, it could not be resurrected.

From the opening years of the century, when they made their dramatic re-entry into the political arena after a generation of relative quiescence, until the 'thirties, when their pretensions to continued authority were put to the ultimate test, Nonconformists provided a valuable index to successive shifts in popular attitudes and party compositions. By instinct and vocation, they were keen students of public questions. They were intimately associated with many of the leading politicians of the day, whose attentions flattered them, and with whom they often joined as eagerly in intrigue as in prayer. Convinced of their personal qualifications and, above all else, of the moral righteousness of their cause, they zealously employed whatever channels were open to them: the pulpit, denominational conferences, the Free Church Council movement, the press, campaign platforms, and Parliament itself. All along, there were critics within as well as outside their ranks who cited the discrepancy, perhaps more potential than real, between direct political involvement and spiritual responsibilities. Gradually and grudgingly, the point was taken.

Men of faith are not to be censured for an unwillingness, in some cases even an inability, to resign themselves to a position of ineffectualness. Nor, for that matter, are politicians to be condemned for seeking to exploit the idealism of their followers. Because the two categories were never mutually exclusive, their interrelations were complex, and dominant motives are sometimes difficult to ascertain. The problem is intensified by the tendency, especially prevalent during earlier years, to sublimate issues in religious terms.

For reasons which are not nearly so arbitrary as they may appear at first glance, religion is considered here only in its institutional forms, and more specifically those with defined political preferences. To the extent that Nonconformity was (or aspired to be) a determinant of political change, it operated within a relatively small number of concentric circles, and its programme was advanced (or appropriated) by a nucleus of top-ranking personnel. To focus upon these leaders of opinion ought not to be taken to imply that they alone counted, but only that they set the procedures and dominated the structure through which Nonconformists acted. Because our essential concern is with developments in the parliamentary arena, and those that happened to impinge significantly upon them, it has been deemed neither mandatory nor practicable to take seriously into account a welter of factors that may have vitally affected Nonconformity, but not appreciably its electoral impetus.

Similarly, the decision has been taken to impose certain chronological limitations. It is further asserted that political Nonconformity was essentially a twentieth-century phenomenon, differing qualitatively and quantitatively from the activism of previous generations of Dissenters. By the time that it attained political maturity, Nonconformity was already on the wane as a social dynamic, and its theological verities had been called into question: in 1881, when 'Mark Rutherford' published his classic *Autobiography,* his was already a ' race . . . which . . . is fast passing away'. Yet, like the great landed proprietors of the eighteenth century, whom they did not otherwise resemble, Free Churchmen ' found their vocation for commanding solid phalanxes of borough members sitting in Parliament ' only after they had forfeited the greater part of their tradition.[3]

The preoccupation with the political process is itself responsible for determining those religious communities to whom closest attention will be paid. Those Nonconformists who organised to intervene in electoral and parliamentary affairs were overwhelmingly, although not exclusively, Congregationalists, Baptists, Presbyterians, and Methodists of one variety or another. Unitarians, who had enjoyed an influence out of all proportion to their small membership during the early Victorian period, seemed to have spent their energies and possibly their illusions. Like Quakers, they now participated chiefly as the affiliates – and sometimes as the benefactors – of the larger, more disciplined bodies. One must keep in mind that the Nonconformist effort did not involve all the denominations simultaneously or to the same degree.

On another level, one encounters obstacles no less formidable. Because clergymen tended to be self-effacing individuals, conceiving of themselves as mere agents of a higher authority, their contributions frequently elude documentation. They rarely preserved private correspondence, and the books written by or about them, mostly inept, concentrate on devotional or ethical themes. Much the same holds true for their lay colleagues, who vigorously pursued their goals through committees, denominational and parliamentary, and who were reluctant to assert an identity apart from that of ' one of the band of brothers '.[4] To compensate for this deficiency, one is forced to rely on the testimony of prominent politicians, whose archives survive in greater plentitude. Although such an approach is not inappropriate to an exercise in political history, it is possibly an injustice to the lesser figures, who may be depicted in a light different from that in which they saw themselves.

Presumably an historian, writing with the benefit of hindsight and with access to published and unpublished sources, is better equipped than contemporaries to distinguish between successes and failures, between pious aspirations and false presumptions, and, where necessary, between godliness and self-delusion. Focusing on developments within the parliamentary framework, the present work must inevitably put greater emphasis on public performance than on matters of private belief. As an analysis of changes in attitude that presaged new voting patterns and party constellations, many of its conclusions will be speculative in nature. The intention is to examine, critically but respectfully, the fitful process by which Nonconformity ceased to operate as a viable and fairly homogeneous tactical unit in modern British politics, and to evaluate the repercussions in relation to transformations elsewhere in the electoral sphere. As no single volume can attempt to encompass all aspects of Free Church thought and activity, it is consciously left to other scholars to attend to the vast realms of inquiry which remain uncharted.

1 *The Victorian Prelude*

Conjuring up the memory of seventeenth-century struggles, which were never far removed from the popular mind, political debate during the nineteenth century was strongly tinctured with religious controversy. In part, the situation reflected the pervasive moral earnestness of the age; more acutely, it reflected the tensions that persisted between those who took their position within the established Church, and those who belonged to the conglomerate of dissenting churches, and who therefore stood self-consciously and defensively outside. Augustine Birrell, the son of a Liverpool Baptist minister and himself a member of successive twentieth-century Liberal Governments, likened this division in Victorian society to ' Offa's dyke . . . , broad, deep and practically impassable, cutting clean through social life'.[1] This underlying dichotomy found expression not only in electoral preferences, but also, often enough, in parliamentary divisions. ' In these days when religious issues excite so much interest,' Lord John Russell observed dourly in 1855, ' many a vote is determined by the last appointment to a Bishoprick.'[2]

Anglicanism, never the monolithic force it seemed to its avowed enemies, held a latitudinarian creed that encompassed a variety of divergent tendencies. To an even greater extent, Dissent consisted of a panoply of sects, some theologically irreconcilable, and each endowed with its own strong sense of fraternity. In politics, where superficial characteristics often count for most, each side manifested a cohesion it lacked in other spheres. It is the evolution of such an attribute on the part of late-Victorian Nonconformists that the present chapter undertakes to chronicle and evaluate.

With the franchise reforms of 1867 and 1884, Nonconformists came belatedly to assume a place in political society commensurate with their numerical and economic strength in the country.[3] That they no longer called themselves Dissenters was itself indicative of their enhanced status: Nonconformist seemed to suggest a greater element of choice, and Free Church – which became common usage at the close of the century – implied even more positive attributes. As much for sentimental as tactical reasons, their loyalties were overwhelmingly at the disposal of the Liberal Party, under whose enlightened auspices compulsory Church rates had been abolished, the Irish Church disestablished, and the older universities were opened to them. As is shown by the case of Dr (later Sir) Henry Lunn, whose ' Liberalism was derived not from Manchester but from Nazareth',[4] their allegiance was usually more instinctive than rational. But their confidence in the party was not, on the whole, misplaced. True, the Liberal front bench continued throughout the century to be as Anglican dominated as the Tory one, but the Liberal leaders tended to be Churchmen with a difference, responsive to greater diversities in thought and background, and less committed to the abstract principle of Establishment. Besides, there were as yet insuperable obstacles to a Nonconformist affiliation with the Tories, who defended sectarian education, scorned temperance reform, and were thoroughly identified as the champions of a corrupt and irrelevant Anglicanism.

This compatibility between the Free Church movement and the Liberal Party, less inevitable than it may appear in retrospect, eventually took the form of an electoral dependence, which was mutual, but never equiponderant. It evolved slowly, and in defiance of various principles and personalities on both sides. The political experience of nineteenth-century Nonconformists paralleled and occasionally overlapped that of nineteenth-century temperance reformers, whose motives and strategies Brian Harrison has painstakingly investigated.[5] In each case, Liberalism was embraced as the less unsatisfactory of the rival parties, neither of which fully accommodated their aspirations. Given the alternative, however, the Liberals offered certain virtues, not the least of which was the promise of an unlimited potential. ' Tories and Liberals contrasted markedly in their attitude to extra-parliamentary pressure groups,' Harrison pointed out.

While Tories like Disraeli or Salisbury publicly explored the deceptions and distortions involved in mobilizing a public agitation, Liberal leaders deferred to, and even on occasion stimulated, such movements. This contrast sprang from two distinctive features of the Liberal outlook: the desire for moral progress and the belief in popular control.

Furthermore, ' Liberal distrust of irresponsible power-wielders made their party always suspicious of monopolies ', and therefore a logical base of operations not only for prohibitionists who opposed the licensing system, but more generally for Nonconformists who agitated against the Anglican establishment and its control over education. On the question of schools, like the question of public houses, the issue of popular control was crucial.

Above all else, the Liberals boasted, in the person of W. E. Gladstone, a leader of indisputable character and courage. On the one hand, Gladstone's High Anglicanism made him an unlikely candidate for Nonconformist adulation; on the other, his intense faith inspired respect and trust. ' Who is Mr Gladstone?' the Rev Hugh Price Hughes, the self-appointed keeper of the Nonconformist Conscience, was asked by his precocious children. ' A man who says his prayers every morning ', came the reply.[6] As a God-fearing statesman, Gladstone boasted credentials sufficiently unimpeachable that he could worship one Sunday at Spurgeon's tabernacle, and then, a few months later, attend the funeral at Oxford of Dr Pusey, the tractarian.[7] Whether Gladstone returned Nonconformity's high regard remains a moot point. In matters of dogma, to which he attached paramount importance, they were poles apart. John Morley, his Cabinet colleague and biographer, recalled that ' Mr G.' had once recounted, ' with horror in his voice, how he was terrified to hear Drummond Wolff say in a Bradlaugh debate, " You know, Mr Speaker, we all of us believe in a God of some sort or another " '.[8] Their theological differences notwithstanding, Gladstone and the Nonconformists justly recognised each other as servants of a common religious impulse.

The alliance between Nonconformity and Liberalism, like that between Anglican interests and Toryism, had long been axiomatic. Yet it was not until the turn of the century that the ramifications were fully felt. Before such an alliance could become operative, there had had to occur fundamental changes within the various denominations, in the relationships between them, and in the national political structure. Not least, religious bodies had had to acknowledge the fact, humiliating to some, that ' they had to work with more secular factors if they were to effect anything which was to have comprehensive results for the whole

B

country '.[9] These changes began tentatively during the 'seventies, when, not coincidentally, Gladstone exerted his strongest appeal. After the turn of the century, they saw a culmination that could not have been anticipated.

To the extent that the alliance worked at any given time, what were its characteristics, and, more problematically, its practical effects? Nonconformity, with its broad provincial base, helped the Liberal Party to expand its social frontiers. Through the chapel, it was possible to recruit electoral support from among the newly enfranchised working classes: Primitive Methodism, for example, yielded high returns for Liberalism in the mining constituencies, much as it later did for Labour. No less important, the chapel provided access to local commercial and industrial magnates, often men of vast wealth and a comparable sense of public duty, who gave generously to campaign expenses and in particular assumed the obligation of subsidising the party press. By the last decades of the century, when landed wealth was defecting to Conservatism, these plutocrats were a prized acquisition.

As a party of the left, Liberalism was fated to be a coalition of disparate elements. But, so long as these internal differences remained a more or less faithful reflection of social realities, they were more a source of strength than weakness to the party. Non-conformity, itself a congeries, found a natural haven beneath the proverbial Liberal umbrella. There, it interacted with other groups, some inherently antagonistic to it, but all imbued with a similar theory of human progress. In their capacity as Liberals, Nonconformists were quick to find secular justification for their doctrines of personal salvation. With equal ingenuity, they propagated a spiritual justification for Liberal doctrines of individual enterprise.

Accustomed to regard itself, and indeed to be regarded by others as the backbone of nineteenth-century Liberalism, Non-conformity is best approached in terms of its component vertebrae. Since the seventeenth century, there had been Baptists, Independents (Congregationalists), and Presbyterians, as well as Unitarians (some of whom long continued to classify themselves as Presbyterians) and Quakers who stood some distance apart, sharing – if little else – a negative attitude to the Sacraments. Since the eighteenth century, there had also been Methodists, who subsequently fragmented into separate connexions. There were a seemingly infinite number of variations within each fold, particularly when one considers the Welsh context. The Scots, equipped with an independent ecclesiastical establishment and educational system, were involved only peripherally in the disputes that engaged the attention of their brethren to the south. Sometimes bonds of sympathy bridged the Tweed, but Scotland was a religious world unto itself. When Halley Stewart campaigned for a seat at Greenock by attacking the 1902 Education Act, he was tartly informed that it was inappropriate ' for an English politician to cross the Border and try to influence the Scottish mind with quarrels in England with which Scotland has nothing to do '.[10]

Each the product of a unique set of historical circumstances, the Anglo-Welsh Free Churches had evolved peculiar social attributes and intellectual attitudes. The Wesleyan Methodists, who boasted a greater number of communicants than any other Nonconformist church, provide a useful case in point. Conscious of their origins within the establishment, which their forefathers had left involuntarily and relatively recently, they were reluctant to throw in their lot with the older dissenting sects. Likewise, they disdained the smaller Methodist denominations, variously estimated at a dozen or more, that had since splintered from the Wesleyan trunk. Obsessively middle-class and traditionalist, they were not easily roused from a half-thinking conservatism. Not surprisingly, their intermediary position on the social and theological spectrums inhibited their political performance. Unlike the Congregationalists, Baptists or certainly the Unitarians, all of whom stood well to the left on both counts, Wesleyans were loath to join in direct agitation, which they equated with heterodoxy and disruption. Consequently, as late as 1868, there were fewer Wesleyans than Jews in the House of Commons, and a further generation had passed before they made a token appearance in the Cabinet, the Privy Council, or the House of Lords. Compared to the other Nonconformist denominations, the Wesleyan commitment to the Liberal Party evolved slowly, and it had no sooner been proclaimed than it showed definite signs of retreat. While it lasted, theirs was a Liberalism of a distinctly different hue, stoutly opposed to the secularist and egalitarian tendencies of the party's Radical wing.

Less dramatically than the Wesleyans, who had the furthest distance to travel, each of the Free Churches strove to adapt itself to the conditions of the new age. On the secular side, the creation of a democratic electorate and the coalescence of mass political parties posed an obvious challenge. On the theological side, there were other developments, no less momentous. As evidenced in 1874 by the furore over the Public Worship Regulation Bill, the perpetual struggle between 'Protestants' and 'ritualists' had entered a new and intensified phase. Although the major battles were fought within the Anglican establishment, there were numerous skirmishes outside. In any case, Nonconformists did not have to be directly affected to join the fray. Issues were at stake with which they had been identified for centuries.

To a degree that would be difficult to exaggerate (although the phenomenon tended to exaggerate itself), Free Churchmen reacted to the threat, half real and half imagined, of a Roman Catholic menace, which they saw everywhere and, particularly, in the higher echelons of the State Church. Although the last great outburst of anti-Catholic rioting had occurred in 1850–51, with the restoration by 'Papal aggression' of the Roman hierarchy in England, the fear of Catholic intentions was constant and surfaced whenever educational proposals were debated. W. E. Forster, who brought down the wrath of Nonconformity by his 'Erastian' Act of 1870, sadly concluded in 1874 that 'the only belief much felt is that we are not and will not be papists.' It is significant that Forster volunteered his observation to Archbishop Tait, himself a vigilant opponent of ritualist tendencies in the late-Victorian Church. If the Archbishop of Canterbury saw cause for alarm, can one blame those who claimed spiritual descent from the Puritans? 'The years from the 'eighties to the First World War', far from bringing an abatement of anti-sacerdotal passions, have been described as 'great years for . . . bodies, Anglican or Nonconformist or mixed, devoted to the preservation of protestant truth.'[11]

While churchmen of every persuasion acrimoniously disputed the forms of Christian observance, others defiantly proclaimed their rejection of Christian belief. The founding of the Metaphysical Society in 1869, with T. H. Huxley among its charter members, signalled the growing respectability of agnosticism. With it came a new militancy. According to John McKinnon Robertson, who celebrated the events he catalogued, the 'seventies witnessed 'the turning of educated intelligence from the current creed to unbelief'.[12] Goldwin Smith offered testimony to the same point: ' Nothing has struck me more in revisiting England after a long absence ', he declared in 1874, ' than the vast growth, not merely of Scepticism but of blank Materialism among the most highly educated and intellectual classes.'[13] On the whole, Nonconformists stood in little immediate danger. To the extent that they kept their distance from the universities, where free thought flourished, they enjoyed a relative immunity.

As yet more implicit than actual, the threat nonetheless could not be ignored. Therefore, in response to rationalists on the one side, and to anti-rationalists on the other, Nonconformists proceeded to modify, and, in no small measure, to discard inherited dogma. During the last quarter of the century, there occurred a trans-denominational shift ' to broader positions about the inspiration of the Bible and the eternal decree of the Creator '.[14] Among Wesleyans, an aggressive Forward Movement gave thrust to the reaction against Calvinist orthodoxy. Similarly, Baptists and Congregationalists repudiated aspects of systematic theology, putting new emphasis on private conscience and local authority. ' I do not object to creeds as statements of belief', Dr John Clifford proclaimed as president of the Baptist Union during the ' downgrade' controversy of 1877. ' It is coercion through and by the creeds that I object to.' Unitarians moved even further from any fixed doctrinal position. Quakers, for whom ' regulations and sound doctrine' had previously been ' the order of the day ', after 1860 ' switch[ed] in church affairs from legalistic self-scrutiny to citizen concern with the surrounding world '.[15] However it manifested itself, and for whatever reasons, this general trend to theological individualism proved an incidental spur to political activism.

To what extent was politics a suitable, let alone a legitimate realm for Christian endeavour? The question, one of basic definition, had engaged the best theological minds for centuries. Nonconformists, deprived of their full civic rights until Victorian times, came relatively late to the debate, but waged it with an ardour that made up for lost time. In simplified terms, opinion was divided between those who eschewed any involvement that threatened to divert attention and limited resources from the service of Christ, and those who remonstrated no less eloquently that spiritual vitality could be best measured, and indeed stimulated, by its application to public affairs. It was mutually agreed

that churchmen, as individuals, had the right and duty to partici-
pate in the concerns of the wider community; the dispute was
whether they had a corporate influence to exert, and, if so,
through what channels.

The debate found vivid reflection in the pages of George
Eliot's *Felix Holt* (1866), where Mr Lyon, an Independent
divine in every sense, declaimed

> my own view, which I maintain in the face of some opposition
> from brethren who contend that a share in public movements
> is a hindrance to the closer walk, and that the pulpit is no place
> for teaching men their duties as members of the common-
> wealth. I have had much puerile blame cast upon me because
> I have uttered such names as Brougham and Wellington in the
> pulpit. Why not Wellington as well as Rabshakeh? And why
> not Brougham as well as Balaam?

Why not, indeed? The only stipulation was not to offend canons
of taste, as did an old Baptist minister, whom Lloyd George
laughingly recalled from his Welsh youth, who had prayed for
deliverance from Disraeli: 'Kill him, O Lord, kill him. We
cannot kill him without being hanged ourselves, but Thou
canst kill him.' Without going nearly so far, countless divines
upheld the theory that political activism was a facet of spiritual
ministration. 'Politics are one of the organs and instruments by
which true Christians hasten the coming of the Kingdom of God ',
Clifford once assured an apprehensive colleague.[16] For men of
Clifford's stamp, Gladstone and Lloyd George were not only
names to invoke in a sermon, but comrades in arms.

Still, a vague uneasiness persisted, which even Clifford occasionally articulated. Men of hard vanity and brooding introspec-
tion, Nonconformist leaders were never entirely certain whether
they were successfully infusing political life with a Christian zeal,
or whether politics was instead vitiating their Christianity. The
upheavals of the seventeenth century, which had given birth to
Dissent, continued to provide alternately an incentive to action
and a warning against its possible consequences. Dissenters, at
any rate according to their own interpretation of history, had
deliberately separated from a Church whose worldliness repelled
them. Two hundred years later, the hegemony of that Church remained unbroken (except in Ireland), and many of its abuses

survived. While Anglicanism had lost the means, and possibly the inclination, to inflict hardships upon its antagonists, its pretensions remained the source of grievous humiliation. Late-Victorian Nonconformists were sorely tempted to use their newly obtained electoral resources, which they were inclined to overestimate, for an all-out offensive against Anglican privilege. The danger was that, in meeting the enemy on his own ground, the cause might be sullied and the troops corrupted. Some were more prepared than others to take the risk, but few minimised it.

The seventeenth-century religious settlement, modified in practice if not in theory during the first half of the eighteenth century, also bequeathed to Dissenters a mechanism of sorts for inter-denominational cooperation. Since 1733, the body of Protestant Dissenting Deputies had annually brought together ministers from the Three Denominations – Baptist, Congregational, and Presbyterian – in the greater London area. Loosely structured, and without a lay component, this organisation had traditionally addressed itself to theological matters or to questions of civil disabilities. In 1841, however, departing from normal procedures, committees were established in each of the metropolitan boroughs to help secure the return of M.P.s who had been certified as predisposed to the Deputies' interests. By 1847, operations had been extended to the provinces, and the Deputies promulgated a national roster of ' approved ' candidates. Thereafter, this body abruptly reverted to its earlier policy of collective non-intervention, only to resume its electoral activity after 1902, when ' their disgust with the Liberals had given way to fury with the Conservatives '.[17]

During the mid-Victorian decades, Nonconformists were usually content to share in the nation's growing prosperity, and to rely on others, whom they expected to defend and extend their hard-won rights. To the extent that it manifested itself, Nonconformist politics was restricted to the municipal level, and tended to assume an *ad hoc* character. During its formative stages, the new Liberal Party was assured of Nonconformity's communal allegiance, which was as yet something quite different from its electoral support as an organised pressure group. The change came during the parliamentary session of 1869–70, when Forster introduced the Liberal Government's proposals for an extensive overhaul of the system (if indeed it can be dignified as such) of elementary education. There was universal agreement that pre-existing arrangements were inadequate to the needs of the new democracy, but contemporaries differed profoundly in the remedies they prescribed.

For neither the first time nor the last, education provided the battleground for Anglicans and Nonconformists, as well as for secularists and the advocates of religious instruction. It can be said, at least in retrospect, that Forster's Act provided a reasonable solution to a problem that remained fundamentally insoluble so long as sectarian animosities ran high. Given the strong feeling on all sides, it was inevitable that Forster should have failed to satisfy one faction or another. Given his own Quaker upbringing, it is perhaps not surprising that he could have incurred fiercest enmity among Nonconformists.

Why should education have sparked off such burning controversy then and again a generation later? Rightly or wrongly, Nonconformists were convinced that nothing less was at stake than their right to survival. That they were the guardians of a minority creed, with its own social conventions, was plain enough. But, in a more profound sense, they also saw themselves as the patrons of a unique culture, marginal but inherently superior. They boasted their own popular literature, periodical press, academic institutions, commercial empires, and recreational enthusiasms, all of which helped to temper any feeling of alienation. Far from rejecting the prevailing system, they were confident that they could work it with better purpose and greater equity. ' It is hard for any one to be an honest politician who is not born and bred a Dissenter ', declaimed William Hazlitt, who had been trained for the Unitarian ministry. Like him, late-Victorian Nonconformists believed without false modesty that they owed it less to themselves than to the nation-at-large to preserve and propagate their time-honoured values. In a period of rapid social and intellectual change, they were therefore particularly defensive about the institutions to which they entrusted their children, who were their mortgage on the future. Anglican-run schools posed a genuine threat to Nonconformist recruitment, and, more directly, to the achievements of Nonconformist Sunday schools, which had undergone tremendous expansion during the 'seventies and 'eighties. Their support from public funds was viewed as a deliberate affront to the status of Nonconformity. In addition, there is reason to suppose that then, as in 1902, not a few Nonconformist spokesmen positively welcomed an unacceptable bill as a focus for their political discontent.

Irate to discover how easily they could be discounted and their interests betrayed by a government they had ardently supported, Nonconformists vented their fury on the twenty-fifth clause of Forster's Act, which authorised a continued subsidy out of public funds for Church-sponsored voluntary schools. As yet lacking sufficient strength within the Commons, they resorted to a strenuous agitation outside. It emanated, as did so many Victorian political movements, from Birmingham, where, in 1869, the National Education League was founded. Its driving force was Joseph Chamberlain, a Unitarian manufacturer who was soon to be launched on his public career as mayor of that city. He employed the services and reputations of two local divines, R. W. Dale (a Congregationalist) and H. W. Crosskey (a fellow Unitarian), who commanded vast influence in their respective denominations. The League's petition against the Education Act was quickly signed by more than two-thirds of all Nonconformist ministers in England and Wales. Chamberlain, at the head of a League deputation, presented it to Gladstone, but came away from Downing Street with only a deepened sense of resentment.

Nonconformists had at last organised, but, contrary to previous expectation, against the Liberal Party and not on its behalf. Their indignation induced them either to sit out the 1874 General Election, or else to vote for Radicals who were outspokenly critical of the party leadership. It is unthinkable that many would have cast protest votes for Conservative candidates: that would have been not so much foolhardy as suicidal. In any case, the Liberals suffered heavy losses, and Disraeli was returned to office. In later years, Nonconformists often gloatingly recalled that they, like latter-day Samsons, had brought down the Gladstonian temple in 1874. In point of fact, their act of revenge would have achieved considerably less impact had not the Liberal Government, by its adventurous policies on Ireland and the universities, forfeited other means of support. But it is doubtless asking too much of Radical Nonconformists that they share credit with recalcitrant Whigs and perfidious Anglicans.

To be sure, not all Free Churchmen responded with the same vehemence to the 1870 Act and the government that sponsored it. One historian has made a useful distinction between ' Soft ' bodies like the Wesleyan Methodists, who tended to side with

Forster, and ' Hard ' ones: ' the bulk of Baptists, Congregationalists, other Methodists, and Unitarians '.[18] If the events of
1870–74 testified to the extent of Liberal disunion, they also
pointed to the centrifugal forces at work within Nonconformity.
Never completely overcome, these forces grew more pronounced
before they were eventually brought temporarily under control.

It took nearly a generation for Nonconformist tempers to cool,
and for Forster's Act to be forgiven, if not forgotten. In the
interim, the Free Churches, as organised entities, kept strictly
to the sidelines. Their representatives stood shoulder to shoulder
with Liberal politicians in the agitation against the ' Bulgarian
Horrors ' in 1876, but their co-operation was geared to a specific
issue and not intended to imply acceptance of an entire party
programme. For the most part, they were unconcerned with the
partisan advantages that might accrue from the situation. Without
repudiating their fidelity to Liberalism, they had become more
qualified in their allegiance to the Liberal leaders. Worshippers
were less likely to hear overtly political sermons or, if they did,
to pay them heed. Except in Wales, few Free Church luminaries
appeared officially on Liberal Party platforms. Voting patterns were
generally left undisturbed, but the tenor of political life had
changed.

Already strained, relations between Nonconformity and the
Liberal Party were put to a further test in 1886, when Gladstone
embarked on his crusade for Irish Home Rule. Joined by a number
of Unitarians, mostly clustered around Chamberlain, a sizable
body of Wesleyan Methodists promptly registered their disapproval. Proclaiming themselves Liberal Unionists, they were
thereby able to oppose party policy without going so far as to
throw in their lot with the Tories. Most eventually returned to
the Liberal fold, at least temporarily, after Home Rule had been
revealed as impracticable; some, however, proceeded by stages
into the Conservative camp. Even those who stood by Gladstone
tended to regret his decision as a sell-out to Roman Catholics and
hooligans (the two being more or less synonymous), who usurped
the priority of more legitimate Nonconformist claims. Then,
too, it was recognised that Gladstone was already advanced in
years, that Home Rule was likely to exhaust his energies, and that
the next generation of Liberal leaders lacked men of his calibre:
John Morley was an avowed agnostic who celebrated the rational-
ism of Voltaire and Rousseau; Sir William Harcourt, the grand-

son of an archbishop of York, had too often acted as an apologist for Anglican interests; and Lord Rosebery flirted with godless collectivists, married a Rothschild heiress, and worst of all, bred and raced horses.

Under the circumstances, Nonconformists felt unmitigated frustration. Despite their steadily increasing representation in the Commons, they neither advanced to key front-bench positions, nor did they carry weight in party councils. It was not so much the case that they were betrayed as that they betrayed themselves by their undue deference in the constituencies and at Westminster. Lloyd George, whom one would not accuse of such failings, was incensed to find that ' these snob Churchmen should be allowed to rise on Nonconformist votes into the House of Commons to oppose Nonconformist principles '.[19]

On occasion, Free Churchmen managed to exercise a negative influence, but it was more the shadow than the substance of political power. Their moral outrage – or, more precisely, other people's anticipation of it – was a potent factor in shutting Sir Charles Dilke out of ministerial office after 1886, when he was cited as co-respondent in a well publicised divorce suit. In the same vein, but with vastly more far-reaching effect, the pangs of the Nonconformist Conscience militated against continued alliance with Charles Stewart Parnell, another reprobate, four years later. J. J. Colman, a manufacturer of mustard and yet a Liberal M.P. of ' mild ' Baptist sensibilities, gravely warned that, if Parnell remained as leader of the Irish parliamentary party, the Liberals would lose no fewer than five seats in puritan East Anglia.[20] The Rev Hugh Price Hughes and others threatened consequences even more dire. Conveniently, Parnell was relieved of his command by a higher authority before the next general election fell due. Nonconformists, tempted to see his tragic end as an act of divine retribution, were otherwise afforded little consolation. By combining with priests and gutter journalists, they had been able to ruin a man's career, and even to cast into disrepute the Home Rule policy for which he stood; but they lacked sufficient impetus and support to achieve more positive results. It was painfully evident, for example, that the drive for disestablishment was losing steam throughout this period. Even with regard to the education question, on which Nonconformists were unyielding, they failed to impose their views on the Liberal Party, let alone on the nation.

As the long imminence of Gladstone's retirement drew to a close, steps were taken to remedy the situation. At the instigation of Hughes, who edited the *Methodist Times* as the official organ of his Wesleyan Forward Movement, Dr J. Guinness Rogers, a respected Congregational divine, issued a call for a Free Church congress. It was published in February 1890, and, in November 1892, an invited cross-section of Nonconformist leaders met at Manchester. There was a second gathering at Leeds two years later, attended ' in the main ' by ' personal members ', and a third in 1895 at Birmingham, where nearly three hundred representatives from two county federations and sixty-eight town councils overwhelmingly approved a motion to create a National Council of Evangelical Free Churches.

R. W. Dale – perhaps repenting for his youthful activism during the early 'seventies, but more probably indicating his latter-day Unionism – took a dim view of the Council scheme, insisting that ' social or political platforms, however desirable or necessary, . . . were not specifically the concern of the Church '. His position received strong backing from, among others, Dr Richard Glover of Bristol, who ' urged that the Free Churches should keep out of all disputes between employer and employed, and should concentrate all energies on the proclamation of the Gospel '.[21] While such arguments were not lightly dismissed, they failed to deter younger men. Hughes, who suffered no such scruples, celebrated the formation of this ' Nonconformist Parliament ', and gladly accepted an invitation to preside at its inaugural session in 1896.

The antithesis between Hughes and Dale was made more interesting by the fact that Hughes was curiously unable to conceive of himself as a political activist, however actively he engaged in politics. In this respect, he stood ' much nearer to the Non-Juror Bishops of the seventeenth century than to their contemporaries among the Puritans '.[22] His daughter could recall only one occasion, ' a private dinner at the house of a Liberal member ', when he had taken ' any part in what might be termed political affairs '. Like her father and many members of his generation, Wesleyans particularly, she confused political with partisan activity. In his public capacity, as the minister of an important London congregation and as editor of the *Methodist Times,* Hughes attempted – not nearly as successfully as he made out – to take an impartial approach to topical issues. ' . . . Our Churches as such must not take sides, must observe a strict neutrality,' he privately averred, ' or they will be involved in a greater disaster than that which has stunned and paralysed the Roman Church in Italy.'[23] But, as Hughes demonstrated in the Parnell episode and again during the Boer War, he was not averse to taking impartial action which might be expected to have definite political consequences. Furthermore, in his super-charged vocabulary, ' impartial ' was used increasingly as a synonym for ' imperial ', with political implications he chose not to recognise.

Those who shared Dale's qualms instead of Hughes's enthusiasm held aloof from the National Council. Eventually, in 1916, they founded a Federal Council, which was not so much a rival as a complement to its predecessor. Essentially a less popular body, the Federal Council was composed of representatives elected by member denominations at their respective conferences. By contrast, the National Council recruited its delegates from a network of local councils and regional federations, as well as directly from individual congregations. The Federal Council addressed itself exclusively to matters of common concern to the denominations, and was intended ' as a step toward organic union '. The National Council, which assumed no ecumenical responsibilities, was avowedly dedicated to the task of ' bringing the spiritual forces of our Free Churches to bear on the public and national life '.[24] In September 1940, the two Councils were fused.

The creation of the National Council in 1896 brings us to the threshold of our proper inquiry. Here we shall embark on a more detailed, perhaps less impressionistic survey. Previously, there had not existed the mechanism to canalise and mobilise Nonconformist opinion, or indeed the leadership to define goals and lay down strategy. The National Council inaugurated a new era, of which it was itself as much the symptom as the cause. Preeminent among a plethora of quasi-religious bodies, it afforded an effective agency – in some ways the first – through which self-designated Nonconformist politicians could advance their cause and often their personal careers. At the same time, it promised to provide a recognised means by which secular organisations, most notably the Liberal Party, might harness the electoral energies of the Nonconformist multitudes.

From the start, the National Council found it easier to proclaim its intentions than to translate them into policy. Its internal dissensions mirrored those in the Liberal Party, which it looked upon automatically, but not always logically, as its parliamentary auxiliary. In 1894, Lord Rosebery succeeded Gladstone as party leader and premier; so far as most Nonconformists were concerned, the situation was not promising. Implored time and again ' to discountenance the influences emanating from the Turf which are demoralising and ruining our population ', Rosebery blandly disclaimed any knowledge of such influences and declined to oblige his petitioners.[25] Wesleyan lay leaders, often men of vast wealth and sophisticated tastes, tended to take a more worldly view of Rosebery's pastime than did more puritanical Baptists, Congregationalists, and Quakers. R. W. Perks, the Liberal member for Louth from 1892 to 1910 and a prominent Wesleyan, headed off a resolution by the London Nonconformist Council, of which he was treasurer, ' saying that no Nonconformist should support political leaders connected with the Turf '.[26] In matters of religious observance, Rosebery was even more out of step with Nonconformity. It was his ' general habit ', he cavalierly informed an irate cleric, to leave a service before the sermon, which could only detract from the sanctity of the occasion. Nonconformist worship, of course, accorded paramount importance to the sermon, and Lloyd George, a keen student of the dissenting pulpit, affirmed ' that the real source of its power was the spoken word '.[27]

Despite these handicaps, Rosebery assiduously cultivated Nonconformist opinion, all the more after he had resigned the premiership in 1895 and relinquished the party command at the end of the following year. He met with a mixed response, but his success among Wesleyans was undoubted, thanks largely to Perks, who was *plus royaliste que le roi* and a relentless intriguer. ' If Scotch Liberals and English Nonconformists hold well together ', he prophesied to Rosebery, who had already stepped down as Liberal leader, ' we shall triumph yet with your aid and guidance.'[28] Requiring little encouragement and receiving less, Perks set to work to build a Roseberian coalition. His first objective was nothing less than to bring round his friend Hughes, who had been put off Rosebery by John Morley's malicious ' story . . . to the effect that you [Rosebery] alleged that it was your set purpose to shake the Liberal Party free from the undue control of the religious communities '.[29] Hughes was not only the most dynamic preacher of his day, but also the first president of the National Free Church Council. Through the *Methodist Times*, he had weekly access to an estimated 150,000 communicants. Under Perks's tutelage, he soon came to see the virtues of Rosebery who sought to jettison the Gladstonian albatross of Home Rule, and who saw national problems, including social ones, from an imperial perspective.

With its wide dispersal throughout the English-speaking world, and its reverence for tradition, Wesleyanism could be said to have laid the foundation for Anglo-Saxon federation. As Hughes's daughter explained, ' Methodists never proselytised, were true to the principles of the Reformation and the necessities of an Imperial ecclesiastical organisation ', and, by her father's definition, qualified as the ordained purveyors of British moral and constitutional achievements. Despite Hughes's professed pacificism (he refused to allow any pictures to be hung in his library ' that might familiarise my children with the horrors of war '), he celebrated the expansion of the British Empire as the triumph of Wesleyan influences. Reading Kipling's ' Recessional ' in *The Times*, he was moved to reflect that the poet owed his inspiration ' to the Methodism in him. You may smile, but it is true.' He even went so far as to credit the glories of the monarchy to the incidental fact that Queen Victoria's ' nurse was a godly Methodist '.[30]

If Hughes ' saw himself as the Cecil Rhodes of the Wesleyans ',[31] which is by no means improbable, Perks may be said to have seen himself as their Starr Jameson. As passionately as his spiritual mentor, he believed in the unique imperial mission of Wesleyanism; as passionately as his political mentor, he believed in the unique imperial mission of Britain. The two impulses reinforced each other until they became inseparable. As a Wesleyan lay leader, ' Imperial Perks ' (as Beatrice Webb loathingly dubbed him) launched his Twentieth Century Fund to raise a million guineas ' to supply the sinews of war for an aggressive movement which, who knows? may be the most far-reaching of twentieth-century developments '.[32] As a Liberal Imperialist, he worked unremittingly behind the scenes to return Rosebery to the helm of the party and national affairs.

Not all Free Churchmen (and not, to give them their due, all Wesleyan Methodists) were so deeply stirred by Rosebery's appeal to imperial emotions. With a few notable exceptions, Baptist, Congregational, Unitarian, and Primitive Methodist leaders inclined in the Little Englander direction. No less anxious than

Wesleyans to sever ties with the Irish Nationalists, who secretly wanted ' not Home Rule in Ireland, but Irish Romanist rule in both countries ',[33] they rightly feared the new quagmires into which Rosebery proposed to lead them. As yet with less enthusiasm than resignation, they pledged their loyalty to Sir Henry Campbell-Bannerman, whom Rosebery's lieutenants wished to displace from the party leadership.

By the time of the Boer War, opinion among Nonconformists was as bitterly divided as that among other sections of the Liberal Party. The Government's policy in South Africa, and the Liberal Imperialist defence of it, received unqualified endorsement from Hughes in the *Methodist Times*, and from W. Robertson Nicoll in the *British Weekly*, an inter-denominational ' journal of social and Christian progress ' that boasted a circulation over 100,000. But the *Daily News*, acquired by a ' pro-Boer ' syndicate at the close of 1900, vigorously denounced the war, and agreed with John Morley (who had close connections with the new proprietors) that Liberal Imperialism was nothing more than ' Chamberlain wine with a Rosebery label '. Commending itself to the Nonconformist community by its refusal to carry advertisements for alcoholic beverages and by its proscription of all racing and betting news, the *Daily News* in its latest incarnation was – as Elie Halévy described it – ' Puritan as well as Radical '.

In the summer and autumn of 1901, the *Daily News* helped to solicit signatures for a ' Free Church Ministers' Manifesto on the War ', and the response was significant in more ways than one. The manifesto was signed by 5,245 of the nearly 10,000 Nonconformist divines in England and Wales, of whom (in approximate figures) there were 1,100 Congregationalists, 1,000 Baptists, 950 Presbyterians, 800 Primitive Methodists, 270 Welsh Calvinistic Methodists, 200 Free Methodists, 100 New Connexion Methodists, 100 Bible Christians, 100 Unitarians, 50 Friends, and 40 Moravians. In only a few cases was there a correlation between denominational strength and ministerial support for the manifesto; the discrepancy was, predictably enough, most pronounced on the part of Wesleyan divines, of whom a mere twelfth signed the document.[34] These statistics lend substance to the impressions which one receives from participants in the anti-war agitation, who pointed up the differences among the various Free Churches : ' The leading Baptist and Independent Ministers are all right ', F. W. Hirst wrote in his diary on the eve of the war; but Silas K. Hocking, looking back on the experience, was not so sure. Himself a product of the Free Methodist ministry, Hocking had been able to count upon the support of the Quakers ' as a body ', most Unitarian divines, ' and a few Congregationalists. The Baptists,' he recalled unforgivingly, ' as a whole ignored us '.[35]

These divisions were revealed even more clearly during the general election, which was called mid-way through the war. Aside from a handful of Unitarians and Wesleyans who stood (with invariable success) as Unionists or Conservatives, the vast majority of Free Church candidates defended the Liberal interest. But that, in itself, said relatively little. Congregationalists usually ranged themselves behind Campbell-Bannerman and kept their distance from either extreme. Baptists, particularly a few Welshmen among them, were more outspokenly critical of the war. Unitarians, perhaps to compensate for Chamberlain's apostasy, were unabashedly ' pro-Boer '. Wesleyan Methodists, unlike the members of any other denomination, did their best to out-jingo the jingoes.

Of the seventeen Methodists who triumphed as straightforward Liberals (instead of Liberal Unionists), twelve were identified by *The Times* as imperialists who ' may be expected to support the Government on questions affecting the war ', one was ' an unmistakable pro-Boer ', another defied classification, and three were newcomers, whose views were not yet properly ascertained. Taking a closer look at the dozen Methodist ' imperialists ' in the new House, one finds that six were full-fledged Wesleyans, four (by the reckoning of the *Methodist Recorder*) were ' more or less closely connected with Wesleyan Methodism ', and two belonged to other Methodist churches. Among the three novices on whom *The Times* suspended judgement, one (T. P. Whittaker at Spen Valley) was a Wesleyan, and he had been ' careful not to identify . . . with the pro-Boer section '. Given the fact that six of the seven Methodist M.P.s on the ministerial side were also Wesleyan, the denomination's imperial allegiance was firmly established.[36]

With Perks and his former law partner, H. H. Fowler, as prominent members of the Wesleyan parliamentary contingent, Lord Rosebery was assured of its support. In return, he served as a patron of Wesleyanism, endowing a chapel and Sunday school on his Bedfordshire estate, and contributing a hundred guineas

C

to Perks's Twentieth Century Fund. Nonconformists of other persuasions, less responsive to imperial rhetoric, were the recipients of other blandishments. In 1899, to commemorate the tercentenary of Oliver Cromwell's birth, Rosebery commissioned Sir Hamo Thornycroft, the celebrated sculptor, to provide a statue of the Lord Protector for a well-placed pedestal at Westminster. Anglican and Irish opposition had precluded the allocation of public funds for the project, but Rosebery sustained total costs amounting to £3200. By his generosity, he endeared himself, if not necessarily his beliefs, to the heirs to the Puritan tradition, who presumably did not trouble to ask themselves whether Thornycroft was paid out of Derby winnings.

Perks ensured that the unveiling of the Cromwell statue, and the benefaction that had made it possible, received extensive coverage in the denominational press. 'Your Cromwell speech has produced a wonderful effect on many Nonconformists,' he told Rosebery, whom he acquainted with his intention to follow it up with a dinner at his house in Kensington Palace Gardens. There were to be two dozen guests, ' all *genuine* Nonconformists ', but half of them laymen : ' Nonconformists don't take their politics from their clergy.' All the same, Perks hoped to include such divines as Alexander Maclaren of Manchester, Thomas Glover of Bristol, P. T. Forsyth of Cambridge, J. H. Jowett, who was Dale's successor at Birmingham, and F. W. Macdonald, who was (among other things) Kipling's uncle.[87] This was not the first occasion on which Perks had extended hospitality on Rosebery's behalf: the previous May, he gave ' a small party ' (by Perksian standards) at which Lloyd George received ' a serious lecture ' on Rosebery's merits from Robertson Nicoll, later his own staunch supporter. The editor of the *Christian World* had also been present, and he, like Lloyd George, was ' not an ardent believer in [Rosebery's] policy '.[88] But, as before, Rosebery declined Perks's invitation, preferring to allow others to plead his case in such company, and possibly aware that they could plead it more effectively in his absence.

In addition to Hughes, with whom he enjoyed a warm relationship, Perks managed to recruit Robert Nicoll, whose influence was exceeded only by his colossal vanity. Nicoll and R. J. Campbell, Joseph Parker's successor as minister at London's City Temple, joined the Council of Rosebery's Liberal League, the latter overcoming a professed reluctance ' to take up duties which would at all tend to draw me away from my own more directly spiritual work'.[39] With Fowler as one of its vice-presidents, Perks as treasurer, and Guinness Rogers an active member, the League had a definite Nonconformist tinge. But, beset by internal contradictions and the waywardness of its leader, it proved no better able to serve Nonconformist than other purposes.

In spite of his slavish devotion to Rosebery, who rarely justified the hopes he inspired, Perks was too restless to work exclusively through any one channel. With Lloyd George, who complained that Nonconformists were ' no longer militant, no longer aggressive, no longer even assertive ',[40] he created in 1898 a Nonconformist parliamentary committee, which thereafter operated sporadically as a pressure group at Westminster. He also accepted a vice-presidency of the National Education Association, established the following year ' to promote a system of national education which shall be efficient, progressive, unsectarian, and under popular control '; its executive, not all of them Free Churchmen, included A. M. Fairbairn, the first principal of Mansfield College, the Congregational foundation at Oxford, Dr Clifford, and an array of Liberal peers and M.P.s. Many of the same individuals were active in the Liberation Society, roused from its torpor at this time, in the body of Protestant Dissenting Deputies, which also recovered something of its old spirit, and in an array of temperance groups.

This proliferation of Nonconformist agencies, some not easily identifiable as such, testified to a renewal of energy, but also, less happily, to a continued fragmentation of personnel and purposes. Obviously the National Council of Evangelical Free Churches provided the best available means to bring together Nonconformists, ministers and laymen, whose denominational differences were overshadowed by secular rivalries. Even so, it was not yet evident on what basis the National Council could either appeal to Nonconformists or act in their collective interest. In 1901, at its annual sessions at Cardiff, there was a sharp but inconclusive exchange between the Revs J. Hirst Hollowell (a Wesleyan by birth, a Baptist by upbringing, and a Congregationalist by choice) and John Scott Lidgett (a Wesleyan), the latter opposing the former's resolution enjoining the Council to take direct action – as did temperance reformers and Fabian socialists – in parliamentary and local elections.

As the war in South Africa staggered to an end, further

attempts were made to unite the Free Churches behind one Liberal leader or another. The practice of the various factions to convene around the dinner table, and to denounce each other in after-dinner speeches, inspired the popular jest that this was political warfare ' to the knife and fork '. Nonconformists wielded the requisite weaponry as skilfully as anybody. Joseph-Compton-Rickett, then Liberal member for Scarborough and a Congregational lay leader, entertained on a scale worthy of Perks, but with different intentions. On 4 March 1902, he tendered the first of two proposed dinners – Rosebery unavailability forced him to cancel the second – to which he invited some thirty Free Church leaders to meet with Campbell-Bannerman and Herbert Gladstone, the party whip. Campbell-Bannerman was thoughtfully provided by his host with an advance list of ' principal guests ', about whom certain salient points were noted :

Rev A. Rowland, Congregational, strong, especially in London.

Rev A. Mackennal, Congregational, C.B., represents Lancashire.

Rev R. J. Campbell, personal friend of C[ompton] R[ickett], . . . Rosebery.

Rev G. Barrett, Norwich, Congregational, Rosebery.

Rev J. Greenhough, Baptist, Imp[erialist].

Rev H. P. Hughes, Perks.

Rev Thomas Law, has helped C[ompton] R[ickett].

Rev W. J. Townsend, sensible man, chairman-elect [of the National Free Church Council].

Rev Silas K. Hocking, C.B.

Among these ' principal guests ', no fewer than four were pledged to Campbell-Bannerman's rival, one was a ' pro-Boer ', and the remaining four were determined – as Dr Mackennal had put it – to do nothing that would ' still further embitter the political conflict '. Compton-Rickett acknowledged that his guest list was weighted with his fellow denominationalists: ' . . . Congregationalists take a more prominent part in political work than Methodists or Presbyterians,' he explained ' and hence it was important to have them fully represented.'

The Rev Silvester Horne, one of the younger Congregationalists at Compton-Rickett's dinner, described how, after the guest of honour had departed, ' the discords developed '. Their host took Campbell-Bannerman's part against Rosebery, who appeared once again to be emerging from the shadows. The Rev J. H. Shakespeare, a Baptist, practically said it must be Lord Rosebery or a split. Robertson Nicoll said that the Irish Alliance had done us no good, and that he dissented from every word that Rickett had spoken. Herbert Gladstone, in a wise and fine spirited speech, tried to throw oil on the troubled waters. But the surges of Imperialism would not be allayed.

As J. D. Jones, another Congregationalist, summed it up, the Free Churchmen were ' as hopelessly divided as the politicians themselves '.[41]

The early weeks of 1902 found Robertson Nicoll in one of those periodic bouts of depression to which Free Church leaders proved unusually susceptible. He threatened to abandon his editorial desk at the *British Weekly* in favour of an armchair in his Hampstead library. 'You must not talk about not being able to stand the strain long', Alexander Maclaren preached to him. 'If you were within a fortnight of being 76, as I am, you might begin to think of retiring. But what would become of the Free Churches if you and Parker and I all subsided into silence 1902?'[42] Joseph Parker died later that year, but the other two were soon invigorated by a radical transformation in Nonconformist public life. In May, the Balfour Government promulgated an Education Bill that unified and mobilised Free Church opinion as never before and never since. Belatedly, Nonconformists crossed the threshold into the world of twentieth-century politics; some of them mistook it for the promised land.

2 Revival and Revivalism

Back in 1870, when Forster's Education Act was thrust upon them, Nonconformists had lacked the means and possibly sufficient self-esteem to resist effectively. By 1902, when A. J. Balfour's Government introduced new proposals for secondary education, the situation had fundamentally altered. It was not simply that Nonconformists refused to accept from Tory hands the same humiliations which, on an earlier occasion, they had brooked from Liberals. Rather, in the course of the intervening generation, they had come to assume a more prominent place in national life, and particularly, in the rank and file of the Liberal Party. They had also evolved institutions which, although embryonic, were capable of giving form and impetus to their protest.

It was the 1902 Education Act, which Balfour presented gratuitously to his opponents, that transformed – seemingly over-night – the Nonconformist commitment to Liberalism from a vague sentiment into an active electoral alliance. Free Church-men in the House of Commons, who had been inclined to sub-ordinate religious to party interests, now saw them as identical. In the constituencies, this tendency was even more pronounced. Until Balfour's *coup de main*, Nonconformist politicians (to the extent that they conceived of themselves as such) had hoped to permeate one or another of the feuding Liberal factions. Now, for the first time in recent memory, they had a vested interest in ' unifying and strengthening Liberalism, not . . . dividing it and weakening it '.[1]

Before 1902, Free Churchmen had experienced much the same difficulties as other Liberals, generally unable to find a place for themselves in the post-Gladstonian order. Confronted with statisti-cal evidence of their relative decline in membership, as well as an unmistakable diminution of ardour, the individual sects responded by tightening their respective structures and by affiliating in inter-denominational agencies of which the most notable was the National Council of Evangelical Free Churches. On the part of some, the motivation was purely theological: to evolve new doctrines as a substitute for discarded orthodoxies and to devise systems of church discipline better able to withstand the pressures of secularisation. To others, the goal was at least partly political: to obtain greater leverage in Liberal Party councils and, thereby, increased influence in public affairs.

In the considered judgement of R. C. K. Ensor, the Education Act ' ranks for England and Wales among the two or three greatest constructive measures of the twentieth century '.[2] Nonconformists, including the few who shared Ensor's Fabian proclivities, were too distracted by their grievance to see anything of the Act's merits. Most galling was the requirement that they contribute through local rates to the maintenance of Anglican schools from which Nonconformist teachers were often barred by tests. The problem was most acute in rural districts, where it almost invariably proved the case that Anglican control was exclusive. And, to add insult to injury, Roman Catholic schools also received a generous measure of preferential treatment.

Although they had moved with the times to the extent that they no longer identified themselves as dissenters, Nonconformists remained – in mentality no less than in rhetoric – children of the seventeenth century. In recent years, they had become more self-consciously anti-sacerdotal: many of their most celebrated ministers declined to use the title ' reverend ' because it smacked too much of clericalism. By contrast, the Established Church had become less distinctly Protestant. Indeed, ' Protestant ' was an appellation that often caused Anglicans considerable embarrassment. Nonconformists were not convinced that the Establishment could be trusted to defend its own vital interests, let alone those of other reformed churches. Their attitude was later typified by Aneurin Bevan, a Welsh Baptist by background, who, as Minister of Health in the 1945 Labour Government, pontifically assured the Archbishop of Canterbury: ' You leave it to me. I'll look after the Protestants.'[3]

True to their heritage, Nonconformists fretted about the undisclosed number of monks and nuns who stealthily slipped across the Channel either as refugees or saboteurs. They helped to circulate chilling accounts of a new Popish Plot which, had it not been foiled, would have planted a Catholic pretender – Mary III

– on King Edward's rightful throne. Rarely did Nonconformist divines miss an opportunity to deplore ' the progress which continues to be made in the Romanising of the Church of England ', or to join publicly ' in prayer to the " Father of lights " that he would prevent the darkness of Mediaevalism from returning upon our land '. Respected Nonconformists mooted proposals for the creation of a watchdog committee to uncover Catholic subversion and to recommend parliamentary counter-measures. John Morley was among those who tried to bring them to reason. ' As far as any designs to make old John Bull R.C. ', he told R. W. Perks, ' you will not, I think, persuade me that they are seriously entertained, or that they can ever have a single atom of success.'[4] But agitated Nonconformists were not likely to take the word of Morley, who, during his distinguished editorship of the *Fortnightly Review*, had scandalously printed ' god ' with a small letter and ' Gladstone ' with a capital.

In terms of organisation and propaganda techniques, Nonconformists obviously had much to learn from those whom they most distrusted. ' We Free Churchmen are only gradually awakening to the value of the press,' observed the Rev Hugh Price Hughes; ' the Roman Catholic Church with its usual astuteness has set itself to train journalists. . . . We shall have to do the same.'[5] The later years of the nineteenth century and the early ones of the twentieth witnessed a dramatic rise in the number and quality of Free Church journals, as well as the conversion of London's *Daily News* into a semi-official organ of Radical Nonconformity. Hughes's *Methodist Times* was flanked on the right by the *Methodist Recorder*, and on the left (from 1900 to 1903) by the *Methodist Weekly*. Other denominational weeklies, either started or revivified at the turn of the century, included the *Primitive Methodist* (soon reincarnated as the *Primitive Methodist Leader*), the *Baptist Times and Freeman*, and the *Examiner* (which became the *British Congregationalist*). There was an efflorescence of literary monthlies and quarterlies, theological reviews, children's and professional magazines, and newsletters published at irregular intervals by individual chapels, leagues, and committees.

Not least, there were two respected inter-denominational weeklies, the *Christian World* and the *British Weekly*, either or both of which were required reading in every manse. Published since the 'eighties, they had had to wait until the Edwardian period to achieve their greatest influence and circulation. The *Christian World* observed a political reticence that owed something to its conservative predilections and more to its shaky financial position. The *British Weekly*, fashioned in the image of William Robertson Nicoll, its longtime editor (1886 to 1923), was livelier and more outspoken politically. Nicoll was an intriguing figure in every sense. Ordained in the Free Church of Scotland, he migrated south into a career in journalism after a throat ailment impaired his pulpit performance. In addition to the *British Weekly*, he edited two monthlies, the *Expositor* and the *Bookman*, and he reviewed books in all three journals and elsewhere under a variety of pseudonyms: Sir Arthur Conan Doyle was outraged when one of his novels was denounced as ' immoral ' by five critics, all of whom turned out to be Robertson Nicoll. But it was not literary taste that Nicoll was most eager to dictate. In political combat he was equally ubiquitous, affixing himself first to Lord Rosebery, and later as passionately to Lloyd George. With one inflamed eye, his Scots pronunciation, and an insatiable appetite for gossip, he provided H. G. Wells with the prototype for ' Dr Tomlinson Keyhole ', the name by which he was called (behind his back) by his cronies at the Reform Club.

There were other techniques, besides journalistic ones, to be borrowed from the Roman Catholics, and again Hughes showed the way. His West London Mission, which opened its doors in 1886, served as a model for a number of similar enterprises, mostly clustered in the greater London area. As much a social centre as a house of worship, it provided meeting and recreation rooms, editorial offices, and halls of residence. Its extensive staff included members of a Wesleyan sisterhood, the creation of which did not pass without comment. South of the Thames, in a more necessitous district, other Wesleyans soon founded the Bermondsey Settlement, with the Rev John Scott Lidgett as warden. The Congregationalists responded with Whitefield's Mission in Tottenham Court Road, and the Baptists with their Bloomsbury Central Mission. Each of these institutions, headed by men who came to appear with equal prominence in the Free Church press and on Liberal Party platforms, combined social and spiritual ministration with unabashed political activity.

But the best gauge of renewed Nonconformist vitality was provided by the ' simultaneous ' or ' united ' evangelical tours, which were multi-denominational ventures under the auspices of the National Council. Earlier revivals had tended to be limited to isolated regions (Northern Ireland in 1859) or particular sects (Wesleyan Methodists in 1874–75); or else, like the Salvation Army campaign of the late 'seventies, they had persevered in the face of opposition from denominational authorities. The new evangelism, born with the new century, differed in origin, scope, and effect.

In the spring of 1900, the National Council laid plans for a ' national mission . . . to reach the masses ' that began early the following year.[6] In London alone, attendance was estimated at 200,000, and the intensive effort yielded a gratifying number of conversions and temperance pledges. Village missions, usually featuring local preaching talent and house-to-house visitations were undertaken in the smaller towns of England and Wales, while special missioners were dispatched to conduct rallies and ' open-air work ' in approximately a hundred of the larger urban centres. Enthusiasm reached so high a pitch that even *The Times* could not fail to be impressed. ' The organizers of the movement,' it observed with unaccustomed warmth on 2 February 1901, ' speak with excusable pride of their achievements.'

The individual entitled to take greatest pride was the Rev Thomas Law, who appropriately served as ' organising secretary ' of the National Council. He employed the services of a trio of itinerant evangelists – Rodney (universally known as Gipsy) Smith, W. R. Lane, and the Rev J. Tolfree Parr – who continued on circuit after the 1901 simultaneous mission was brought to a close. Law, who regarded nothing as impossible, immediately proposed to repeat his success within two years, but caution prevailed, and the second simultaneous mission was deferred until 1904. In the meantime, the Rev F. B. Meyer, whose ' Letter to Missioners ' had set the standard for the first go-round, embarked on a two-month tour through Lancashire and Yorkshire. Delay proved beneficial: according to Gipsy Smith, the second simultaneous mission went even better than the first. Then, in 1905, Dr Robert Forman Horton, the tenth president of the National Council, held a series of eight area conventions in strategically placed cities; each lasted four days, featuring sermons and discussions on topical issues. It was reported back that Horton's ' presidential campaign ' had been ' remarkably successful ' in introducing the Council and its work to Nonconformists throughout the country.[7]

The most phenomenal results of Edwardian revivalism came in Wales, and with no appreciable stimulus from the National Council. Indeed, if local accounts are to be believed, the Welsh revival of 1904–5 was the gift of God and owed little to any earthly agent. Some mention must be made, however, of the two key participants: Evan Roberts, a twenty-six year-old blacksmith's apprentice, and, to a somewhat lesser extent, Joseph Jenkins, a Methodist minister. Thomas Law, Gipsy Smith, and W. T. Stead journeyed like the Magi to Cardiff and marvelled at what they beheld. Stead, describing himself as ' a child of the Revival of 1859–60 ', paid tribute to Roberts's ability to weld an audience of a ' thousand or fifteen hundred persons . . . into a myriad-headed but single-souled personality '. Welsh chapel member-ship, which ' had shown only sluggish progress ' during the pre-ceding decade, now ' mounted rapidly ', with the greatest gains registered by the Baptists, the sect ' perhaps least curbed by ecclesiastical formalism '. In the years between 1893 and 1903, Nonconformity had increased its aggregate membership in the principality by only 66,000; in the next two years, it ' leaped ahead ' by 82,000 to a total of 550,280 communicants in 1905.[8]

Admittedly envious, English Free Church leaders met in the ' closing hours ' of 1905 to consider the ' spiritual awakening in Wales ' and the ' possibility of its spreading to London and the rest of England '. But what could be done to influence events which (in the words of the Rev Thomas Phillips) were ' entirely independent of man '? Hope soon gave way to impatience. ' Is it too much for us to seek that tens of thousands may be converted to God in London, as has been the experience in Wales through the great outpouring of the Holy Spirit?' demanded the Rev J. H. Shakes-peare, president of the Metropolitan Federation of Free Churches. Although the National Council received and, in turn, disseminated persistent reports that ' waves of spiritual blessing ' had begun to roll upon various provincial towns, England proved stubbornly resistant to the Welsh variety of evangelical enthusiasm.[9]

The closest that Englishmen came to sharing the Welsh ex-perience was the work of two American visitors, Dr R. A. Torrey, a former Congregational minister who held a degree from Yale University, and Charles M. Alexander, his musical assistant. They had initiated their travels in Chicago, and, moving westward across Australia, reached London in January 1903. Except for a brief interruption, when Torrey returned home to fulfil a previous commitment, they spent the next three years in Britain. By their own reckoning, their success was extraordinary: their first visit to Liverpool (6–30 September 1903) produced some 4000 converts, their second from November 1904 to January 1905) a further 7000; they saved 4500 souls at Manchester (November 1903), and 7500 at Birmingham (January and February 1904); and they reported satisfactory results at Glasgow, Dublin, Bristol, Bolton, and Cardiff. The leaders of English Nonconformity tended to look upon Torrey as something of an interloper, alternately faulting him for theological vagary and an 'impassive' platform style. By Welsh standards, the mission was certainly a disappointment. A correspondent for the Congregationalist *Examiner* paid a visit to London's Albert Hall and acknowledged the large turnout for Torrey and Alexander, 'but as for spontaneity or spiritual fervour none could be detected'. At the end of a long evening, the crowd made its way to the closest underground station at South Kensington, and 'not a bar of a hymn broke from man or woman'. Later that year, Torrey was himself forced to admit that his Oxford mission was 'a bad record', with undergraduate audiences left unmoved.[10]

Doubtless it was asking too much of English Nonconformists, who differed markedly from their Welsh brethren in social background and national temperament, that they should deliver themselves to Christ with the same communal abandon. Nor were they encouraged to do so. Dr G. Campbell-Morgan, who conducted English-style revivalist meetings at Christ Church in Westminster Bridge Road, London, 'did not propose to have his regular services broken up by anyone save God alone'.[11] And yet it would be a mistake to conclude that a genuine revival eluded English Free Churchmen, whose contribution to the overall increase in communicants was by no means discreditable. The 1906 *Free Church Year Book* calculated a rise from 1,983,650 communicants in 1902 to 2,136,079 in 1905, a larger gain than had been recorded for the preceding seven years; in addition to increases among the Baptists, who were particularly strong in Wales, there were striking advances on the part of Wesleyans and Congregationalists. Within particular areas of England, statistical evaluation is made difficult, if not impossible, by the absence of a religious census, and by such factors as the migration of Wesleyans to the south-east and the general drift of middle-class groups to the suburbs. But the Baptist community in Berkshire, which has been the subject of intensive scholarly investigation, showed a decade-long decline in membership before 1902, and a modest recovery thereafter; in 1905, the Berkshire Baptist Association proudly ' reported 200 baptisms in the previous twelve months and a quickened spiritual life which was widely attributed to the influence of the Welsh revival '.[12] From such isolated situations, it is possible to conclude that, however attenuated its forms, the Welsh revival was not as geographically circumscribed as its popular designation would suggest.

In any case, the intensified commitment on the part of English Nonconformists manifested itself less frequently at revivalist sessions than at the polls in a succession of dramatic by-elections, and ultimately in the general election of 1906. Such a commitment is admittedly more difficult to quantify than an increase in worshippers or Sunday school enrolments. Few, however, would dispute F. B. Meyer's contention that ' Every great revival of religion has issued in social and political reconstruction '.[13] Again, Wales proves the point most conclusively; swept by religious fervour during 1904 and 1905, its thirty-four seats were captured by Liberal candidates in the ensuing election. ' From the first ', the Rev H. Elvet Lewis explained, the spiritual revival in the principality was stimulated and sustained by a national revolt: ' The Revolt without the Revival might have become too political; the Revival without the Revolt might have become too pietistic.'[14] Lloyd George's patronage of Evan Roberts showed him to be alert to this inter-relationship, which he did his best to foster. Although English Nonconformists lacked a comparable sense of ' thwarted nationalism ' (to borrow Henry Pelling's phrase), they too saw themselves as victims of a tyrannous Anglicanism. In response, Free Churchmen temporarily overcame their parochialisms: Wesleyans made common cause with Baptists and Quakers; Welshmen with Englishmen; ' pro-Boers ' with Imperialists; Fabians with Cobdenites; and plutocrats with trade unionists.

Was there a causal relationship between Radical impulses in politics and religion, and, if so, in which direction? Did the 1902 Education Act win adherents for an embattled faith, or did the new devoutness inspire a determination to venture forth in battle? More specifically, were Liberal Free Churchmen the servants of personal and party interests, or were they selflessly seeking to employ their party as a vehicle for religious sentiment?

Priority of motive is difficult to establish, even in the case of most individuals. Suffice it to say that Nonconformity attained a heightened self-consciousness which its leaders exploited most skilfully. Their immediate goal was to obtain redress for a particular grievance. Beyond this, however, they entertained elaborate and sometimes contradictory ambitions to fulfil Lord Palmerston's much quoted prediction that, ' In the long run, English politics will follow the consciences of the Dissenters '.

Nonconformity had always been a force to be reckoned with in British local politics. Now, for the first and last time, it was to achieve a truly national dimension. Four days before Sir John Gorst announced the provision of the 1902 Education Bill to the Commons, Perks – who knew what to expect – invited Lord Rosebery to preside at a massive protest demonstration at the Queen's Hall, London, on 10 June. Scott Lidgett, another Wesleyan and a pillar of the National Council, helped Perks to assemble a set of speakers as diverse as Lloyd George, H. H. Asquith, Sydney Buxton, and such divines as Robert Forman Horton, John Clifford, and J. Guinness Rogers. Rosebery, who did not seem to Perks ' quite [to] appreciate the intensity of the Nonconformist feeling ', was given a lesson in political tactics: ' *Possibly* the Bill may be made to work,' Perks conceded, ' but 9 Liberals out of 10 don't *believe* so: & it is hardly our business, I think, to stem the torrent of popular hostility against the Government.'[15]

As the Queen's Hall demonstration symbolised, education was as yet one of the few issues that permitted Liberals of different persuasions to join in collective activity. Sir Henry Campbell-Bannerman, who officially led the Liberal forces in the lower house, instructed his chief whip to sound out prominent imperialists so that the front bench might ' take such a line on the 2nd R[eading] as may furnish a united attack '.[16] Liberal M.P.s, who had been dissipating their energies and often their credibility in internecine strife, now saved their invective for those few hapless Nonconformist Unionists – like J. S. Randles, the Wesleyan who sat for Cockermouth – who gave their votes to the betrayal of their co-religionists. Whatever their differences on Home Rule, which remained enormous, Liberal politicians were unanimously contemptuous of Irish Nationalists, who supported the Education Bill as Roman Catholics instead of rejecting it as allies of British Radicalism.

The parliamentary opponents of the Bill constituted a forlorn minority in the Commons, where the measure passed its second reading by a thumping margin of 237. Obviously they could not have expected to impede the Bill in the Lords, where their representation was even more pitiable. Nevertheless, they mounted a vigorous campaign, which was implicitly addressed to a larger audience that lay beyond Westminster. There was keen competition for places at the eye of the storm among M.P.s who sought to improve their credentials or to discredit their rivals. Lloyd George, who was not oblivious to either consideration, ' wrote about 15 pages ' of a speech which he did not know whether he would be called upon to deliver, as there were reportedly ' 40 members who have put their names down to speak already on the Liberal Whip's list '. While he impatiently waited his turn, he heard R. B. Haldane audaciously support the Bill: ' It will help as far as it goes ', Lloyd George calculated, ' to damage the Liberal Imperialists.'[17] Perks, who had no such consolation, worked indefatigably to harness the Nonconformist agitation to the chariot of the Liberal League.

Although Lloyd George and Perks, representing two extreme positions, disagreed profoundly on the ways in which the Liberal Party might serve Nonconformist interests and *vice versa*, they were brought into increasingly frequent contact. Founders in 1898 of the parliamentary Nonconformists' committee, which had proved something of a non-starter, both belonged to the executive of the National Council of Evangelical Free Churches, of which Perks was treasurer. Both were also active in the Liberation Society: Perks as vice-chairman (under Sir John Brunner, a Unitarian M.P.) of the religious equality parliamentary committee, and Lloyd George as parliamentary vice-president from 1902. Other Liberal members who carried on the liberationist tradition included James Bryce, J. Carvell Williams, and H. J. Wilson. Despite their advocacy, it was very much a dying tradition, as the Society's avowed objective – ' the liberation of religion from state-patronage and control ' – had lost much of its appeal among Englishmen, if not necessarily among Welshmen.

By July 1902, Lloyd George had come round to Robertson Nicoll's view, conveyed privately as well as in the columns of the *British Weekly*,

that the time has arrived when we should take counsel together as to our next step. . . . The whole fight against the Bill seems to me, to use an educational phrase, to lack co-ordination. There ought to be a more complete understanding between those who conduct the campaign in the Country and the Members who fight the Bill in the Commons. . . . The House of Commons is not yet convinced that the Nonconformists in any part of the country except Wales mean business.

To this end, he invited Nicoll, Clifford, and Hugh Price Hughes to consult with ' two or three of the more active Nonconformist Members in the House ',[18] among whom he presumably counted himself. There is no evidence that such a meeting was ever held; in any case, as Hughes died in November, it would have served a limited purpose. Yet, if nothing else, the proposal portended a growing correlation between the political fortunes of Lloyd George and those of Radical Nonconformity.

The leaders of the various Nonconformist communities knew better than to put too much trust in professional politicians, even those with whom they occasionally appeared on campaign platforms. Their own response to the education controversy was a passive resistance movement, conducted with a zeal worthy of seventeenth-century commonwealthmen. To be sure, only a small percentage of the nation's Nonconformists had the courage as well as the conviction to defy the law. But those who passively resisted tended to be ministers and other men of rank, who commanded widespread sympathy and respect among their neighbours. Duly warned, they were visited by the local sheriff, who impounded some possession – usually a silver inkstand, candlesticks, or a tea service – estimated as equal in value to the unpaid rates. The merchandise, put up at public auction, invariably found its way back to its owner through the good offices of friends, members of the same chapel, or, if all else failed, a servant dispatched to tender a discreet bid. The passive resister thereby managed to keep his principles while his account was settled for him. But one would not wish to suggest that the protest was a charade: often those involved were summoned before the magistrates, convicted, and fined or imprisoned. The *Christian World* was appalled by the unseemliness of the spectacle, but the *British Weekly* warmly applauded, and regularly brought its readers ' news of the persecutions '. Each October, a National Passive Resistance Day was commemorated with ceremonies at the City Temple, where the Hampdens and Eliots of the previous year were commended for their valour.

The initiative for the movement was said to have come from 'Alderman' George White, a Baptist shoe manufacturer, who continued to be known by the local office he had held at Norwich even after 1900, when he graduated to become M.P. for North West Norfolk. Its moving force was, without question, Dr John Clifford of Westbourne Park Chapel, Paddington, who combined Hampden's fidelity to principle with a thoroughly Cromwellian sense of vengeance. The Rev C. Silvester Horne, a young Congregationalist who officiated at Whitefield's Mission, wore the mantle of Ireton, although one can detect traces of Lilburne in the *Crusader*, the penny journal which he edited first as a monthly, and then, from October 1903, as a weekly.

Clifford, though he lived until 1923 and kept active almost to the end, was already nearing his seventieth year. As A. G. Gardiner knowingly described him in a *Daily News* character sketch, he was 'the type of Nonconformist minister of the old days of proscription and disability, with all the merits and all the defects of the stern school out of which he came'. Horne, though Clifford survived him by nearly a decade, belonged to a younger generation and possibly to a newer breed. A match for Clifford in journalistic output and platform oratory, he sat in Parliament from January 1910 until his premature death in May 1914. The discrepancy in the ages of the two men did not preclude their fruitful collaboration and mutual esteem; yet it nonetheless pointed to an essential weakness among Nonconformity's political activists, namely the paucity of middle-aged ministerial talent. One generation of leaders had either died out or entered old age with the turn of the century; the next had yet to prove itself.

The deficiency showed up most clearly among the Congregationalists, in whom public-minded Free Churchmen had traditionally found their spokesmen. J. Guinness Rogers resigned his pulpit at Clapham in 1900, at age seventy-eight, and thereafter kept to the sidelines. 'How the Nonconformists seem to want a man of weight just now like Dale!' Principal James Denny of Glasgow lamented to Robertson Nicoll, one of his few compatriots who successfully made the transition to English religious politics. A. M. Fairbairn, another transplanted Scotsman, 'can never be an Englishman with all his ability', Denny argued, 'and there could not be a more fatal drawback to any one wishing to deal with

D

an English question '.[19] Robert Forman Horton, who lacked Fairbairn's particular handicap, suffered from his own ' fatal drawback ': a ' Puritan engrafted with Oxford culture ' (again to quote
Gardiner), he was immobilised politically no less than theologically by a tendency to ' bitter self-abasement '.

Horton's church at Lyndhurst Road was a magnet for Hampstead intellectuals as well as for artisans who climbed Haverstock
Hill from nearby Camden Town. But the Congregationalist
divine who drew the greatest crowds was indisputably R. J.
Campbell, who presided at the mammoth City Temple. Isaac Foot,
then a young law student in London and later a leading parliamentary Nonconformist, went with some friends to hear Campbell
one Sunday morning: they were turned away, only to return that
evening ' to wait from 6.0 to 7.0 and then fight & struggle
like footballers ' for admission. D. R. Daniel, visiting the metro-
polis from Wales, recounted a similar experience:

> City Temple. 11 a.m. R. J. Campbell whom I now heard for
> the first time. The crowd was immense. I had great difficulty in
> getting in. Disappointed on the whole with preacher and
> sermon. I failed to discover the secret of his popularity. Can it
> be the result of advertisement, log-rolling on the part of
> Robertson Nicoll & c. [?] In style of speaking, R.J.C. sounded
> like Balfour.

There was a resemblance, too, between Campbell's ' new theology' and the metaphysical exercises with which the Prime
Minister amused himself and bemused his contemporaries. All
things considered, it is not surprising that Campbell should have
contemplated conversion to Rome ('After all, that was the real
Church,' he offhandedly remarked in 1911 to Lloyd George, who
thought him ' as unstable as water '), before he ultimately took
Anglican ordination in 1916.[20]

The other denominations fared no better. Apart from Clifford
and possibly F. B. Meyer, the Baptists boasted no one of established reputation. J. Monro-Gibson, a respected Presbyterian, was
not in the same league; nor yet was John Scott Lidgett, later to be
celebrated as the greatest Methodist since Wesley. Unitarian
divines, active participants in mid-Victorian political debate, were
now more than ever eclipsed by laymen; the same held true
among the Quakers. There was a further contrast, even more
striking: during previous generations, political Nonconformity

had operated from a strong provincial base; now its ministerial leaders were men who occupied metropolitan pulpits, and who enjoyed ready access to National Council headquarters at the Memorial Hall, to Westminster, and to Fleet Street.

Once again, Nonconformity broke down into 'hard' and 'soft' components, although the lines were not as clearly drawn as those during the early 'seventies. With reportedly only two votes cast against the motion, the Baptist Union gave its emphatic endorsement to passive resistance; the Congregational Union promptly followed suit; and the Primitive Methodists, who contributed the first passive resister to go before the magistrates – Thomas Charles Smith, a Sunday school teacher at Wirksworth, near Matlock, in Derbyshire – were especially militant. Most Quakers preferred not to respond; Unitarians usually maintained an embarrassed silence; and the Salvation Army held predictably aloof. Within Wesleyan Methodism, there occurred a bitter struggle between those who espoused passive resistance (for others, if not necessarily for themselves), and those who categorically denounced it. The *Methodist Recorder*, as the organ of the Wesleyan old guard, was scandalised by the essential illegality of the movement; the *Methodist Weekly*, which provided a forum for 'progressive' views, strenuously defended it; the *Methodist Times*, perpetuated by Hughes's successor, tried its best to reconcile Protestant principle and political necessity. Opinion at the 1902 and 1903 Wesleyan conferences was, as one historian has put it with classic understatement, 'not unanimous'. Finally, to preserve a semblance of unity, a resolution was carried 'without expressing an opinion on what is known as Passive Resistance'.[21]

Perks, who was as much compromised by some of his fellow Wesleyans as by certain Liberal Imperialist allies (most notably Haldane), found himself in the uncomfortable position of siding with the proto-socialists who edited the *Methodist Weekly*. He fired off a letter to the *Methodist Recorder*, a copy of which he pointedly sent to Campbell-Bannerman, in which he vowed undying opposition to the Education Act, and castigated those Wesleyans who agreed to work it.[22] This was tantamount to a declaration of war against such august personages as the Revs D. J. Waller, J. H. Rigg, W. L. Watkinson, and F. W. Macdonald, with whom Hughes had formerly done battle. True to form, these conservative divines identified more strongly with the Established Church than with Nonconformity. Far from maintaining a political neutrality, which Perks would have considered sufficiently blameworthy under the circumstances, they affiliated with Sir George Hayter Chubb's Nonconformist Unionist Association, a predominantly Wesleyan group, which was more a source of irritation than accomplishment.

The split among Wesleyans left a legacy of inter- and intra-denominational resentment. Lloyd George was incensed by their back-sliding on ' the policy of " No Rates ". The leaders of the Free Churches', he told Robertson Nicoll, ' have committed themselves too deeply for reconsideration. They must go through with their threats – otherwise they will make themselves contemptible in the eyes of the nation.'[23] Primitive Methodists had further reason, if any were needed, to deplore their parent connexion's social pretensions and Tory bias : the Rev A. T. Guttery, minister at Newcastle's Primitive Methodist Central Church, reported in his denominational weekly (3 November 1903) that he had been locked out of a neighbouring Wesleyan school, where a protest meeting had been scheduled. More generally, there was a fierce dispute whether political groups – including trade unions – should be allowed access to Wesleyan facilities, including those at the new Central Hall, Westminster, which had been built with the proceeds of Perks's Twentieth Century Fund.

To an appreciable extent, Wesleyans were divided between those who imbibed London's intoxicating influences, and those in the provinces who abstained. Isaac Foot, the son of a local preacher from Plymouth, formed his closest friendships with several Congregationalist students, who took him to hear Silvester Horne (' It was electrifying!'), and to passive resistance meetings. His fiancée, who stayed behind in the West Country, was not subjected to the same radical influences, and consequently adhered to a more orthodox Wesleyan line on public questions. ' Your reference to the Education Bill has quite depressed me to-day ', he scolded her :

> I am very sorry to read your views of the passive resistance resolve on the part of the Free Churches. I am afraid that you are not very staunch in your Free Church principles. ' Absurd ', ' mean ', and ' contemptible ' are strong words to use but if they are to be used at all they should be applied to the *reputed* descendants of Puritans & Dissenters who are prepared to pay to support the schools of a grasping, greedy, arrogant and

largely corrupted church. . . . I am afraid, dearie, your descent from William Wallace does not show itself in your present attitude. I am quite certain that if I become a rate-payer before this Bill is overthrown I shall not pay it and shall be glad to get the privilege of refusing to do so. I quite agree with you that some great Educational measure is necessary, but the present Bill is a remedy worse than the Evil itself. . . . I am sorry to see that you have been wheedled . . . into holding your present views.[24]

Miss Eva Mackintosh presumably recanted, for she and Isaac Foot eventually married and gave issue to a political dynasty. Other differences between Wesleyans, and between them and other Free Churchmen, were less easily reconciled.

With qualified support from its Wesleyan component, the National Council of Evangelical Free Churches proceeded to organise opposition to the Balfour government and its education policy. Various members of its executive occupied key places on the National Passive Resistance Committee. By the end of 1903, a network of some 430 citizens' leagues and committees was in operation throughout England and Wales; many of these groups were offshoots of local Free Church councils, some duplicated in personnel, and all drew their financial sustenance from Council benefactors. Their object was not so much to incite others to rebellion as to publicise and justify the action of those whose consciences had impelled them to rebel. Nonconformity, its sense of mission and identity weakened by the concessions it had won during the mid-Victorian period, had to be taught anew how to defend its own vital interests. For this reason, Robertson Nicoll was not perturbed when passive resisters were sometimes disenfranchised as criminal offenders: '. . . Where one vote is lost ', he reasoned, ' at least ten will be gained by public demonstration thus afforded of the iniquities and injustices of the Act.'[25]

What did the passive resisters hope to accomplish? There are indications that, at least at the start, they acted more out of desperation than out of any belief that they could achieve positive results. Obviously, they could not expect to bankrupt the exchequer by non-payment of rates. There was equally little chance that they might impose their will on a government whose tyranny they likened to that of Strafford and Laud. Nor were they particularly sanguine about the electoral potential of the Liberal Opposition, still grievously afflicted by leadership quarrels. ' Is there anyone optimistic enough ', the *Crusader* asked its readers on 15 February 1903,

> to believe that the swing of the pendulum would be so great as to enable the Liberal Party to go back into power with a majority, independent of even the Irish, sufficient to secure the repeal? And, even granting that, is the great Committee of the Anglican Church (as Dr Clifford aptly styled the House of Lords) to be overthrown?

Within three years, the Liberal Party was returned with a massive majority that afforded, among other things, temporary relief from a dependence on Irish Nationalist votes; and, within a decade, the House of Lords was shorn of its powers. Yet these developments, to which Free Churchmen contributed significantly, failed to bring them the benefits which, not unreasonably, they might have expected.

3 Nonconformity Redivivus

Swathed in 'khaki', the general election of 1900 had renewed the Unionists' lease on office with a handsome majority. True, in the final tally, the victors had gained only three seats, and the Liberal showing had proved ' better rather than worse than [one] would have expected '.[1] But, if the Liberals managed surprisingly well to hold their ground, it must be borne in mind that the ground was already considerably eroded. In qualitative terms, the opposition suffered heavily: many respected stalwarts and promising newcomers (particularly those tainted as ' pro-Boers ') either went down to defeat or else scraped through by slim margins.

Less than six years later, the Liberal Party made a phoenix-like recovery and scored an unprecedented electoral landslide. How is one to explain this remarkable resurgence? The 1902 education controversy, and the Nonconformist agitation to which it had given rise, was doubtless a crucial factor. But how crucial? In the opinion of a great many contemporaries and not a few later historians, Free Church militancy counted as the single most important weapon in the 1906 Liberal armoury. The present study, more modest in its claims, assigns the Nonconformists credit less for the fact of the Liberal victory than for its magnitude. That in itself pays them high tribute and should entitle them to scholarly attention.

Even before the Education Bill passed into law, Liberal candidates had begun to score spectacular successes at by-elections. In May 1902, Bury was wrested from Tory hands by George Toulmin, a journalist of Wesleyan background. His strong views on the education issue may have had no direct bearing on the situation at Bury, where (as in some other Lancashire cotton towns) there were no board schools; but Bury's Nonconformist population would not have been insensitive to the plight of their brethren elsewhere, and, in any case, would have reacted against the presence in the constituency of a large and tightly organised Roman Catholic community. In July, North Leeds fell to the Liberals, and here the Nonconformist factor was even more pronounced. R. W. Perks rejoiced ' that the Education Bill is the cause of [Rowland H.] Barran's victory, & that the victory is that of the Nonconformists & School Board advocates. It is the first time for 35 years that the chapel bell has rung.' Months later, Free Churchmen continued to bask in the glory of the North Leeds result. Strolling through Kensington Gardens in October, Silvester Horne met Dr Clifford, with whom he ' compared notes on the campaign '. They agreed that North Leeds, won ' magnificently ' by a prominent local Methodist, ' has been *the* feature of the fight so far '.[2]

More incredible in its way was the outcome in August at Sevenoaks, always regarded as one of the safest of Conservative seats, where a Baptist stood in the Liberal interest and was returned on a 24.1 per cent swing. Despite the constituency's unlikely social composition, the education controversy was ' the main topic' of the campaign: Beaumont Morice, celebrating his upset victory, expected to ' put another nail in the coffin of the Education Act on which the battle was fought '.[3] Joseph Chamberlain, who nursed profound misgivings about the education policies of the government to which he belonged, took fright. '. . . I do not think ', he advised the Prime Minister, ' that any seat, where there is a strong Nonconformist electorate, can be considered absolutely safe '.[4] That winter brought further Liberal gains at Newmarket and Rye, both traditional Tory strongholds with Nonconformist entrenchments. Perks petitioned the National Free Church Council to assist C. D. Rose's candidacy at Newmarket, and addressed campaign meetings for Rose at Ely. There were certain problems, he confided to Lord Rosebery, posed by the fact that Rose (like Rosebery) was a breeder of racehorses. But the Nonconformists at Newmarket were nonetheless ' working hard for Rose " regarding him not so much as a man as the embodiment of a principle " ! '[5]

Campbell-Bannerman, taking the waters at Baden-Baden, had ample time to ponder the situation. While he had no wish to appear intractable, he shared James Bryce's view that Liberals should resist any compromise which, one way or the other, would deprive them of valuable Nonconformist support. Like those

Tories with whom he engaged in holiday conversation, he found it impossible to understand why the government had decided to ' meddle with this hornet's nest' instead of applying itself to pressing problems of higher education and technical training.[6] Not for the last time, he imputed to his opponents a strategy they did not have. Balfour, never a particularly good judge of popular opinion, took for granted that the Nonconformist ' fever will be allayed in twelve months ',[7] and that the Act would be vindicated by its efficient implementation. The experience of his predecessors might have taught him (in the words of Norman Gash) that ' a civil government faced by rebellious churchmen, acting however intemperately on grounds of spiritual conscience, is at a disadvantage in any liberal-minded society '.

There was serious apprehension among Nonconformists that they might be sold short by their parliamentary allies, whose vision often did not extend beyond Westminster. Bryce, speaking more as a Baptist than as a member of the party hierarchy, communicated to Clifford his uneasy ' impression that Liberals outside Parliament, especially Free Churchmen, are clearer and stronger in this matter than many Liberals in Parliament, and that outside opinion . . . might have the greatest weight '.[8] The education committee of the National Council, taking a similar view of the situation, ' resolved to recommend the [local] councils to make Education a test question at all elections and to carefully watch the selection of candidates '. There were public meetings and rallies, culminating on 23 May 1903 with a demonstration in Hyde Park. More directly, Nonconformists applied pressure by sending successive deputations to wait upon Campbell-Bannerman and Lord Spencer, the leader of the Liberal peers. Lloyd George, yet to take his place among the party mandarins, introduced one such deputation in August, when Clifford declared that the more than 800 Free Church councils in England and Wales ' would make Education a test question at the next election '.[9]

Taking their lead from the National Council, other Nonconformist agencies overcame their scruples against electioneering. The general body of Protestant Dissenting Deputies, politically mute for more than a half century, recovered its voice. At its annual meeting on 28 March 1904, the Rev W. D. McLaren submitted a motion 'declining to discuss any matters not directly touching questions of Protestantism & Dissent'. It was quickly dropped, 'finding no seconder'. Instead the meeting proceeded to pass vehement resolutions on such remotely theological themes as education, licensing, and Chinese indentured labour in South Africa.[10] The last issue, coming in the wake of the Boer War, touched the Nonconformist Conscience to the quick. ' Every little Bethel,' L. S. Amery wrote facetiously to his chief, Sir Alfred Milner, ' is an anti-Chinese assembly room.'[11]

It was on the golf links that Silvester Horne asked Arthur Porritt, a writer for the *Christian World* (and later its editor): ' Don't you think the Free Churches ought to put up a hundred candidates at the next election?' It was not enough to elect a Liberal Parliament; it had to be a Parliament that contained a healthy complement of Free Churchmen who conceived of themselves primarily as such. At Horne's suggestion, Porritt went to see Herbert Gladstone, the chief whip, who ' was not enthusiastic ', and who made it brutally clear that ' he did not want to be encumbered with men with bees in their bonnet over one issue'.[12] Where, Gladstone asked, were a sufficient number of qualified candidates to come from, and who was to finance them?

In the cramped pages of his diary, where he made brief reference to an interview with Porritt on 16 July, Gladstone pretty much answered his own questions. On 17 June, for example, he had seen James Gibb, who was soon adopted to stand successfully at Harrow in the next election. Willing to 'put down a certain amount' for his campaign expenses, Gibb was typical of many Nonconformists who, though they had always taken a keen interest in politics, 'never before thought of standing but Educn. and F[ree] T[rade] bring him out'.[13] Other Nonconformist hopefuls, less able to pay their own way, were promised support from a fund raised by the National Council in collaboration with the *Christian World*. With landed wealth solidly behind the Tories, and trade-union subscriptions diverted to Labour candidacies, Herbert Gladstone was in no position to spurn the offer of Free Church support. Besides, from the little that we can piece together about Liberal Party finances, he already depended heavily on the generosity of Nonconformist businessmen, including Sir John Brunner, George Cadbury, W. P. Hartley, W. H. Lever, and Albert Spicer.

Gladstone, according to his own terse account, ' encouraged [the] proposal for a Noncon. Com. (Silvester Horne, Guinness Rogers, etc.) to put pressure on desirable men to fight constitu-

encies '.[14] But the constituencies he had in mind were those
'forlorn hope seats' (as Arthur Porritt called them) which no
one else would have wished to fight. A case in point was Bath,
where Donald Maclean, a Presbyterian solicitor who practised
at Cardiff, sought to reverse the judgement he had received from
the electorate in 1900. 'By the way,' Maclean cautioned his
fiancée,

> the 'M.P.' business is a very open thing indeed. Bath is a
> veritable stronghold for the other side, and they only came to
> me again because . . . they could get nobody else. As I live on
> forlorn hopes, there was, of course, nothing else for me to do
> but take it on once more which I did with no sense of martyr-
> dom or any rot of that kind.[15]

Whatever his subsequent victory owed to his fortitude as a Nonconformist, it owed appreciably less to any assistance he received
from the chief whip.

There ensued a series of colloquies between Gladstone and the
Rev Thomas Law, whom some partisans have cited as the real
architect of the 1906 Liberal triumph.[16] There can be no doubt,
however, that Law was no match for Gladstone, who always got
the better of him. On 11 August, Law proposed names which
Gladstone agreed to consider for possible vacancies. But, on the
morning of 23 September, Law and three other Free Church
leaders (the Revs J. Monro-Gibson, Meyer, and Scott Lidgett)
complained bitterly to Perks 'that Herbert Gladstone had given
them 25 hopeless constituencies to fight with Nonconformist
candidates (if they can be found).' For Rosebery's amusement,
Perks recounted how the four 'reverences' had explained

> that Hartley (a Methodist) has given them £5000 provided I
> will do the same – & they said if I would do this they saw
> their way to another £10,000. I told them . . . that they were
> foolish to take Herbert Gladstone's leavings. . . . They took
> this all in very good part – admitted that they were 'like
> children' at the business, but were supremely anxious to put
> into line all the fighting forces of dissent, and then to see that
> they are not thrown overboard as in 1870 when the battle is
> won.[17]

Rebuffed by Perks, and presumably unable to collect Hartley's
£5000, Law (this time accompanied by the Rev W. J. Townsend)

returned to Gladstone's office, hat in hand. Asked to allocate £25,000 for the promotion of Free Church candidacies, Gladstone 'undertook to contribute' no more than £5000, and that in several instalments. 'Much satisfied with this arrangement,' he minuted, and he had every right to be.[18]

Any evaluation of the Nonconformist electoral effort must take into account the question of Tariff Reform, which intruded in the spring of 1903. Joseph Chamberlain, who soon resigned from the Colonial Office to lead a full-scale crusade for protection, admitted that he had propounded his scheme with a view to winning back support alienated by the government's education policy. As Lord George Hamilton, his erstwhile Cabinet colleague, put it: 'If we had had no Education Bill of 1902, we should have had no Tariff Reform in 1903.'[19] Historians, much like contemporaries, have heatedly debated whether the Liberals owed their eventual success more to enraged Nonconformists or to steadfast Free Traders. The situation is further complicated by the fact that there was considerable overlap between the two groups. For what it was worth, Campbell-Bannerman (who had had the benefit of a conversation with 'a Unionist ex M.P. from Yorkshire') was firmly of the opinion 'that Education is far before Tariffs in the public mind. Tant mieux!'[20]

There was the distinct threat that Chamberlain, himself the product of a dissenting background, might outbid his Liberal rivals for Nonconformist support. In a previous incarnation, 'Radical Joe' had led the assault against the 1870 Education Act. It was not inconceivable that Nonconformists would accept Tariff Reform as the price of his explicit promise to work for a repeal of the 1902 measure. 'Law gave me a hint,' Perks wrote nervously to Rosebery, 'that Chamberlain has been making some overtures to the Free Church Federation re Education of a somewhat advanced nature. Protection & Disestablishment would sound curious.' Not so curious, some Nonconformist leaders might have retorted, as the combination of Free Trade and 'protected' schools. Perks subsequently had good reason to fear that R. J. Campbell, for one, had 'completely gone over to Chamberlain,' who was said to be 'quite ready to give to the Nonconformists what they want.'[21]

The Liberal Party leaders were on the horns of a dilemma. As they perceived it, Chamberlain's latest tack made it both logical and expedient for them to strike an alliance with Free Traders on the Unionist side. But, unfortunately, several of their potential allies were among the most infamous defenders of the Education Act. However dextrous, Liberals could not pick up the support of the Unionist ' Free Fooders' without dropping their Nonconformist parcels. On this score, Perks and Lloyd George stood in rare accord. ' Perks wanted to see me on a proposed agreement with the Duke of Devonshire and the Free Trade Unionists as to the Education Bill,' Lloyd George reported to his wife on 23 December 1903. ' Glad I saw him for we cannot accept their proposals at any price & Asquith – who was prepared to agree – must be stopped at once.' On the same day, Perks served notice to Rosebery and Asquith that ' it is the bounden duty of the Nonconformists, thru every agency in their power, to oppose every candidate be he Unionist Free Trader or anything else who will not accept our Education policy.'[22]

Herbert Gladstone hoped that Nonconformists might be induced to give ground, but Asquith, who had personal experience to guide him, was doubtful. ' The Nonconformists are in a difficult mood & require special handling,' he observed, sounding more like a future chancellor of the exchequer than like a former Congregationalist. ' They don't sufficiently realise that it is all important to defeat J. C., & for the moment to concentrate on that.' Gladstone broached the subject at a meeting with Law, who would go no further than to say that the case of each candidate ' wd. be considered on its merits. Eg. He wd. support Winston [Churchill] against a Tory,' provided of course that Churchill ' stepped forward on Temperance & on Educn. accepted Public Control & No Tests.' At Gladstone's suggestion, Campbell-Bannerman deputed Bryce (who was warmly remembered as a former president of the Nonconformist Union at Oxford) to ' try to feel the pulse of the Non Cons' and to convince ' Clifford & Co. . . . that this is as much their games as ours '. Bryce accepted the assignment, but not without demur. ' You are right in thinking that they [the Nonconformists] are suspicious,' he told his chief, ' not of you, nor of Spencer (though they don't know him as well as we might wish) but of others in our party: we must therefore be careful not to arouse a suspicion that the N. C. grievance is being sacrificed for the sake of Free Trade. . . . It would not do, when we are going into battle, to blunt the edge of the Puritan sword.' Bryce patiently put the case to Clifford, who consulted ' several friends ' and replied much as one would have predicted: theoretically, Nonconformists might endorse selected Unionist Free Traders, but on stringent terms that put a formal electoral pact out of the question.[23]

Largely ignorant of these top-level deliberations, Nonconformist candidates prepared for the fray. They were armed with copies of *The Education Act: A Handbook for Free Church Workers*, a primer of facts and figures culled by Law from the *Daily News* and published under the imprint of the National Council of Evangelical Free Churches.[24] In the closing days of 1903, Fred Horne, Silvester's brother, made an unsuccessful attempt to revive Liberal traditions in the Ludlow division of Shropshire. It was not a constituency in which Nonconformity ran particularly strong, but Horne, a local farmer, was virtually the only man both willing and able to take the field. Perhaps he and his sponsors anticipated an overspill from the Welsh revival.

Fired with enthusiasm, Free Church spokesmen assured an incredulous Gladstone that even Rutlandshire, where no Liberal had stood in the last four general elections, ' can be won on the Educn. question!'[25] Their self-confidence was better justified in the case of several more imminent contests: J. Williams Benn, the son of a Congregational minister, won a seat at Devonport by a majority of 1,040 votes; Philip Stanhope, not himself a Nonconformist, increased the Liberal vote at Harborough in Leicestershire by capitalising on the ' strong feeling in many of the villages about the Education Acts '; and J. S. Higham, a Congregationalist married to the daughter of W. P. Hartley, the Primitive Methodist jam manufacturer, romped home at Sowerby by ' put[ting] the Education Act and its repeal in the front of his election address, and refus[ing] to vote for a Roman Catholic University.'[26]

On 2 February 1905, Jesse Herbert, secretary to the chief whip, calculated that the Liberal Party had won no fewer than sixteen seats and had lost only one since the introduction of the Education Bill. The most recent breakthrough had come at North Dorset, where A. W. Wills had professed ' strong Nonconformist sympathies ' and was accordingly rewarded by the Free Churches with ' substantial aid in canvassing and on the platform.' An even greater upset occurred in April at Brighton, where E. A. Villiers, a renegade from Anglican orders, declared himself ' in favour of vitally amending the Education and Licensing Acts '. The Local Free Church council rendered him strong assistance, and Villiers self-consciously ascribed his surprise victory to ' fear of Protection and the Priest '. His Tory opponent was even more explicit that the ' crusade against the Education Act [was] one of the chief causes of his defeat '. In June, Noel Buxton became the first Liberal to sit for Whitby, his candidacy actively supported by Dr Clifford and the Rev J. Hirst Hollowell. During the same week, the Conservative majority at Chichester was sharply reduced by J. E. Allen. The election committee of the National Free Church Council was gratified to report that its agents

> had been in full evidence at . . . Brighton, Whitby and Chichester. Leaflets had been delivered throughout each constituency and cartoon-posters used in connection with each election. The candidates had testified to the fact that the co-operation of the Free Churches and the help they gave on the Education question had been a powerful factor in the elections.

Within weeks, East Finsbury and Carlisle were both captured from the Conservatives, the former by J. Allen Baker, a Quaker, and the latter by F. W. Chance, whom the Free Church Council had prodded to take a more vigorous stand on the education issue.[27]

Not unnaturally, Free Church activists were inclined to posit a direct correlation between their interventions and Liberal by-election victories. Doubtless there were instances in which they either exaggerated their contribution or purposely overlooked extenuating circumstances. By the same token, there were occasions, which they did not deign to publicise, in which their ' assistance' hurt more than it helped. Steadfastly opposed to Unionist candidates, Free Trade or otherwise, the leaders of militant Nonconformity were seldom machine Liberals. Many celebrated Will Crooks's Labour win at Woolwich, and, less legitimately, claimed a share in the glory. ' In that contest,' the *Crusader* told its readers on 14 March 1903, ' Free Churchmen were well to the fore, and the Education Act went a long way towards that stupendous victory. Of course Dr Clifford had a hand in the fight, as also did Rev John Wilson and many another stalwart.' Some of the more progressive also supported Arthur Henderson, a temperance reformer and Wesleyan local preacher, who stood successfully in July as an Independent Labour candidate against a Liberal at Barnard Castle. The *Methodist Weekly*, the *Primitive Methodist*, and even the *Daily News* endorsed Henderson, none seeing their decision as incompatible with genuine Liberal principles or Nonconformist aspirations. But despite Henderson's personal credentials, it required a feat of imagination to depict the result at Barnard Castle as a credit to Free Churchmanship: the victorious candidate himself drew no such conclusion. There were no fewer than two additional contests in which Nonconformist influence worked, perhaps indirectly to the detriment of official Liberalism: Perks, by his maladroit tactics, was said to have ruined the chances of the Liberal contender at Chertsey in July 1904; and, two months later, Joseph King, a member of the executive of the Liberation Society, failed in his bid to capture the Isle of Thanet by waging a campaign too truculent for the sensibilities of middle-class Kentish electors.

Where did the Nonconformists obtain the funds to carry out their ambitious programme? Financial assistance was required not only by most aspiring candidates, but more desperately by passive resisters, particularly those in Wales, who had to improvise alternative educational facilities for children withdrawn from Anglican schools. 'This we cannot do without money,' Lloyd George reminded Robertson Nicoll, 'and so we propose appealing to the English Nonconformists.' The *Christian World* had initially proposed to raise £50,000, but total receipts fell far short of this goal. On 4 February 1904, Law revealed that £10,629. 6s. 6d. had been pledged, of which only £1566. 9s. 6d. had been collected. Arthur Porritt told the committee that ' as far as the "Christian World" was concerned the fund could not be regarded as having been successful.' Within a fortnight, prospects had improved. George Cadbury, the Quaker cocoa manufacturer, gave £2500 (which he subsequently increased by a further £1000), and Hartley promised ' £5000 if £20,000 were raised or ten per cent on all sums up to £50,000 '. A director of fundraising was appointed at an annual salary of £200, and appeals were henceforth addressed to wealthy individuals instead of to congregations. The response was sufficient to leave a surplus of £836 after all election expenses had been met.[28]

There are also indications that, as the Nonconformists proved their usefulness, the Liberal whip became more open-handed: Gladstone was willing to put up as much as £400 if Silvester Horne, a modern Daniel, could be persuaded to beard the Chamberlain lion in his den at West Birmingham. He was not alone in entertaining such extravagant hopes of the Congregational firebrand. Lloyd George heard secondhand from ' a very cool and experienced Labour man ' in the constituency, who said that, in the event of a Horne candidacy, ' he would not be at all inclined to bet long odds on Chamberlain's victory. The Nonconformist and Labour votes are both powerful there, and combined could carry the decision.' Horne's ultimate failure to stand has been variously ascribed to the opposition he met from either the London Congregational Union or the local Liberal association. Yet he was undeniably tempted by the prospect of a parliamentary career, which he launched elsewhere in January 1910.[29]

The longer Balfour clung to office, the greater the likelihood that the Nonconformist offensive would lose steam or turn against its Liberal auxiliaries. One may safely assume that such possibilities entered directly into his calculations. Admittedly, his 1904 licensing proposals – scorned by the *Crusader* as ' the Brewers' Endowment Bill ' – intensified Nonconformist hostility to the Unionist government. But, throughout 1905, the Nonconformist-Liberal coalition was subjected to increasing strain, which in turn threatened to create rifts between one section of Nonconformists and another. J. F. Cheetham, a Methodist trying to tip the scale in a January by-election at Stalybridge, complained to Bryce that the party's official line on education was costing him support. Might he perhaps ' hint at exceptional treatment for Catholics and Jews?' Bryce vetoed the idea, but, writing to Gladstone, betrayed a consciousness of the responsibilities that would soon devolve upon him: ' Whatever course we may ultimately have to take, promises made now would make great trouble with the N.C.s. . . . They would think we were deserting them.'[30]

Lloyd George, another Liberal politician on whom Free Churchmen relied, was even more intoxicated by the scent of impending office. Seeking to protect and, at the same time, to extend his base of political operations, he was subject to diverse pressures to negotiate a settlement to the education dispute. Some of his compatriots, while recognising the political advantages to be gained by continuing the struggle, concluded that the price was too high:

Meanwhile the Educational Machinery is thrown into chaos, the interests of children and teachers are wantonly sacrificed, and, worst of all, the very existence of any religious instruction

E

in day schools is endangered. . . . The Lloyd George policy threatens to bring the Liberal Party into disrepute with all those serious minded Nonconformists who value daily religious instruction for their children & who feel that the Bible must be the root and soil of a real education.[31]

Such misgivings were felt most acutely among the Calvinistic Methodists, whom Lloyd George – perhaps taking his in-laws as prototypes – adjudged ' on the whole a Conservative force in the Nonconformist life of Wales '.[32]

In March 1904, Lloyd George communicated to a meeting of top-ranking Free Churchmen the terms of an ' educational compromise ' which he had worked out with the Bishop of St Asaph. Perks angrily denounced it as ' a surrender that would take the heart out of the Dissenters,' and he reported that the others – including Joseph Compton-Rickett, Albert Spicer, Percy Bunting, Dr John Massie, Clifford, and Townsend – ' all agreed with me.'[33] Lloyd George was discouraged but not deterred. On 13 December, he informed Herbert Lewis, his parliamentary sidekick, that he ' had just been on the telephone ' with J. H. Yoxall, a Wesleyan member whose stand against passive resistance had put him ' in hot water with the Nonconformists at Nottingham.' Yoxall, who lamented ' that the chances of his retaining his seat are rather meagre,' proposed ' a bargain ': he would support any accommodation which Lloyd George might reach, in return for Lloyd George's promise to ' go down to speak for him ' at Nottingham. ' The worst of it,' Lloyd George confided to Lewis, ' is [that] the Free Church Council will be disappointed. Law, especially, . . . is keen for a row.'[34] All the same, he accepted the challenge. A few weeks later, he gave his compromise formula a second airing in the course of an interview with Porritt in the *Christian World*: Nonconformists, he prophesied, would have to make some concession on the vexing question of clerical instruction during school hours, and furthermore could not expect complete redress from any future Liberal administration. His remarks created an uproar he had clearly not expected. On the pretext that he had been misrepresented, he obtained ' clarification ' in the next issue. Porritt, who insisted that Lloyd George had seen (and tacitly approved) a proof of the article, kept his distance from the Welsh Wizard for the next quarter century.[35]

Lloyd George's motives, and certainly his strategy, can perhaps

be better deduced from another interview which he gave on 23
June to officials of the Liberation Society, whom he declined to
satisfy by giving notice of a motion for disestablishment during
the current session. '. . . Such a step,' he explained,

> might suggest the addition of another great question to the
> Liberal Party's programme in the next General Election, and
> might detach some Liberal Churchmen, who resented the
> Education policy of the present Government, and so prevent
> that perfect union of forces which it was hoped to secure.[36]

This parley was testimony to a growing fear in Liberal parliamentary circles that Nonconformists were running away with the
show, and stood to alienate more support than they were capable
of attracting. The chief whip's office, which had never taken
enthusiastically to the idea of trafficking with the Free Churchmen, resented profoundly the way that the Rev Thomas Law
and his ilk arrogated the right to speak for the party. Nonconformists, on the other hand, considered themselves 'the predominant partner in the Liberal firm', and uniquely equipped 'to
save Liberalism from its peril'.

On 21 September 1905, Perks joined Clifford, Law, and others
at a Cheltenham rally. 'There were 3000 people present,' he
told Rosebery. 'Evidently these worthy Nonconformist divines
mean to give the next Liberal Government a pretty lively time.'[37]
Not that it was seriously threatened that Nonconformists would
gravitate in any number to the other side: although there existed
an agency known as the Nonconformist Unionist Association, the
Unionist chief whip dismissed its members as 'mostly a self
advertising lot'.[38] But, as the general election drew closer, Free
Churchmen let it be known that they were not to be taken for
granted. According to Law, the National Council required 'a
very clear and definite understanding with the Liberal leaders'
on the education problem before it would consent to throw its
weight behind them. And the Liberation Society put the case
directly to 245 Liberal parliamentary candidates in England and
Wales, all of whom professed support for amending the Education Act, and 195 of whom proclaimed themselves in favour of
the principle of disestablishment.[39]

In October, the Congregational Union met at Leeds, and
delegates divided their time between the sessions there and the
by-election campaign nearby at Barkston Ash. Silvester Horne,

possibly breaking his own record, delivered fifteen speeches in a few days, five of them from Liberal Party platforms. ' Let the Liberal leaders go back on their word in regard to the [Education] Act,' he warned, ' and I for one will be the first in the new revolt. And if we leave the ship because she has turned back on her course, . . . we will fire the torpedo which will blow the Liberal Party sky-high.' The Rev J. H. Jowett, chairman-elect of the Congregational Union, echoed these sentiments : ' Freedom of Trade is important,' he acknowledged, ' but it is infinitely more important that we should have free communion with the Highest without the intervention of any priest.' Horne subsequently revealed that he and Jowett received ' some mild rebukes ' for the ' threats ' they had uttered at Leeds, but he insisted that it would do the Liberal leaders no harm to hear the truth : ' . . . To be forewarned is to be forearmed.' Clifford, too, saw no need to mince words. Although he welcomed Campbell-Bannerman's ' lucid and decisive ' statement on 16 November, he deplored the fact that ' there are some Liberals so faithless to the central principle of Liberalism as actually to say that the Roman Catholics must have preferential treatment.'[40]

Barkston Ash, which the Liberals had previously contested only twice, was a great victory. In Lloyd George's opinion, the Education Act ' did more to win [it] . . . than any other single cause '.[41] The Free Church performance was notably more restrained at Hampstead, which the Tories held in November with a diminished majority. Local factors were largely responsible, but the estrangement between party and Nonconformist leaders played its part. As the days passed, it became increasingly probable that Balfour intended to resign office, leaving his Liberal successor with the unenviable task of forming a government before an election. Gladstone, among others, advised Campbell-Bannerman that acceptance of office under such circumstances 'wd. bring upon us all the difficulties which we are entitled to avoid. Labour men, Irishmen, cranks of all sorts, & last but not least the *Noncons* wd. hammer at you & all our candidates to extort their pounds of flesh.' He instructed Robert Hudson, secretary of the Liberal Central Association, to gather opinions from ' 15 or 20 of the most representative men ' who were ' in touch with the constituencies & with the Noncons. . . . The Clifford school I suspect wd. be for acceptance.'[42] In case Nonconformists required any further proof of Gladstone's sentiments, he was heard to speak

of the education question as a ' 2½d. one'. Small wonder that
Clifford admitted to Perks, whom he met at Derby, ' that he
sincerely distrusts Gladstone, & that he believes C. B. will not
go straight on Education.'[43]

To the relief of the ' Clifford school,' Campbell-Bannerman
not only accepted the King's invitation to form a Cabinet, but
also filled a majority of its nineteen places with Nonconformists
of one variety or another. Exactly how many was a moot point:
the Liberation Society counted a total of eleven (' 7 Methodists,
2 Baptists & 2 of the Society of Friends ');[44] the *Free Church Year
Book* counted only ten. Although Free Churchmen had expressed
a preference to have either Bryce or Lloyd George at the Education Office, they were more than satisfied with Augustine Birrell,
a Baptist minister's son who (although few suspected as much)
had lost the habit of chapel-going as an undergraduate at Cambridge. Lloyd George, after a perfunctory reference to Welsh
disestablishment, went to the Board of Trade. Dilke was excluded
on personal grounds, but his Nonconformist critics were allowed
to think that it had been on moral ones. Compton-Rickett, who
advertised his availability for a government post, was solemnly
advised that the Prime Minister would pray for divine guidance;
when his name did not appear in the published lists, Compton-
Rickett had only to conclude that the Almighty had let him down.
Perks, less ambitious for himself than for other Liberal Imperialists, congratulated Campbell-Bannerman on assembling ' a very
powerful government'. And Clifford, unable to contain his enthusiasm, exclaimed ' I almost feel as if I were in the Cabinet
myself.'[45] There was something pathetic about the tendency of
Nonconformist spokesmen to embrace Cabinet ministers as fellow-
communicants : Asquith, Birrell, Burns, Haldane, and even
Morley showed up on various lists of ' Free Church statesmen.'
Obviously, they felt less compunction to scrutinise confessional
loyalties than to assert vicariously their own importance as against
that of a hegemonic Establishment.

Gladstone need not have worried. Nonconformists had waited
too long to stint their labours. ' The opportunity of the Passive
Resister and the Free Churchman has come!' the *Crusader*
trumpeted on 14 December. Everything depended on the Government's amassing a majority ' absolutely independent of Unionist
and Irish votes'. Sir Edward Grey, who usually held aloof from
domestic controversy, shared the ' hope [that] . . . the size of the

majority . . . will be large enough to carry a reform of the Education Act; if we aren't strong enough to do that we shall do very little good.'[46] To this end, the National Council of Free Churches implemented plans that had been held in readiness for years. Its fifty-one district federations and nearly 900 local councils were hives of activity. There were conferences and demonstrations in virtually every major city. Some of the most celebrated names in Nonconformity took to the road on motor tours; in the more remote villages, their disembodied voices were heard giving ' phonographic speeches . . . supplied . . . through the Federations '. Quantities of literature were distributed by local councils, which assisted in canvassing. ' The contribution of the Free Churches is magnificent in its scope of public spirit,' the *Daily News* wrote on 6 January 1906. ' It is not only the Education Act that will be discussed. The message will also include a statement of the entire case for a purer, better informed, less unscrupulous national life.'

There were some Nonconformist clergymen who thought that the pulpit and denominational press had become too blatantly partisan, and that the National Council had been reduced to ' an adjunct of the Liberal Party '.[47] Their complaints were not wholly without foundation. Reports proliferated of ' unscrupulous ' divines who led their congregations in prayer for the defeat of sinful Tories, and who proclaimed that ' in voting for the Liberal . . . electors would be voting for Christ Himself.' Still, as one historian has cogently argued, Nonconformists' ' passionate moral fervour exalted the election more than their bigotry sullied it.'[48] To what degree, if any, did either their fervour or their bigotry have an effect?

It is understandable that Free Churchmen should assign them-selves credit for singlehandedly delivering the massive Liberal majority. ' It may be said,' Birrell wrote with philosophic detach-ment, ' that just as Free Traders are perhaps too apt to attribute all increase of material prosperity to the open market and to forget railways and electricity, so the zealous Christian sometimes places to the credit of his faith the whole of the humanitarian move-ment.'[49] To some extent, Nonconformists were encouraged in their self-delusion by Tariff Reformers, anxious to divert attention from the adverse electoral effect of their own doctrines. While it is clear that Nonconformist militancy was only one of several factors that fortuitously coalesced to produce the 1906 result, it cannot be denied that Nonconformists infused the campaign with a moral fervour, giving secular issues an evangelical appeal that proved irresistible. Free Trade, for example, was espoused not so much as an economic theory as an article of faith; the transportation of Chinese 'coolies' to the Transvaal was decried as an affront to God, who had presumably reserved South Africa for free white labour; and, not least of all, the 1902 Education Act was attacked on neither pedagogic nor administrative grounds, on either of which it was eminently defensible, but essentially on spiritual ones.

Regarding the outcome in certain areas – Wales, the West Riding, and Northumbria – as 'a foregone conclusion', the National Council concentrated its effort 'upon the weaker places'. Occasionally, the results were negligible. Accompanied by the Rev J. D. Jones, Silvester Horne conducted a motor tour through Buckinghamshire, Shropshire, and East Anglia, speaking on behalf of many candidates, not one of whom managed to win. In the Birmingham area, which was Chamberlain's fief, the Unionists professed abiding sympathy for Nonconformist grievances and held their ground. It has been said that the Liberals owed their phenomenal success in Lancashire to Free Trade, which they emphasised to the virtual exclusion of other issues; but Nonconformist spokesmen there pointed proudly to the fact that A. A. Haworth, 'the only out-and-out evangelical Free Churchman in the field,' garnered a majority at Manchester South that exceeded any other in the city. F. E. Smith, who successfully defended the Unionist interest in the Walton division of Liverpool, was (for quite different reasons) equally critical of the view that Free Trade had been decisive: 'He had heard the majority on the other side of the House described as the pure fruit of the Cobdenite tree,' he taunted in a brilliant maiden speech. 'He should say they were begotten by Chinese slavery out of passive resistance.'[50]

Elsewhere, the Nonconformist achievement was incontestable. Donald Maclean, in another maiden speech, legitimately claimed to have 'had a great deal to do' with the Liberal campaign in the West of England, and felt 'sure that had it not been for the education question we should not have had such a large majority in that part of the country'. The Rev G. Campbell-Morgan toured the eastern counties and Lincolnshire with Dr Clifford, and, in 'four-and-twenty years . . . of religious campaigning' had never experienced anything 'more deep and remarkable'. (Clifford seems to have been equally impressed with the automobile, in which he gamely rode for the first time.) The Liberals swept all but two of the seats in the area. Perks did comfortably at Louth: ' The Anglican clergy, and the Roman Catholics made a dead set at me,' he boasted to Rosebery, ' otherwise my majority would have been 1500.' Hull and Spalding gave particular satisfaction to the Passive Resistance League. Richard Winfrey, a self-styled ' political Dissenter ' and another passive resister, became the first Liberal to sit for South West Norfolk. And, more astoundingly, the eccentric Arnold Lupton was returned at Sleaford. ' We didn't win it,' Lupton's agent told those who proffered congratulations; ' it was an act of God.'[51]

The situation in and around London had greatly changed since 1885, when party professionals had taken the view that, in the metropolitan boroughs, ' the Church could beat the noncons out of the field.'[52] The *Daily News* religious census for London (published on 9 July 1903), which otherwise offered little satisfaction to religious authorities, ascertained that the Established Church led in sabbath attendances ' with a bare total of 15,000 over the combined Nonconformist Churches.' The same year, London, which had hitherto enjoyed exemption from the provisions of the recent Education Act, was subject to supplementary legislation which Lloyd George thought ' altogether worse than 1902.'[53] As signalled by the action of the President of the Baptist Union, a former Unionist who signed the nomination papers of the Liberal candidate at Islington, London Nonconformity swung solidly behind the Liberal Party and its Labour allies.

It was the authoritative opinion of C. F. G. Masterman, who entered Parliament as Liberal member for West Ham North, that protection was probably not ' in any degree responsible for the winning of London.'[54] During the 1906 campaign, the Metropolitan Free Church Federation was unremittingly active, drawing its support from 843 chapels organised into 65 local councils. Gipsy Smith had been conducting missions in the weeks that preceded polling, and the revivalist spirit ran strong. In addition to Horne and Clifford, there were a number of Radical divines, including the Revs Charles Ensor Walters, Alexander Connell, and Thomas Phillips. Whitefield's Mission, where the *Crusader* and the *Signal* had their editorial offices, attracted thousands to its open meetings. A virtual campaign headquarters, it was the scene of frenzied jubilation on the night that the first returns poured in.[55]

By attracting countless middle-class Nonconformists back to the Liberal fold, the education issue ' helped to turn the balance in many [London] constituencies, and, in a few, such as Brixton, East Islington and North Hackney,' provides ' the most convincing explanation for the Conservative defeat.'[56] Whitefield's took an especially keen interest in the contest at South St Pancras, a constituency which the *Daily Mail* had had the effrontery to label a ' Tory pocket borough.' The Liberal candidate was P. W. Wilson, the labour (and subsequently parliamentary) correspondent for the *Daily News*, who belonged to Horne's congregation and contributed his journalistic talents to the *Signal*. There were an estimated 2000 electors in the district who had sat out the previous general election, and Wilson's goal was to win them back to Liberalism. The pundits gave him little chance, but he confounded them with a majority of 61. ' I could have fought Wilson,' his defeated opponent stated, ' but I could not fight Whitefield's.'[57]

When the dust had settled, somewhere between 180 and 200 Nonconformists had been elected, not a few to their own astonishment. They could not agree among themselves on an exact number: some included Unitarians and/or Scottish Presbyterians in their tallies; most chose to ignore the presence of a half dozen or so dissenters, mostly Unitarians and Wesleyans, on the Unionist side. Arthur Porritt, who based his count in the *Christian World* on a questionnaire he had addressed only to prospective Liberal and Labour candidates, acknowledged the imperfections of his method: ' Men who had always relied on their wives' church membership to get them into heaven woke up to the political advantage for the moment of having some slender link with Methodism, or Congregationalism, or Presbyterianism.'[58] Nevertheless, Porritt's figures are as good as any and better than most. All that he – or anyone – could say with precision was that fifteen passive resisters and 83 members of the Liberation Society had won seats.

The return of a sizable phalanx of Free Church M.P.s had been assumed. Sixty-five Nonconformists were defending English or Welsh seats which they (or, in a few cases, their party) had won in the 1900 general election or in by-elections since. With few exceptions, these constituencies were classified by the chief whip[59] as ' certain wins ', and were located in the traditional areas of Nonconformist electoral strength. The most remarkable results were achieved by Nonconformist candidates who were not incumbents. Porritt put their number at 112, or whom 55 (including all five who stood in Wales) were reckoned by Gladstone to have an even chance or better: 'certain win', 'probable win', or, most usually, 'possible win'. Of the remaining 57, eight do not appear in Gladstone's forecast: six candidates for Scottish or Irish seats, and, inexplicably, two contenders in England. Seventeen Nonconformist challengers were given an 'off chance' of success, seven were regarded as probable losers, and twenty-five were written off as certain casualties.

Gladstone, however skilfully he managed other aspects of the campaign, wholly failed to anticipate the Nonconformist performance. Thirty Free Churchmen, whose candidacies he had dismissed more or less as exercises in futility, won majorities, some of them quite respectable; they included no fewer than ten of the twenty-five from the 'certain loss' category. The achievement may be better appreciated if one considers that forty per cent of Nonconformist candidates in this bottom group attained success, as compared to only twenty-two per cent of other 'certain loss' Liberals, who won in eighteen of the remaining 81 contests. Was it the case that these Free Church hopefuls were simply carried along by the Liberal landslide, or do they deserve credit for helping to create that landslide? Would they have offered themselves, sometimes standing where no Liberal had previously dared, without an indomitable belief in the righteousness of their cause? Who, save other Free Churchmen, would have given them the necessary financial and moral support? Could they have roused the electorate with anything less than their messianic zeal?

'We have been put into power by the Nonconformists,' averred Campbell-Bannerman.[60] Making due allowance for the fact that he was attempting to fend off an importunate Roman Catholic prelate, his statement carries a fair measure of conviction. Admittedly, the Liberal Party would have enjoyed a comfortable majority without thirty some odd additional backbenchers, and Free Church leaders would have been no less entitled to boast that the 1906 Parliament contained a greater number of chapel-goers than any since the days of Oliver Cromwell. But the parliamentary party would have differed in spirit and, to some extent, in social composition without the membership of men whose own inconceivable success inspired the belief that the Fifth Monarchy was near at hand. Among Labour as well as Liberal M.P.s the Nonconformist ethic predominated, a fact that helps to explain not only the policies which were thereafter pursued, but also many of the difficulties that were encountered.

4 *Pilgrims' Progress*

'There is no getting away from the fact', Edwin Montagu rebuked H. H. Asquith, who had committed the indiscretion of inviting a lady of dubious virtue to a Downing Street reception, 'that ours is a Nonconformist Party, with Nonconformist susceptibilities and Nonconformist prejudices.'[1] The point was no less well taken in that it was made by a lapsed Jew to a Congregationalist who had come a long way from his antecedents. What, however, did it mean in concrete political terms?

During the 1906 political campaign, the assurance of victory had induced Radical Nonconformity to subordinate, if not ignore, its differences with official Liberalism. After a decade in the political wilderness, the promised land at last seemed to lie within reach, and it was not to be jeopardised by continued wrangling. If Liberal Imperialists consented to make common cause with 'Little Englanders', and Cobdenites with social reconstructionists, it was only to be expected that Nonconformists, too, should clamber aboard the bandwagon. Yet, like other factions, they did so with profound apprehension about some of their fellow passengers.

The ardour with which they promoted Liberal candidacies ought not to obscure the fact that Free Church leaders bestowed their blessing selectively, and often with gnawing doubts. Writing in the *Primitive Methodist Leader* on 23 November, when the general election was 'at the doors', Dr John Clifford candidly assessed the situation:

> If only the demon of division can be kept out of the constituencies, the Progressives, composed of Labour representatives and Liberals, will be returned with an overwhelming majority . . . independent of that Irish party to whose action on a critical occasion we owe the iniquitous Education Act.

That being so, the new Government will have to deal with the Education Act at a very early juncture. It is to be its first *real* business. . . . But how far they will travel towards a completely satisfactory and final settlement of the points which most dearly concern Passive resisters, will depend upon the democratic forces behind them. . . . Nor may we forget that Liberalism has never dealt firmly and frankly with this subject of sectarianism in Education. Its history is a history of compromises and concessions. . . .

Paradoxically, Liberalism's spectacular success at the polls created precisely those conditions and attitudes which Clifford had most wished to avoid. The very size of the parliamentary Liberal party gave licence to its discordant elements, at the same time that it encouraged a spirit of intransigence on the part of the hereditary Unionist majority in the House of Lords. Both developments hamstrung the government, necessitating further ' compromises and concessions ' at the expense of vital Nonconformist interests.

On the face of things, the position of Nonconformity in the 1906 Parliament was unassailable. Approximately 200 Free Churchmen – outnumbering the Unionists in the House – packed the Liberal back benches. All of them were *de facto* members of the Nonconformist Parliamentary Council (or Committee), which R. W. Perks had been instrumental in founding in 1898. Perks was inclined to glorify this agency, to ascribe to it credit for amending the Burials Act and other miscellaneous pieces of legislation, and, not least of all, to exaggerate his own influence in it. ' This group of members ', he later proudly recalled, ' was the mouthpiece of political Nonconformity not merely at Westminster but throughout the country. Moreover they had powerful allies in the London and Provincial Press.' When he retired from parliamentary life in 1910, Asquith reportedly told him : ' Perks, I am thankful you have left the House of Commons. With those 200 Nonconformist M.P.s behind you we never knew where we were.'[2] If the story is to be believed, it proves only that Asquith, elevated to the premiership two years earlier, had lost neither his sense of humour nor his measure of Perks's vanity.

The truth of the matter was that the Nonconformist Parliamentary Committee never justified Perks's expectations, let alone Asquith's alleged fears. Unlike the Liberal Unionists, the Irish Nationalists, or the Labour men, its members did not sit together in the Commons chamber. Nor did they cohere in the lobbies. On 25 February 1910, a newly-elected 'Baptist M.P.' revealed the fiction to readers of the *Baptist Times*:

> The number of Nonconformists in the last Parliament was vastly over-rated, many who were claimed as such were Nonconformists only in name, and during the whole four years took absolutely no part in helping the work of the Nonconformist Committee. The denominational papers bragged of 200, but of these, I am told, not more than seventy or eighty at most could be relied upon.

Perks, by exercising a proprietary right over the committee, doubtless helped to reduce its active membership and inhibit its performance. In the wake of the 1906 election, a concerted attempt was made to push him aside. 'Compton-Rickett, George White, & (in some degree) Albert Spicer were at the bottom of this little intrigue,' he wrote bitterly to Lord Rosebery. 'My friends told me that they feared my " Imperialism ". What that has to do with the business I don't know.' As the weeks passed, he detected signs that the plot had been masterminded by Herbert Gladstone, who was acting through Compton-Rickett and J. A. Pease, a Quaker M.P. and future chief whip. Unable to evict Perks from the chair, they tried ' to frustrate my plan of an active committee of 20, & lastly to get control of the Secretariat. I am glad to say that on all 3 points I have beaten them.'[3] So long as Perks sat in the House, he could not be dislodged. Yet his experience testified to the antagonisms that prevailed within his ' Council of Two Hundred ', as well as between it and the party leadership.

It is difficult to feel sorry for Perks, an arch intriguer who was only getting a taste of his own medicine. One cannot, however, consider his predicament apart from that of political Nonconformity as a whole. In the aftermath of the general election, various attempts were made to neutralise or rechannel the Free Church agitation, which had recently proved a boon to the Liberal Party and now quickly threatened to become an embarrassment. Standing at North Bristol, Augustine Birrell, the new minister for education, had made some casual pronouncements which received wider coverage and elicited more vehement protest than he had anticipated. At its first post-election meeting, the general committee of the National Council of Evangelical Free Churches heard from the Rev Thomas Law that he was 'constantly receiving' communications from local affiliates 'calling attention to Mr Birrell's speeches on Education and stating that these speeches had caused great uneasiness in the country'. On behalf of the Liberation Society, Dr John Massie (newly elected as M.P. for Cricklade in Wiltshire) wrote to Birrell, 'giving him a word of warning' that 'nothing mischievous' would be tolerated. 'I am surprised', confessed Perks, who was preoccupied with his own troubles, 'to find that Dr Clifford, Lidgett, & the Noncon. leaders are by no means sure of the treatment they will get.'[4]

The 'Noncon. leaders' had their answer on 9 April, when Birrell introduced an Education Bill that left them divided and, on the whole, profoundly disappointed. The system laid down by Balfour's 1902 Act was modified in detail, but not in essentials: the Anglican and Roman Catholic churches were still permitted to make limited use of 'ordinary facilities' in the rural districts, and might take advantage of 'extended facilities' in those urban districts where four-fifths of the parents requested them. Containing a proposal for a separate council to co-ordinate educational policy in Wales, the Bill went further to allay discontent in that part of the kingdom than elsewhere. J. H. Jowett, who had uttered dire threats at the previous Congregational Union, was incensed: 'It was not the Bill he expected, nor the Bill for which Free Churchmen had been struggling.' Passive resisters, encouraged by the Liberal landslide to relax their efforts, considered themselves betrayed. Scott Lidgett, not himself a passive resister, invited Lloyd George to a meeting of the National Council executive at the Memorial Hall, where Clifford wanly defended the proposed compromise, and J. Hirst Hollowell railed against it. With all the casuistry at his disposal, Lloyd George managed to head off a resolution condemning the Bill. 'What a strategist you are!' Scott Lidgett whispered to his guest, who repaid the compliment in kind: 'Yes, and so are you, or you would not have seen it.'[5]

Dissatisfaction with the measure was not confined to a few English divines. On his way to a Cabinet meeting, Lloyd George was handed a letter from Herbert Lewis, who reported intense anxiety in the lobby on the eve of the Bill's promulgation:

I heard a man express what I think is the general feeling when he said, speaking of the safeguards for denominationalism which are talked of, ' If we are to be asked to do the dirty work of the Tory party in the House of Lords, we may as well leave the job alone.' This sort of feeling is not merely entertained by the Nonconformists in the House. It is held even more strongly by many Churchmen who know the feeling of their Nonconformist supporters.

Whatever happens the introduction of the Bill must not be the signal of agitation against the Government by its staunchest, most strenuous and most self-sacrificing supporters. . . . Standing as I do at the mouth of the crater, I can hear ominous rumblings which portend a disastrous eruption if the Bill is unsatisfactory.[6]

Birrell soon received the same admonition from Hirst Hollowell, who particularly condemned the failure to repeal the infamous fourth clause of the 1902 Act:

Clause iv. sacrifices Nonconformists who did largely get the Government in, to Lancashire Catholics, who did not. Free Trade and resentment against the Balfour Act aroused and carried Lancashire. Free Trade will be here next election, but if Clause iv. is forced upon us, Nonconformist enthusiasm will have been killed. . . . We love the Government, but we cannot bear to see it make a worse mistake than was made in 1870.[7]

Obviously, Liberal policymakers were not unaware of the resentment that emanated from the back benches and from many leading pulpits. Why, then, did they elect to persevere with the measure? For one thing, they felt obliged to produce quickly an education scheme, however slightly it improved upon the previous one. For another, they believed that they could capitalise on a fund of Nonconformist goodwill that had been denied to their Tory predecessors. Their confidence was proved justified by the action of the general body of the Three Denominations, which accorded the Bill its ' general approval', and trusted to see ' amendments' which would restore the *ad hoc* principle & remove tests from training Colleges & introduce modifications in Clause 4 '.[8] Clifford and Horne each took a similar position, the latter writing in the *British Congregationalist* (2 August 1906):

We like Clause Four as little as ever – as little, we fancy, as [Birrell] does himself – but we have no manner of doubt that the Bill as it stands marks an enormous educational advance, and hastens the day when the nation will be mistress in her own schools.

With a few prominent exceptions, Congregational leaders adopted the same posture for which they had previously taken Wesleyans to task: 'Nonconformists . . . will do well to remember', the same journal pontificated in a leader of the following week,

> that, though they are among the most numerous of the Government's supporters, that does not give them the right to direct the policy of the country in their own interests. Their aim should not be religious privilege for themselves, but religious equality for all. Some of them would be none the worse for a few lessons in the higher patriotism.

Perhaps, like Balfour in 1902, Birrell and his Cabinet colleagues were persuaded that the Nonconformist opposition would soon exhaust itself. If so, it is easy to see how they were misled. ' Have you any feeling that people are getting sick of the Education Bill, and that the Government will suffer neither for the goodness nor the badness but for the abhorred presence of the thing?' Principal James Denny asked William Robertson Nicoll in June. ' The poor Government', he went on, ' are much to be pitied when friends and foes conspire to prevent them from acting on principle, and then unite to denounce their unprincipled action.'[9] J. D. Jones, without going nearly so far as Denny to exonerate the government, saw in retrospect that Free Churchmen had weakened their cause by trusting too blindly, if not to politicians, then to fate: ' That is not because we have acquiesced in the provisions of the 1902 Act ', he maintained,

> it is not because we have ceased to resent its injustices, it is because we believed time was on our side & that slowly but surely all schools would come under popular control & sectarian tests for the teachers would consequently disappear.[10]

For whatever reason, Free Churchmen unwittingly helped to create the impression, even among themselves, that their demands could be discounted with impunity by a Liberal administration.

Before political Nonconformity could divide irretrievably against itself and against the government, the Unionist majority in the House of Lords lumbered to its rescue. In the course of its stormy passage through the upper house, Birrell's Bill

F

was amended beyond recognition. Its Free Church critics and defenders were equally outraged. The question was no longer whether the Bill had been satisfactory, but whether an assembly of territorial and (still worse) ecclesiastical magnates possessed the constitutional right to overrule the policies adopted by the accredited representatives of the nation. 'The fight must come ', vowed Horne, who conveniently forgot the immediate issue, ' and when it does come it will reunite all the forces of progress and exhibit to the full the enthusiasm and energy which only a great cause can generate.' The general body of the Three Denominations was no less relieved to widen the scope of the debate : its committee met on 5 December to adopt unanimously a resolution ' declin[ing] to recognise the right of spiritual & temporal peers, constituting an unrepresentative House, to set aside the mandate of the people so strongly pronounced at the last general election '.[11]

Nonconformist spokesmen, like Cabinet ministers, could not agree on the next step to be taken. Some of the more weary favoured an inter-party compromise, which might yield a measure of relief from the disabilities of the 1902 Act. Most, however, stood firm, seeking to precipitate a constitutional showdown in order either to save the present Bill or to clear the way for a more comprehensive measure. Perks heard with mixed feelings ' that the Prime Minister means to support the Noncon position on the Education Bill, & to reject the Lords amendments en bloc '. The worst that could happen, in his opinion, would be for Campbell-Bannerman to dissolve Parliament and go to the country over the fate of a Bill which ' is hated by the Noncons ' and ' creates no enthusiasm . . . even among Liberals. . . . If there were an appeal to the electors ', Perks predicted, ' the Free Church Ministers would refuse to take the field.'[12]

Lloyd George, certainly no friend of aristocratic privilege, wished to sacrifice neither the Bill nor the government to which he belonged. He recounted to Herbert Lewis, with whom he enjoyed ' a walk along the Plage ' at Biarritz on 29 December, ' that, when the Cabinet recently considered the position as to the Education Bill, Burns made a speech advocating complete surrender '. Lloyd George, by his own telling, was stung into delivering ' the only formal speech he had ever made in the Cabinet '. Lewis dutifully recorded a transcript :

I did not threaten to resign, I have never done that. I spoke quietly but as gravely and impressively as I could, and they saw I meant it. I recalled the action of the Cabinet in 1870 and reminded them that although the Government survived until 1874 there was no life in it and that it was the defection of the Nonconformists which chiefly caused its ruin at the polls. At this a vehement ' hear! hear!' came from C.B. and I then remembered that part he had played in 1874. They (members of the Cabinet) were rather apt to run down the Nonconformist leaders and to regard them as extreme and impracticable men, and I told them that I had been in touch with them all along, that they were not merely interested in Education from the Nonconformist point of view, but were Liberals, keenly anxious that the Government should live, and that the Government had no more loyal supporters.

This carried the Cabinet, and from that time on there was no question of surrender. If I had not made that speech they would have given way all along the line on the question of the teachers.

A question subsequently arose as to the nomination of a member of the Cabinet to negotiate with Balfour. The Chancellor of the Exchequer (Asquith) was named, but I was determined that he should feel he was suspect, so I said, ' No, I suggest the Foreign Secretary '. Asquith turned round to me with a smile and said, ' You are afraid that I shall give way on the question of the teachers '. ' That is just what I am afraid of ', I said. The result was that in the negotiations, Grey fought hard on the question of the teachers. He had previously been willing to give way (and the Chancellor heartily agreed with him) to the extent of allowing all the teachers to give denominational education, which would have been absolutely fatal to us.[13]

Lloyd George's seaside testimony, intended as much to regale as to impress Lewis, offers some illuminating sidelights: one is usefully reminded of Campbell-Bannerman's Radical sentiments, and of both the difference in outlook and the candour that characterised Lloyd George's official relations with Asquith; one can also discern the basis of Lloyd George's emergence as the foremost parliamentary spokesman of Nonconformity.

The private negotiations with Balfour, which the government had undertaken with Lloyd George's sanction, led nowhere.

On 17 December, their lordships voted by a majority of 152 to 53 to uphold their amendments. The Prime Minister, seeing no alternative, allowed Birrell's Bill to perish ignominiously. In later years, it became common practice for Nonconformists to blame the House of Lords, that bastion of Anglican privilege, for killing the 1906 Education Bill and thereby denying them the prize for which they had fought. In point of fact, conspicuously few of them mourned the measure at the time of its demise, and many confessed to feelings of intense relief. The ' Rev T. Law & Co.' had all along proclaimed their displeasure with the Bill, displeasure intensified but not created by the Lords' amendments. When the Bill was finally withdrawn, ' scores of Noncon M.P.s ' confided to Perks that they were glad to be relieved of the obligation to vote for it. Although Perks disapproved of their compliance, he could appreciate their predicament: ' The Government whips have stooped to some rather low tricks to break up our Noncon. group ', he informed Rosebery, to whom he enumerated cases in which backbenchers had been threatened with retribution if they failed to toe the party line.[14]

Without achieving tangible results in terms of legislation, the 1906 struggle had far-reaching effects. On the secular side, it foreshadowed the constitutional conflict of 1909–11, in which Free Churchmen now had a vested interest. In the religious sphere, it exacerbated a variety of tensions: between Nonconformists, who thoroughly identified with the rights of the Commons, and Anglicans, whose prelates sat ostentatiously in the Lords; between Nonconformists and Roman Catholics, who had used their entrenched position in the upper house to oppose the Bill; and between left-wing Nonconformists and Wesleyans, who, as a rule, had shied away from the fight. A ' Bothered Brother ' wrote indignantly to the *British Congregationalist* on 18 October about the utter impossibility of cooperation with ' High Church ' Wesleyans, whose attitudes differed so markedly from those of Baptists, Primitive Methodists, and Congregationalists. On 13 December, the editor of the same journal inveighed against those, outside as well as inside the Established Church, who were ' tied to an unprogressive theology ', and whose servitude to ' medieval doctrine ' rendered them ' impotent against the Romanists '. A convenient scapegoat was found in Thomas Lough, the Wesleyan M.P. for West Islington who served as undersecretary to Birrell at the Education Office, and whose few interventions in debate had been singularly ineffective.

Lough, despite truculent demands for his removal, retained his place for the duration of Campbell-Bannerman's premiership. But Birrell was soon transferred to the Irish Office, where he replaced Bryce, who was dispatched to Washington as ambassador. His successor at the Board of Education was Reginald McKenna, a Congregationalist who sat for North Monmouthshire. The *Baptist Times*, reporting the appointment on 1 February 1907, confessed to ' a feeling of surprise and disappointment ': it had hoped for George White, whose nomination ' would have shown that the Cabinet was in earnest on the Education question, and . . . would have recalled and fixed the somewhat wavering allegiance of Nonconformists '. Perhaps, it was reasoned, McKenna's appointment was intended as a sop to Wales, where Nonconformists ' are discontented almost to the point of revolt against the Government ' over disestablishment as well as educational policy.

Angered by the government's pusillanimity, which had been reflected as much in the content as in the treatment of the previous year's Education Bill, Nonconformist leaders were scandalised by intimations that the government contemplated concessions to Ireland before mitigating Free Church grievances. ' The line I am going to take with the Noncons is that Disestablishment must take precedence of Irish R. Catholic reforms ', Perks notified Rosebery. ' I don't think the English or Welsh Dissenters will stand Ireland being thrust into a foremost place this session.'[15]

It was not Perks's style to press too far, especially when he could depend on others to press further. At the start of the new session, the ' extreme left of the Noncons ' in the House ' put down an amendment to the address – in order to extract from the Government their views on Passive Resistance & the administration of the Education Acts '. Disclaiming personal responsibility, Perks defended the move to Sir Henry Fowler, the chancellor of the Duchy of Lancaster, to whom he remonstrated

that the Government could hardly expect the Nonconformists to denounce the Lords for rejecting a Bill which they (the Noncons) hated & in proof of this I reminded [him] that not a single Nonconformist, or indeed Liberal organisation, had passed any resolution regretting the failure of the Bill or asking for its reintroduction. C.B. was standing close by & listened carefully to all I said, but I did not address my remarks to him, & he said nothing.[16]

Perks's attention was riveted on the Brigg division of Lincolnshire adjoining his own constituency, where a by-election was scheduled for the first week in March. His ' agent and sub-agents ' reported from Brigg ' that the Wesleyans, who are very strong, would not vote, fearing Home Rule '.[17] They were not mistaken. A Tory was returned on a reduced Liberal vote, and the government was dealt its first clear-cut reverse in a by-election. Richard Winfrey, who sat for South West Norfolk and served as private secretary to the president of the Board of Agriculture, ascribed the defeat at Brigg to the fact that ' Free Churchmen, and especially the Primitive Methodists in the rural districts, are anything but satisfied with the way in which the Government has handled the Education question '.[18]

McKenna inaugurated his brief tenure at the Board of Education by introducing a single-clause Bill designed to relieve local authorities of the cost of religious instruction in non-provided schools. Icily received by all sides, it was not pursued. By early spring, it had become evident that his primary concern was to avoid another confrontation with the House of Lords. The *Daily News* denounced the government's timidity on 14 March and the next day published an appreciative letter from George White, whom many Free Churchmen had favoured for McKenna's job: what the party most urgently required, he agreed, was ' a really bold policy to give it the inspiration which alone can lead to real success ', and he added that ' the rumours as to forthcoming legislation are disquieting '. A few weeks later, the Baptist Union held its annual assembly at the Bloomsbury Central Church. The Rev Samuel Vincent, a former president, moved a resolution that acknowledged McKenna's ' sincere attempt ' to grapple with isolated problems, ' but inasmuch as this measure is only a very partial contribution to a just solution of the Education question ', member churches were urged ' not to relax their efforts '.

Baptist critics of the government received strong and sometimes overpowering support from Primitive Methodists, who were preparing to celebrate their denominational centenary. By 9 May, the *Primitive Methodist Leader* had been ' forced to the conclusion that the clerical influence in the Government is dominant, and that it is adopting the surest way for driving Free Churchmen out of the Liberal Party. We are betrayed again, as in 1870.' During the preceding week, a series of Primitive Methodist district meetings had manifested anti-government sentiments : at Sheffield, for example, Free Church M.P.s ' were subjected to considerable satire on account of their failure to keep the Government up to its pledges at the General Election '; and in the Carlisle and Whitehaven district, the Rev F. E. Thistlethwaite ' raised the meeting to a high pitch of excitement ' by proclaiming ' " There is a limit to the Nonconformists' patience " . . . to which the whole house said " Aye "!' The Rev A. T. Guttery, in his regular column for the *Leader*, asserted that the Prime Minister ' has had our blank cheque long enough and it is quite time that it was dated and made payable '. He plaintively enjoined some Free Church parliamentarian, preferably a Primitive Methodist, to step forward as ' a Nonconformist John Redmond ', which would have made an interesting hybrid. ' One thing is certain ', he concluded, ' and it is that Primitive Methodists all over the country are making up their minds that they will not submit to a regime of disloyalty and fear.'

The *Baptist Times*, usually more circumspect, expressed confidence on 17 May that ' Free Churchmen generally will endorse the attitude already taken up by the Primitive Methodists '. The Rev J. Hirst Hollowell, one of the more militant Congregationalists, took the opportunity to ' congratulate the Primitive Methodist Church on the quickness with which its leaders have discerned the signs of the times '. Rejected by the electors at South Birmingham, he was all the more contemptuous of those who had succeeded, and to no effect. ' We have had to refuse rates ', he wrote to the editor of the *Leader* on the 23rd, ' and now there is every likelihood that we shall have to refuse votes. Men have gone to Parliament in our name who have trifled with our mandate.'

The Nonconformist reaction against the government attained new proportions on 30 May, when the *British Weekly* devoted its frontpage leader, usually reserved for theological subjects, to ' The Losing of the Legions '. Hollowell and Guttery were snipers who often missed their targets, but Robertson Nicoll aimed his artillery with deadly accuracy. ' The Government have reached a very critical stage in their short history,' he began regretfully :

The situation is extraordinary. There are in England about eight million Nonconformists, and it is safe to say that ninety-nine out of every hundred voters among them support the Liberal Party. In the Liberal Associations best known to the present writer, nine out of ten of the active workers are earnest Nonconformists. . . . The Nonconformists constitute the Liberal Party to three-fourths of its extent, but when they raise the party to power the honours and emoluments fall to others. . . . So far as Nonconformity itself is concerned, it may be very gravely doubted whether, since the disestablishment of the Irish Church, any advantage whatever has accrued for it when a Liberal victory was won.

History proves that Liberalism goes under whenever a strong section of Nonconformists revolt. . . .

With a catalogue of extracts from the Free Church press, Nicoll illustrated his point 'that Nonconformists are profoundly dissatisfied with the present Government, and especially with the Education Minister, Mr McKenna'. As he saw it, a large measure of blame attached itself to Nonconformist M.P.s, of whom only 83 out of an approximate total of two hundred took seriously their responsibilities as Free Churchmen. A week later, he fired another salvo, this one aimed at particular ministers – Lloyd George included – who had 'nipped rather than gripped' essential problems. The correspondence columns of the journal overflowed with letters that left no doubt that the editor's views were widely shared.

According to Herbert Lewis, Nicoll's outburst reflected nothing more than that he had suffered a slight from Lloyd George, who had either declined a dinner invitation or, worse, had accepted and then failed to turn up.[19] It is not difficult to credit such an interpretation, given Nicoll's *amour-propre* and his obsessive complaints about the honours list, on which his own name did not appear until 1909. But, whatever Nicoll's motives, his intervention gave force and focus to prevailing discontents.

The stinting nature of McKenna's Bill had inflicted a humiliation that was exceeded only by the circumstances of its retraction. Although Nonconformists had belittled its provisions, they had not wished to surrender without a fight. Nicoll told an anecdote to account for the apparent perversity of their attitude:

A very tyrannical Scottish laird had the most subservient of retainers. Once, at breakfast, the patron remarked that the client had a very bad egg, and tried to take it away. 'Mony thanks, Sir Andrew,' was the reply, 'but I *prefair* them rotten.'

Nonconformist backbenchers decried the perfidy of Cabinet officials, who retaliated by faulting their followers for 'luke warmedness'. Denominational spokesmen were unable to decide which had shown greater weakness, the Liberal Party or the Non-conformist Parliamentary Council. 'Ministerialists who are not Nonconformists', the *Economist* observed on 15 June, 'lay the blame on the Unionist Party, and on the House of Lords'; but that argument did not carry weight in Free Church circles: 'A man may easily be more angry with the friend who leaves him in the ditch than with the enemy who threw him into it.' In effect, there had occurred a complete breakdown in communications between Nonconformist politicians inside and outside the government, and more seriously, between those inside and outside Parliament.

The repercussions were felt almost immediately in the mining constituencies, where Primitive Methodism was congregated. In a July by-election at Jarrow in Durham, local passive resisters re-fused to support S. Leigh Hughes, the Liberal candidate, 'owing to the failure of the Government to go on with Mr McKenna's Bill'. The *British Weekly,* mindful of its reputation, cautiously endorsed Hughes, 'who has never in his voluminous writings, so far as we know, written one word in disparagement of the Non-conformist cause'. But R. J. Campbell, who had joined the Labour Party earlier that year, backed Pete Curran, a socialist of Irish extraction. 'No Government ever began with better pros-pects than the present Liberal administration', Campbell wrote to Ramsay MacDonald,

> but so far its achievements have been poor in comparison with the promises given at the General Election. Old Age Pensions are postponed for the present. Nothing more is to be done for the starving child or the unemployed. We are to hear nothing more of the Miners' Eight Hour Bill or of Education until next year. What is to be done for Temperance nobody knows. The House of Lords is stronger than ever. . . . What is wanted before the next session begins is a large increase in Labour representation. . . . It is no use trusting to either Liberals or Conservatives for measures which will go to the root of the social evils of the day.

Curran triumphed at Jarrow, and Hughes placed a poor third, behind a Tariff Reformer. The *Primitive Methodist Leader* ventured the opinion that passive resisters had voted Labour ' as a protest against the inaction of the Government on the Education question. Other Nonconformists ', it reckoned, ' will no doubt have followed their example.' No one attempted to depict the Free Church contribution to the Jarrow result as more than marginal. That in itself was significant. The contest had been waged almost exclusively on secular lines, much to the advantage of Labour and the consequent detriment of Liberalism. A fortnight later, the pattern was repeated at Colne Valley in Yorkshire, where Victor Grayson, a more incendiary socialist than Curran, captured the seat from the Liberals. The *Baptist Times* confessed to a ' disagreeable surprise ', but the *Primitive Methodist Leader* welcomed Grayson's return as an ' outstanding lesson to ministerialists . . . that they have neither gone far enough nor fast enough to satisfy the country '. At the end of the month, the Liberals fared better at North West Staffordshire, where Albert Stanley trounced a Unionist challenger. But Stanley, it deserves to be pointed out, was himself a Primitive Methodist who eventually defected to Labour.[20]

Coming from humble stock, Primitive Methodists had the most compelling reasons to address themselves to social considerations above strictly religious ones. Then, too, their theology encouraged that tendency. Other sects followed more tentatively along the road to secular politics, some diverging towards Conservatism instead of Labour. This reorientation, which antedated the war, reflected a general loss of self-confidence as well as a disillusionment with traditional electoral alliances. The evangelical revival had proved nearly as ephemeral as Nonconformity's post-election euphoria. According to the statistics which David Caird, the secretary of the Liberation Society, compiled for successive editions of the *Free Church Year Book,* the aggregate of Free Church communicants fell by some 27,000 from 1906 to 1907, and by a further 37,000 in the years between 1907 and 1910. As the war approached, the decline in chapel membership was slowed, but not the decline in Sunday scholars. One may postulate that, just as the Free Churches had attained an unprecedented vitality in conjunction with the Liberal resurgence, their numerical subsidence was in some way correlative with their retreat from Liberalism. By the same token, the shift away from Liberalism was intrinsically linked to the simultaneous attenuation of the evangelical impulse. Without going so far as to suggest that either weakness led inexorably to the other, one may safely conclude that there existed a reciprocity between them.

As usual, Wales reflected the situation most acutely. Here, revivalism had scored its most phenomenal successes, and the ensuing Liberal victory had been unalloyed. But on both the spiritual and political fronts a reaction quickly set in. As early as February 1906, there were disconcerting reports that drunkenness and attendant vices had crept back into the Rhondda valleys; sixteen months later, the Rev Thomas Phillips heard ' from a London layman who has paid a visit to the field of the late Revival . . . that many of the young converts have relapsed, because of the lack of shepherding and care, due to the pachydermatous conservatism of some of the elder brethren '.[21] No less apparent was ' the crumbling machinery of Liberalism in the constituencies ', where there was an increasingly pronounced threat from Labour.[22]

Along with their burning grievance over education, Welsh Nonconformists retained their preoccupation with disestablishment. Again, the government proved unobliging. Instead of introducing legislation, the Prime Minister appointed a royal commission to investigate the problem. D. A. Thomas, the senior member for Merthyr Tydvil (and later Viscount Rhondda), complained that it was taking evidence after the verdict had been given. Although four of the nine places on the commission were allotted to Nonconformists – Samuel Evans, M.P. for Mid-Glamorgan, Principal A. M. Fairbairn, Professor Henry Jones of Glasgow University, and John Williams, a former M.P. and an active Liberationist – there were complaints ' that while a Welsh Church dignitary [Archdeacon Owen Evans] was appointed member, Welsh Nonconformity had no such direct representation '. After six months of fruitless wrangling, Evans, Fairbairn, and Jones resigned.[23]

Lloyd George, who had worked feverishly behind the scenes to save the commission, now redoubled his labours to conciliate opinion outside. He wrote at uncharacteristic length to the Rev H. M. Hughes of Cardiff, whose ' evidence committee ' had urged the Welsh Congregational Union to deny further support to the government until disestablishment had been acted upon. ' . . . If the report is adopted in its present form ', he contended, the Congregationalists will find the following morning that there will be more joy in the camp of the enemy over a report issued by them than over a hundred speeches delivered by Mr Arthur Balfour or a myriad Articles appearing in the ' Daily Mail '. . . . The whole tone, direction, and argument of the report, in so far as it refers to the questions of Disestablishment and Education, [are] calculated to sow distrust and suspicion of the Government in the minds of Nonconformists. . . . Why weaken the hands of the leaders by these petty attacks on what are purely tactical points in the campaign? . . . Can the Congregational Committee not trust them [the Cabinet] that they are doing their best, and that, if they adopt a course which tactically does not seem to the Congregational Committee to be the best, that they may have sound reasons of strategy for doing so?

The president of the Board of Trade tartly reminded his friends ' that the present Prime Minister [had] voted in the House of Commons for Welsh Disestablishment when many of them were sitting on a form at school '. More to the point, he attempted to allay Celtic jealousies with assurances that neither the Scottish Small Holdings Bill nor the Irish Councils Bill had preempted ' the place which ought to have been given to Welsh Disestablishment in the present Session '. In closing, he implored Hughes ' to use your great influence to induce the Congregational Union to pursue the path of restraint '.[24]

Meeting at Neath on 25 June, Welsh Congregationalists discountenanced Lloyd George's appeal. Any misgivings they might have entertained had been dispelled three days earlier, when Campbell-Bannerman flatly informed the Commons that a Bill for disestablishment was not on his agenda for 1908. Josiah Thomas, who took a leading part in the Neath proceedings, revealed that the resolutions had been tempered only to the extent that they spoke of governmental ' slowness ' instead of ' apathy '; but the intention remained firm: ' Disappointment, broken pledges, indifference, and utter ingratitude on the part of a majority of our representatives has caused our hearts to grow sick,' he wrote to the *British Weekly*; ' but Wales will rouse itself once more, not so much Liberal Wales as Nonconformist Wales. . . .' Thomas would presumably have exempted from his censure Ellis Griffith, M.P. for Anglesey, who likewise penned a stinging letter to the *British Weekly*: ' I am fully persuaded that Welsh Nonconformists, and especially Welsh Nonconformist ministers, can even now induce the Government to pass the Welsh Disestablishment Bill through the Commons in this Parliament.' In early September, the Welsh Baptist Union passed resolutions similar to the Congregationalist ones.

None of these developments reflected to the credit of Lloyd George, who was able neither to discipline his troops nor (assuming that he tried) to influence his Cabinet colleagues. Increasingly distrusted, he was put down by Nicoll on 6 June as ' a supremely clever man, with a quite ecclesiastical turn for manoeuvre '. Although the characterisation must have rankled, its validity was confirmed by the speed with which Nicoll was converted from a reproachful critic to a devoted ally. The two men met in early August, ' and had a long conversation . . . on the Welsh and Nonconformist situation. Many correspondents ', Nicoll pointedly revealed, ' had written bitter and abusive letters about L.G. to the British Weekly, but as they did not sign their names for publication he had not inserted the letters.' He professed anxiety ' that the Government should *introduce* the [Disestablishment] Bill during the fourth Session. He . . . would be quite satisfied with that.' But Lloyd George, who gauged more accurately the dimensions of the problem, ' was sure the Nonconformists of Wales would not be satisfied with the mere introduction of the Bill.'[25]

His parley with the editor assured Lloyd George of more favourable treatment in the pages of the *British Weekly*. On 26 September, while absent from the Board of Trade ' on a well earned holiday ', he received belated praise in the ' Notes of the Week ' for his heroic efforts on behalf of disestablishment during the 1892 Parliament. More recently, Lloyd George had ' proved himself an administrator of the first rank '. Perhaps, occasionally, he had ' yielded to the breath of officialism ', but Nicoll was ' convinced that in his inmost heart he is as faithful as ever to the Free Church principles the advocacy of which has made him famous '. The defence came none too soon. The same issue of the *British Weekly* carried the announcement of

a great representative Convention of all the Nonconformist organisations of the Principality to consider the situation, its possible dangers, and the duty of those who have so long relied upon the promises of Liberal leaders for the fulfilment of our national hope.

Summoned to meet at Cardiff on 10 October, the ' Welsh National Convention ' was jointly sponsored by, among others, the Welsh Congregational and Baptist unions, and the general assembly of the Welsh Calvinistic Methodists.

As soon as he was back from Switzerland, Lloyd George entertained an interviewer from the *British Weekly*, most probably Nicoll himself. The previous week's issue of the journal had been ' the first thing I read on landing in England ', he averred. The government was fully alert to its responsibility to Wales, and on its behalf, he promised that Welsh disestablishment would be ' press[ed] through ' at the earliest possible opportunity. He recounted that the Prime Minister had been eager to promulgate a Bill, ' but that the action of the Lords on Education especially had upset all such calculations '. On no acount would he have it said that the government had defaulted on its pledges:

> What [was] the very first great measure introduced and pressed through the Commons by the Government of 1906? An Education Bill which constituted the greatest and most dramatic measure of Disestablishment and Disendowment of the State Church ever proposed in this country.

Last but not least, he warned Welsh M.Ps that they risked the support of English Nonconformists if they rebelled over disestablishment at a time that an ' Education Bill is under consideration ' in the Cabinet.

The Rev H. M. Hughes read the *British Weekly* interview with inestimable pleasure. ' It is just what was needed to counteract the " schemes " and machinations of two or three persons who have in every way tried to stir up a revolt ', he assured Lloyd George, for whom he had pulled strings to obtain an invitation to the following week's convention:

> Now, I hope you will come, and say what you have uttered in the B. Weekly. As I have already told you, more than once, there is a deep feeling in Wales concerning Disestablishment, which amounts to bitter resentment with regard to the Commission. This is really the *fons et origo* of the mischief.[26]

Lloyd George replied by expressing satisfaction that ' you approve of the interview. It would be quite impossible', he confided,

> for any minister to go further at this stage. . . . I am anxious
> to meet the Committee on Wednesday afternoon to talk things
> over so as to encourage perfect unanimity at the Conference.
> Any appearance of dissension or disunion would injure the
> cause. I hope the Convention will be a success. A good confer-
> ence with wise resolutions would strengthen my hands.[27]

To Nicoll, whom he sent a copy of Hughes's letter, Lloyd George
paid lavish tribute for helping to subdue those ' who a few weeks
ago were in full revolt against the Govt.'. He mentioned a confidential correspondence with Welsh Wesleyan and Congregational leaders, several of whom had ascribed ' the whole of this
agitation to the desire of a few men to " trip Lloyd George
up " '.[28] With the assistance of the *British Weekly,* the attempt
was foiled, and the Cardiff convention netted him a personal
triumph. ' His peroration was magnificent ', J. Glyn Davies reported in the *British Weekly.* ' It swept the audience into ecstasy;
not a man but shouted and wept.' Welsh indignation continued
unabated, but Lloyd George had made himself its master instead of
its object. ' I never felt more confident of Wales than I do now ',
he boasted to Herbert Lewis a few months later.[29] In large
measure, he owed that sense of confidence to the support of a
Scotsman which, once secured, he sedulously maintained.

To give him his due, Lloyd George did not exaggerate when
he asserted that English Nonconformists were too gravely concerned with the education question to tolerate a diversion over
Welsh disestablishment. Roused from its torpor, the Nonconformist Parliamentary Council – with Perks standing conspicuously
aloof – held ' numerous meetings ' over the summer to prepare
suggestions for the next Education Bill, which could not be long
delayed. George Hay Morgan, a Welsh Baptist who sat for Truro,
headed the committee that presented an outline scheme on 22
August. Joseph Compton-Rickett, who served concurrently as
chairman of the Congregational Union, undertook a public explanation of the resolutions and the ' difficult circumstances ' in which
they were framed. ' The storm centre was the continuance of
simple Bible instruction . . . in the elementary schools ', he told
the readers of the *British Weekly* on the 29th. The hurdle could
have been surmounted most easily ' by a stride towards Secular-
ism ', which he would have found acceptable, but which would

have left a serious division in the Free Church camp . . .: An overwhelming majority of Methodists, as well as many Congregationalists, Baptists, and others, would demur to any such sacrifice.' In consequence, the committee fastened upon the expedient of ' contracting out', whereby particular schools (with the stipulated approval of ' a sufficient number of parents or electors of the district ') might declare their independence from the national system, retaining a ' purely denominational ' character and foregoing an endowment from the rates.

Clifford confessed to misgivings at these proposed arrangements. Yet he went so far as to admit that the ' suggestion [of contracting out] is one that deserves the fullest consideration as perhaps the nearest approach we can make at present to a perfectly civic system of elementary education '.[30] His guarded approval embarrassed Lloyd George, who ' had opposed contracting out and had carried the Cabinet with him ', but who had to give way when McKenna invoked Clifford's preeminent authority. ' I think contracting out is a mistake,' Lloyd George told Herbert Lewis during the Christmas recess, which they spent together in the south of France. ' It will be 1870 all over again.'[31]

On 24 February 1908, McKenna introduced his lengthy Bill, clause by clause, to the Commons. Despite the elaborate groundwork that had been laid, he evidently did not know what to expect. Three days before, he had ' begged ' Perks ' almost with tears in his eyes not to oppose his Education Bill " especially in the present crisis in our party " '. Then, when his supplications proved unavailing, he issued a stern warning that ' the party would resent my opposition ', to which Perks testily replied, ' I am not in the market '.[32] Nicoll, who was always in the market, received a corresponding share of the cajolery. ' There is no paper which exercises a wider influence than yours ', McKenna flattered him:

> Indeed a recent Prime Minister has been known to avow that there is no more powerful factor in creating and guiding opinion than your articles. In the case I refer to, perhaps the exact words used may have been ' misguiding public opinion '; but I need hardly say that I recognise not only the power but the permanent value of your organ.[33]

McKenna met his most formidable opposition from the Anglican episcopate, one of whom – the Bishop of St Asaph – introduced alternative legislation in the House of Lords. Organised Nonconformity, whose response to McKenna's Bill was tepid at best, declined to rally to his defence. J. Hirst Hollowell found the 1908 measure ' in . . . some ways more objectionable than Mr Birrell's in 1906 '. Enumerating a long list of criticisms, he waxed most indignant about contracting out, which, ' combined with right of entry and other provisions, would make every school in the land, to a certain extent, sectarian '.[34] The annual meeting of the general body of the Three Denominations, while recording ' its gratification that His Majesty's Government has introduced an Education Bill which is, in many respects, and improvement upon that of last year ', nevertheless regretted

> the insertion in the Bill of a contracting-out clause, inasmuch as this will prevent the realisation of what has always been the ideal – the establishment of a complete and efficient system of National Education, free from all sectarian influences, and under effective popular control.[35]

And the Liberation Society, welcoming McKenna's Bill as ' an honest attempt to deal with existing difficulties ', felt ' bound to object that the Bill continues the system of teaching religion under the authority, and at the cost, of the State '.[36] This indeed was damning with faint praise.

The situation was further complicated in April by the resignation and death of Campbell-Bannerman. As expected, Asquith ascended to the premiership, although the *Methodist Times* had had the temerity to recommend Sir Henry Fowler. McKenna was shifted to the Admiralty, leaving a legacy of unfinished business at the Board of Education to Walter Runciman, a Wesleyan. In a vain attempt to save his predecessor's Bill, Runciman entered into prolonged negotiations with the Archbishop of Canterbury. Eventually, these discussions were joined by several bishops and Nonconformist divines including John Scott Lidgett and Silvester Horne. That, however, was not sufficient to allay the suspicions of more militant Free Churchmen. In October, the education committee of the National Council requested an audience with the Prime Minister, whose intentions were as much a subject for speculation as his theological commitments. Asquith curtly declined to receive them, and they had to rest content with written assurances from Runciman ' that the paragraphs which had been in the press, asserting that a compromise with the denominationalists had been arrived at, were quite untrue '.[37]

On 10 November, Runciman summoned a meeting of Nonconformist M.P.s, whom he briefed ' as to the course, & present position, of the negotiations '. H. J. Wilson, a Congregationalist who sat for Holmfirth in Yorkshire, repeated the salient points in a letter to members of his family. In return for various concessions, ' the Archbishop of Canterbury and his friends ' were to be allowed an opportunity for contracting out as well as ' the " right of entry " for sectarian teaching in all schools. . . . The last condition is an abomination to me ', Wilson confessed,

> & to most of us. But the arrangement seems to be all we can get at present. If rejected, we shall probably have to endure the existing state of things for half-a-generation. If accepted, it is quite probable that an Education Bill may pass before Christmas. In common phrase we are ' between the devil & the deep sea '. The conclusion come to by a very great majority was that we had better not refuse it.[38]

Ten days later, Runciman introduced his compromise Bill.

The grudging endorsement that Runciman had obtained counted for less than he assumed. Hollowell, true to form, ridiculed the government for accepting ' some of the very worst amendments made by the Lords in Mr Birrell's Bill, and which were so bad that the Prime Minister withdrew the Bill of 1906 rather than include them '.[39] But Free Churchmen of his ilk were not alone in repudiating the policies of their official representatives. On 3 December, the Representative Church Council, an assembly of Anglican clergy and laity, resoundingly voiced its disapproval which, in effect, constituted a vote of no-confidence in the prelates who had helped to negotiate the measure. The next day, the Bill was hastily withdrawn. The *Manchester Guardian*, disgusted with extremists on both sides, maliciously pictured Hollowell dancing for joy around a Christmas bonfire in the company of Balfour, the Bishop of Manchester, and other Church stalwarts.

At the close of another year, Nonconformists still had nothing to show for their vast expenditure of time and effort. A Licensing Bill, introduced in the Commons in May, came to grief in the Lords in November. Disestablishment was a dead letter, and the prospects of another Education Bill were virtually non-existent. With the wisdom that comes from hindsight, Lloyd George contemplated the advantages that would have been gained if his Cabinet colleagues had heeded his advice ' to dissolve on the Lords in 1907. . . . That was the moment for attack ', he reminded Nicoll. ' We should have won easily – with a few insignificant electoral casualties . . . & we . . . could have gone on passing Licensing Bills & *real* Education Bills.'[40] Having lost one opportunity, Lloyd George was determined to create another. As chancellor of the exchequer, he was uniquely placed to force events. On 29 April 1909, he presented his ' People's Budget ', provoking the Lords into battle. The question in many minds, including his own, was whether Nonconformity would again rally to the colours.

5 *Decline and Disenchantment*

Delving into his rich treasury of boyhood memories, David Lloyd George vividly recalled ' an old ex-sergeant of police ', who had hunted foxes in the Caernarvonshire hills with the help of two or three doughty little Welsh terriers. From this neighbour, Lloyd George acquired two stuffed foxes, as well as a valuable political lesson, which he shared in 1913 with a group of his fellow-Baptists: ' If there are any of you contemplating a hunt for wild beasts of any sort anywhere, just take in your pack the little terriers bred under the auspices of the little chapelers.' Dr John Clifford, who took the platform with him on this and innumerable other occasions, was a champion specimen of the breed, whose spiritual pedigree could be traced to Oliver Cromwell. ' They are the men to root out things ', Lloyd George exclaimed. ' They never get tired. They will follow you over rock and crag, these terriers, whilst the spaniels, daintily fed, will leave you directly you quit the comfortable highway. They are never daunted by snarls; they never fear opposition.'[1]

At each stage in his ' tempestuous journey ' over the rocks and crags of twentieth-century politics, Lloyd George attempted to keep the little terriers obedient to his will. As usual, his motives were as much sentimental as tactical. Here was an organised body of opinion on which he could draw for support, and for which, as a result of his pious upbringing, he nursed a genuine reverence. Even after he had apparently discounted the content of religious belief, he retained a zealous devotion to its outward forms. Not himself a saintly man, he enjoyed the companionship and earnestly sought the approval of many to whom such a label would not be misapplied. A lay preacher, he took delight in singing Welsh hymns and reciting the perorations of sermons which he had heard in his youth. Rarely did he miss an opportunity to address a denominational assembly, to congratulate a divine who celebrated an anniversary, or to unveil a statue or portrait of one of the heroes of Nonconformity, including those who had been his political antagonists.

To an extraordinary extent, the political history of post-Victorian Nonconformity was linked, inexorably and avowedly, to the fortunes of this single and singular individual. The relationship, progressively less advantageous to either side, was never without its incongruities. Flattered by Lloyd George's attentions, Free Church leaders tended to overlook the disappointments they suffered at his hand. Justly proud of his rapid advancement, which they took as a credit to themselves, they tried their best to ignore the naked opportunism with which he pursued his goals. Occasionally, he went too far; but he was always able to restore himself in their good graces by a fervent appeal to their common inheritance, or, better still, by a rousing attack on privilege, ecclesiastical or otherwise.

A Baptist married to a Calvinistic Methodist, Lloyd George knew firsthand the theological and social tensions that prevailed within the bosom of Nonconformity. A Welshman at Westminster, he knew equally well the discrepant national interests that were embraced by British Liberalism. His task, as he saw it, was to transcend these incompatibilities, which were manifest in the 1906 debate on education, the 1907 debate on disestablishment, and the 1908 debate on licensing. In his first year in office, he called for a ' Holy Alliance ' of Free Churchmen ' against drink and injustice. . . . No influence, no monopoly could stand against it ', he promised.[2] It went without saying that he proposed himself to lead such a crusade which, had it materialised, might have deflected the Nonconformist agitation into those amorphous areas where it could have no conceivable quarrel with the government. Not until after his elevation to the Exchequer did he receive the first of several opportunities.

With the rejection of his omnibus Budget of 1909 by the Unionist preponderance in the House of Lords, an appeal to the electorate was unavoidable. In the parlance of the day, the cup was now filled, and among the discarded Liberal measures that had gone to fill it were several that had dealt specifically, if less than satisfactorily, with Nonconformist grievances. Free Churchmen were urged to put aside their resentment against the government, and to join the Welsh David in his efforts to fell the Anglican Goliath.

Some held back. In an anonymous pamphlet, a ' Nonconformist Minister ' strenuously argued ' simply this – that modern Nonconformity, in making corporate political action bulk so large in its programmes, is forsaking its first ideals, substituting a smaller thing for a greater '. Professing himself a staunch Free Trader and an opponent of the 1902 Education Act, the author deplored the fact that,

> since the beginning of the education struggle, Nonconformity has become more political than ever, and this quite apart from the education question itself – more given up in all its meetings to political discussion, more ready to give forth *ex cathedra* pronouncements on any and every political argument of the day.[3]

The pronounced decline in denominational memberships seemed to give substance to his case.

One could depend upon William Robertson Nicoll, who was due to receive his knighthood before the year was out, to counter such blasphemies. In a series of *British Weekly* articles, which ran continually from 1 July through 30 September, he implored his readers to engage in ' One Fight More ' for the rewards that had thus far eluded them. Under that heading, his pieces were promptly reprinted in pamphlet form, and received wide distribution. If the Lords triumphed, he gravely intoned, the path would be eased for protection, conscription, drink, and other evils. ' We recognise this as a far more serious crisis than even that in which we fought – and won ' in 1906. ' We shall so use it that, as the storm rises into a hurricane, the voices of Free Churchmen shall be heard.' Lloyd George, himself no slouch at hyperbolic rhetoric, thanked Nicoll for giving him ' much inspiration and support '. He agreed that Nonconformists had a particular vendetta against the House of Lords, and a crucial role to play in the forthcoming campaign:

> Without their active and zealous cooperation in every constituency, we cannot hope to win; at least the victory would be such a doubtful one as to leave us weak, embarrassed and impotent.
>
> I believe the Budget has secured the enthusiasm of the vast majority of the working men of the Kingdom; but it is Nonconformity alone that can bring the middle class to our aid. . . .

As to the organisation itself, the start is everything. Clifford is a first-rate fighting man, and there could be no better General appointed to command the Nonconformist Forces in this expedition against the House of Lords; but it is highly important that all the picked men of the Free Churches should be associated with him from the start. . . . They might assist us even to procure a few candidates : we are still short, and we want really good men to fill up the vacancies. There are many excellent Nonconformists, with some leisure and just enough means and who are excellent speakers. . . .[4]

If Free Church backing was less substantial than Lloyd George would have wished, the government must bear some measure of the responsibility. On 29 September, the organising committee of the National Council met to consider ' the question of what action, if any, should be taken . . . in connection with the next General Election '. The reticent phraseology was itself ominous. Sir Joseph Compton-Rickett (who had been knighted two years before) tried to retrieve the situation by ' pointing out that the Committee must of necessity, in view of the repeated resolutions of the General Committee and of the Annual Council, continue its agitation in favour of its Education and Licensing policy '. After a ' lengthy discussion ', his view carried, and he and Clifford were appointed to draft a manifesto urging Nonconformist voters ' to make Education and Licensing a definite test question for candidates '. At the same time, the committee decided to remit its message directly to Downing Street, and Compton-Rickett undertook to make the necessary arrangements. A week later, he reported back that the Prime Minister ' was not receiving any deputations on any subject ', and had requested the committee to state its case in writing.[5] Asquith's brusqueness was inevitably contrasted with the accessibility of his predecessor during the 1905–6 campaign.

The National Council's performance was further inhibited by the absence of the Rev Thomas Law, its organising secretary, who was convalescing from a nervous breakdown. His deputy, George S. Hirst, lacked his pertinacity and possibly his commitment. On 26 November, Hirst announced ' a plan of electoral organisation ': the Council's manifesto was to be issued to 120 London and provincial newspapers and digested for publication as a broadsheet; district conferences were scheduled throughout

England and Wales, with ' expenses to be borne locally '; a massive
London demonstration would feature Lloyd George, who ' had
agreed to speak as a Free Churchman to Free Churchmen dealing
only with Free Church questions '; and finally, it was proposed to
raise a campaign fund of £2,000. The Liberation Society adopted
a similar strategy, taking the precaution of predicating its action
on ' a definite statement ' from Asquith on the future of Welsh
disestablishment and education.[6]

The campaign, one of gruesome duration, was officially opened
on 10 December with a speech from the Prime Minister at the
Albert Hall, from which women were carefully excluded to guard
against suffragette disruption. During the hectic weeks that
followed, Asquith must often have wished that he could deal as
summarily with the Nonconformists, who bridled at the reintroduction of Irish Home Rule into practical politics.

Lloyd George quickly stole the spotlight. On Thursday evening, the 16th, he made his scheduled appearance at a Free Church
demonstration at the Queen's Hall. It was a curious spectacle.
A prayer was offered by the Rev J. H. Shakespeare, and hymns
were sung. Gracing the platform were such divines as Scott
Lidgett, Meyer, Horne, Monro-Gibson, Jowett, and Guttery, and
such laymen as Compton-Rickett, W. T. Stead, and J. Allen
Baker, the ' fighting Quaker ' M.P. for East Finsbury. Clifford,
who had a previous speaking engagement in Berkshire, sent a
laconic message: ' This election is our Waterloo: let us fight
like men for the cause of the people.' He neglected to specify
whether he saw himself as Bonaparte or Wellington; but, in view
of the disrepute in which dukes were held at the Queen's Hall that
evening, that was probably just as well. Law wrote from a rest
home at Margate that he hoped presently to ' be at the centre of
things ' again. Sir Robert Perks, who had been created a baronet
the previous year, was another conspicuous absentee.

The huge crowd greeted Lloyd George with wild enthusiasm,
and roared with laughter when he deigned to describe himself
' not as a Liberal Minister or member of a political party ', but
only as ' a quiet and retiring Free Churchman taking counsel
with his fellow-members of the Free Churches '. Thereupon, he
launched into a fiercely partisan attack on the House of Lords,
wherein dwelled the hereditary enemies of Dissent, ' those
Philistines who are not all uncircumcised '. Holding the Lords
exclusively responsible for the misfortunes of Nonconformity,

he adamantly rejected Perks's suggestion that the government was at least partly to blame. 'The mention of Sir Robert's name', according to a graphic account in the *Christian World* (23 December),

> provoked loud hisses from all sides, but Mr Lloyd George would have none of them. 'Sir Robert Perks', he said 'has rendered great service to Nonconformity, and I do not want to say a word against him.' Then he quietly added, with curling lip, 'But I do wish that he (Sir Robert) would not always talk as if the Nonconformist conscience were locked up in his City safe' – a thrust which the meeting drove home by its almost deafening cheers.

By the end of an hour's oration, Lloyd George had effectively disposed of his enemies and not a few of his erstwhile friends. With a comparable display of false modesty, Perks replied 'as an ordinary Wesleyan Methodist layman' through the correspondence columns of *The Times*. Having declared his intention not to seek re-election to the Commons, he had already relinquished the chairmanship of the Nonconformist Parliamentary Council to Sir George White, yet another recently honoured Free Churchman. For the time being, he continued as treasurer of the National Council, though he now protested that it had 'no authority whatever officially, or even indirectly, to represent the Free Churches; and least of all does it represent the Wesleyan Methodist Church'. His letter, written on the 20th and published the next day, pointed with satisfaction to the absence of Wesleyans from the platform at the Queen's Hall demonstration. He counted two exceptions (the precise number was five), whom he characterised as 'avowed Socialists of a somewhat nebulous type' and therefore obviously susceptible to the Chancellor's demagogic appeals. The vast majority of his co-denominationalists, he confidently predicted, would prove more discriminating. Denied 'the explicit pledges which Nonconformists are entitled to receive from the Government', some would choose Tariff Reform as a lesser evil than socialism, while others, devoted to Free Trade but opposed to Home Rule, would choose to abstain.

The Rev William Perkins, president of the Wesleyan Conference, gave amplification to Perks's statement. 'I have always held that the Wesleyan Methodist Church is a free church – free to everybody – and that our freedom must be maintained', he preached at the New Year. ' I have also held that my position as a minister of that Church is not my own, but a position to which I have been called and appointed by Christ and his Church, and which, therefore, I cannot use for party purposes.' The *Methodist Times* agreed that Wesleyans ought proudly ' to bear the inevitable reproach of being " mugwumps ", or whatever is the current slang for those who will not allow religious organisations and high moral principles to be exploited by party wire-pullers '. More surprisingly, similar sentiments were articulated by George Cadbury, a devout Quaker and a benefactor of the National Council since its inception. Recent events had prompted him to question whether the Free Churches, as such, should contract political marriages. He addressed his remarks to the *Daily News,* the paper he owned, and whose own attitude towards the government had cooled perceptibly.

Cadbury's strictures were heard respectfully, but failed to deter a majority of Radical divines. The Rev Evan Jones, president of the National Council, stoutly defended the right of the Free Churches to ' take part in pure political struggles ' when their interests were menaced ' by irresponsible and implacable Peers '. Shakespeare depicted Lords Curzon and Milner as reincarnations of Strafford and Laud, while Campbell-Morgan saw the election as ' a great battle between freedom and feudalism '. Law, returning to his desk at the Memorial Hall, wasted no time on subtleties : ' We are fighting for our lives ', he thundered. Scott Lidgett, J. D. Jones, and Horton were among those who campaigned for particular Liberal candidates, but no one could compete with Clifford, who literally vacated his pulpit at Westbourne Park chapel while he stumped for votes. Speaking at an average of twice daily, Clifford surpassed himself on 11 January, when he addressed three meetings at Watford in the afternoon, and then appeared at Camberwell in the evening. ' He had known Mr Lloyd George as a personal friend for twenty years ', he testified at Wandsworth, where he had come to promote the candidacy of Walter Warren, a Baptist, ' and he told them that Mr Lloyd George was in politics as Mr Gladstone was in politics, that he might serve God in politics.' On one occasion, Clifford got carried away by his ' fervid oratory ' and toppled headlong from the platform to a reporters' table below. ' Not bad for a man of seventy-three ', he resumed.[7]

But, from the Free Church perspective, the stellar attraction of the January election was the candidacy of Silvester Horne at Ipswich. Having been denied – it is unclear by whom – an opportunity to tackle Chamberlain at West Birmingham in 1906, he had since been ' unofficially approached' to stand at Merthyr Tydvil, where D. A. Thomas was slated to retire. Instead he chose Ipswich, another two-member constituency, where the situation was complicated by a local tradition by which the Liberals had always taken care to run a Churchman in harness with a Nonconformist. Inconveniently, Sir D. F. Goddard, who took prior place on the Liberal ticket, was another Congregationalist. It was widely feared that the adoption of two Nonconformists, one of them ordained, would alienate the support of Liberal Churchmen. Happily, this did not prove to be the case.

Horne's Nonconformist friends had other reasons to worry. Fearful that a parliamentary career ' might wean him away from Whitefield's', they sought and obtained his assurances that he did ' not believe it is impossible to combine the two and to keep the religious interest foremost in both places'. Against their better judgement, they were reconciled to the idea. ' We need in Parliament a man who shall give expression to Nonconformity on its spiritual side', J. D. Jones and J. H. Jowett contended in a joint letter to their denominational weekly; they advertised Horne as the Free Church counterpart to Lord Hugh Cecil. Others were not persuaded. ' The general question as to whether ministers of the Gospel should sit in Parliament we need not debate', the *Methodist Recorder* informed its readers when Horne was elected:

> Such cases will probably be very few. How Mr Horne is going to square the claims of Parliamentary life with the demands made upon him at Whitefield's Tabernacle we cannot explain. . . . A man cannot do everything. . . . We hold that not all ministers, perhaps not many, can enter into public political controversy with advantage. Many are temperamentally unfitted for such a part; they are easily roused, and with little provocation speak words of much heat and little judgment. Some have no light at all to shed on political matters, and, if they could believe it, would help more by silence than by speech.

One can imagine how much these remarks must have stung the junior member for Ipswich, all the more because he soon came to realise their essential validity. The brightest star on the Nonconformist horizon, Horne failed to shine in the parliamentary firmament. He held his seat in the second 1910 election, and continued to preach at Whitefield's most Sundays. But in the spring of 1914, as he prepared to embark on a visit to America, he confided his intention to resign either his pastorate or his membership in the Commons: the physical strain was too great and the rewards were too few. His sudden death, which occurred aboard a steamer on the Great Lakes, resolved his dilemma.[8]

According to a recent investigation of the 1910 general elections, certain ' ominous cracks ' began to appear in the substructure of political Nonconformity: ' One ran horizontally, separating clergy from congregations; another vertically, separating the denominations '.[9] The second tendency, as we have seen, was nothing new; but the first marked a significant departure from the norm. Perks, one may recall, had cited the disinclination of Wesleyans to tolerate ' politics in the pulpit '; this attitude became more pronounced, and, at the same time, spread to other sects. The growing divergence between clergy and laity could be seen on many levels. The general body of the Three Denominations, composed exclusively of divines, embraced the Liberal cause with greater fervency than any of the denominational conferences, each of which contained a substantial lay element whose political commitments were increasingly determined by class considerations. In the opinion of one well-placed commentator, the 1906 election had proved the final occasion when the Congregational Union ' stood solidly behind the Liberal – or indeed, any other – Party '.[10]

For the time being, the difference between the spiritual and lay wings of political Nonconformity was essentially one of emphasis: as signalled by Cadbury among the Quakers or W. P. Hartley among the Primitive Methodists, lay elders tempered their customary allegiance with a new restraint. Often, however, the estrangement was more complete: in the northern districts and, to some extent, in the Midlands, Primitive Methodist local preachers broke with divines to endorse Labour candidacies, and even to stand in the Labour interest; in the Home Counties, Wesleyan lay leaders flaunted their Tory sympathies. Congregational churchmen who had been pleased to postulate an interdependency between theological and political independency, were confronted by the presence of ' convinced Tariff Reformers and other . . . Unionists of even deeper dye ' among those whom they led in worship. The *British Congregationalist* published a series of letters from chapel-goers who criticised their clergymen's links to the Liberal Party. These complaints emanated not only from the Birmingham area, where one would expect them, but from as far afield as Bradford and Bournemouth, where J. D. Jones was said to have coerced his flock into line by threatening to abdicate his pulpit if a Tory carried the constituency. The *Manchester Guardian* featured a similar correspondence, mostly drawn from Lancashire and the north west. One beleaguered divine acknowledged the existence of ' thousands of Conservatives in our Free Churches ', whom he begged to refrain from attempting to ' muzzle their minister '. Nothing could testify more conclusively to the extent to which times had changed.

Polling began on 14 January and continued for more than three weeks. Approximately two hundred Free Churchmen took the field, the overwhelming majority of them as Liberals. Significantly, however, the proportion of Free Churchmen was higher among the 78 Labour contenders. Here was a common denominator between the parties of the left, although one that imparted more shadow than substance. Despite the drift of Nonconformist voters to the Unionist side, fewer than ten per cent of Unionist Party candidates lacked Anglican credentials, and this segment included Roman Catholics and Jews: ' Only religion, the residuum of an earlier socio-economic and cultural division, provided any sharp contrast in the social background of the major parties' candidates.'[11]

As the returns came in, it became evident that the Liberals had been divested of their magnificent 1906 majority, and could continue in office, if at all, only on Irish and Labour sufferance. Each reverse drove Radical divines to greater frenzy in their efforts to drum up votes. ' Verily the helots are let loose; let Spartan youth take heed ', the Rev J. Morgan Gibbon exhorted the readers of the *British Weekly* after the first week of polling. ' Atheism and the Yellow Press have kissed each other. If these signs are not sufficient for Nonconformists, then neither would they believe, though One rose from the dead.' As the casualties mounted, the editors of the Free Church press sank deeper into despondency. ' A Liberal Government dependent on an Irish majority ', the *Christian World* despaired, ' is not likely to tackle the Education question drastically.' Revealingly, they mourned their losses not as Liberals, but more specifically as Nonconformists: ' A strange fatality seems to have hung over Free Church candidates at this election. Roughly speaking, only half of them have survived the contest.'

Was the picture really as black as it was painted? The decline in Nonconformity's parliamentary membership, although precipitous, was almost directly proportionate to the decline in Liberal seats: Free Churchmen numbered approximately 125 among the 315 Liberal and Labour representatives in the new House, as compared to an estimated 180 among the progressives elected in 1906. It was therefore possible to reason that Nonconformists had managed to hold their own within the intra-party balance. Moreover, one might say that they had suffered less on their own account than to the extent to which they had served as agents of a debilitated Liberalism.

The *Christian World* compiled a roster of Free Church M.P.s, including the names of Labour men, but scrupulously omitting any Unionists ' on the ground that they do not, perhaps cannot, attach themselves to the Free Church M.P.s Committee of which Sir George White is the Chairman'. Among the outcasts were four of the twenty-eight successful Wesleyans, as well as a sprinkling of Unitarians. The editors were better disposed towards Norval W. Helme, a Wesleyan who stood at Lancaster, and who qualified as one of the few Free Churchmen to secure an English county seat for the Liberals:

> Brewers and publicans joined the priests in the fray, chiefly because Mr Helme proved his loyalty to his denomination by presenting the Wesleyans with a fine church in close proximity to that of the Anglicans, and has strongly advocated the licensing clauses of the Budget and public control of education.

In the Louth division of Lincolnshire, where a vacancy was created by Perks's withdrawal, the Liberals tried to recruit first a Wesleyan local preacher and then a Congregationalist, both of whom ' resisted the bait'. In desperation, they adopted a Welsh Calvinistic Methodist, who lost the seat to the Tories, but won it back the next time round.

Its ranks reduced by a half dozen members, the Wesleyan parliamentary contingent could consider itself fortunate. The English Presbyterians, twenty-two strong in the previous Parliament, sent a single member to Westminster: Dr Christopher Addison. The number of Liberal Unitarians was halved to seven. Northwich, where the venerable Sir John Brunner chose not to stand again, was inherited by his elder son, who was in turn succeeded as member for Leigh by a Congregationalist. Elsewhere, however, Congregationalists fared less well. Still the best represented of the Free Churches, their membership in the Commons fell from seventy-three to fifty-three. The denominational journal, applying more rigorous criteria (that excluded the Prime Minister among others), put the total at thirty-nine, of whom three were Labour men. A. A. Haworth, whose Congregationalism was unimpeachable, carried Manchester South by a splendid margin of 2452, Sir Albert Spicer held Central Hackney, and Compton-Rickett scored decisively at Osgoldcross in Yorkshire. Silvester Horne's showing at Ipswich was more modest, but no less prized. His absence from Whitefield's undoubtedly contributed to P. W. Wilson's defeat at St Pancras South, just as Clifford's from Westbourne Park worked to the disadvantage of L. G. Chiozza Money, the Liberal incumbent at Paddington North. Congregationalists took vicarious pleasure in the victory in Merionethshire of H. Hayden Jones, J. D.'s brother, who was himself a Welsh Calvinistic Methodist.

Four or possibly five Baptists in the late Parliament had retired at the dissolution; but, so far as the *Baptist Times* could tell, ' no Baptist member who offered himself for re-election suffered defeat '. At North West Norfolk, Sir George White came within 200 votes of his 1906 record poll. At Derby, the victor was a newcomer, J. H. Thomas, who was billed as ' a typical man of the people '. Edgar Jones headed the poll at Merthyr Tydvil, and G. Hay Morgan fought a stiff battle to retain Truro. But the denomination's most celebrated triumph belonged to Lloyd George, who literally dominated the January campaign. Jane T. Stoddart, who wrote as ' Lorna ' in the *British Weekly*, jostled with the crowds in Aldwych for a view of the screen on which the *Daily Mail* flashed the latest returns: ' A bitter hatred of Mr Lloyd George found expression among a group of watchers near us,' she reported. ' Among the dregs of the population – the class who were frantically beating at the doors of public houses at 1 a.m. on Tuesday – his name is execrated.'

The Primitive Methodist membership in the House of Commons remained fixed at seven, if one includes – as they did – D. J. Shackleton, whose connections with the sect were through his family. All except Shackleton, who had been a cotton operative in his youth, had seen service in the mines. Going against the tide, the Quakers doubled their parliamentary representation, netting fifteen seats. The most promising of their novices was Arnold Rowntree, who was returned for York. The Welsh Calvinistic Methodists had eight M.P.s, as before; and the United Methodists again totalled three, although Silas K. Hocking was no longer one of the trio.

One would not wish to suggest, of course, that all Nonconformist electoral effort was expended on behalf of Free Church candidates. Some of Captain F. E. Guest's most devoted supporters at East Dorset were ' the Nonconformists of the villages, who have worked not only for the Budget, but to abolish the power of the Lords, that the Education and Licensing Bills may become law '. They gathered at Wimborne to sing the Doxology when his election was announced. Guest's cousin, Winston Churchill, was another beneficiary of Nonconformist enthusiasm. There was no limit to the lengths to which Free Churchmen were prepared to go in order to patronise an Anglican ally: at Norwich, for example, Sir Frederick Low was touted as the product of stock that had produced a Smithfield martyr and a victim of the Bartholomew ejections.[12]

To what extent did political Nonconformity influence the outcome? J. A. Hobson, in a speech to the Sociological Society, pointed to ' the larger and clearer part played by definitely economic issues in this election '. It was his contention that religious preferences, like other ideological and emotional considerations, had merely ' reinforced and qualified this drive of economic forces '. More recently, Dr P. F. Clarke has presented cogent arguments to the effect that the general elections of 1910 marked the transition to a system of ' class politics in much their modern form '.[13] Without disputing Hobson's thesis, to which Clarke has given substance, one may ask whether it applies equally well to all geographical and denominational sectors.

In London and the Home Counties, where neither Free Churchmanship nor Liberalism was dominant, the floodtide of 1906 receded: the vast majority of seats which the Liberal Party had won on narrow margins were swept away. Nonconformists, particularly Wesleyans, had continued to migrate in considerable number to the middle-class suburbs of the Southeast, where they tended to assert their social respectability by assuming their neighbours' Tory colouration. By contrast, political Nonconformity continued to manifest strength in the West Country, in

Wales, in the West Riding of Yorkshire, and in the Northeast, where the Unionist revival met varying degrees of resistance. It has been suggested that ' Radical sentiments and militant Nonconformist habits ', the two being mutually supportive, ' probably limited Liberal losses amongst the middle classes in the North '.[14] One may argue more positively that Radical Nonconformity, in such mining constituencies as Merthyr Tydvil and Leigh, enhanced the appeal of progressive Liberalism among working-class electors. Here the predominant churches were, respectively, Baptist and Congregational. In the northern bastions of Primitive Methodism, where theology helped to foster class-consciousness, the drift was decidedly in the Labour direction. The overall effect, therefore, was a chequered one, with political Nonconformity achieving its greatest impact in precisely those situations in which it acted as a catalyst to those secular forces which, even before 1906, had begun to displace it from the political arena.

Admittedly, there were complications, which usually owed as much to personality as to social structure. At Bow and Bromley, Dr Clifford was confronted with a difficult choice: the I.L.P. challenger was George Lansbury, a pious Anglican with impeccable credentials as a pacifist, a non-smoker, and a teetotaller; the Liberal defender was Stopford W. W. Brooke, the son of a famous Unitarian divine. On the temperance issue, Lansbury could not be faulted. On the education question, he was by far the more satisfactory candidate, favouring an arrangement by which elementary schoolchildren, at the discretion of their parents, might receive religious instruction ' through the denomination to which they belonged '. Clifford, fearful of a split in the progressive vote, urged Lansbury to withdraw. His advice rejected, he awkwardly pledged his support to Brooke, who finished in third place.[15] One might have expected a more open response from Clifford, whose name had graced the title-pages of Fabian Society tracts. But, like many Nonconformist elders, he had a tendency to subordinate future requirements to past connections.

The *British Weekly* echoed Clifford's apprehension about three-cornered contests, but made a better effort to come to terms with the electoral transformation. Its editor, Robertson Nicoll, had gravitated from Perks's orbit into Lloyd George's. Like his new mentor, he did not regard traditional party lines as inviolable.

H

Without specifying who was to give way, he called upon ' Progressives ' to unite against the Protectionist foe. As the results were declared, he went so far as to endorse the ' idea of a coalition of Liberal and Labour members ' on the ground ' that joint action in some form would be natural enough '. It seemed to him that Arthur Henderson, Ramsay MacDonald, and D. J. Shackleton were eminently qualified ' to receive, even for a short time, the responsibility of office '.[16] It went without saying that such an arrangement would have augmented the Free Church component within the government. The Liberal chiefs, however, preferred to collaborate less formally with their Labour and, for that matter, Irish Nationalist allies.

In the history of the National Council, the first of the 1910 elections closed a chapter that had opened with the 1906 Liberal victory. The change could be seen most clearly in terms of personnel. On 27 January, Perks announced his resignation as treasurer. Pleading that business commitments would take him abroad for extended periods, he showed his good faith by remitting his usual subscription of £100. The Rev Thomas Law, to whom Perks addressed his letter, soon effected a less dignified departure. Returning (perhaps prematurely) from his convalescence, he encountered the bitter reproaches of those who opposed the policies which he, as organising secretary, implemented. In reply to his critics, he offered assurances that the forthcoming Council sessions at Hull would adhere strictly to ' devotional ' themes. A reporter from the *British Weekly* sought clarification. ' Political questions will have a place in the programme, I suppose,' he asked. ' Excuse me ', Law replied impatiently,

> political questions, as such, have no place in our programme and never have had at any of our meetings. Your surmise is beside the mark. True, we discuss questions of national life so far as they raise great moral issues and affect deep religious convictions, but we have no place for matters of a purely political character to be discussed with the political spirit.[17]

The Hull sessions ran smoothly, but opposition to Law continued to mount. On 30 March, the executive of the National Council met at the Memorial Hall, and notice was given of a motion of censure. Law scurried to Westminster, where he implored several leading Nonconformist M.P.s – Compton-Rickett reportedly the first – to intercede on his behalf. They refused, ' owing to their duties in the House '. Disconsolate, Law wired his colleagues that he was feeling unwell, and left for Brighton. There, a few days later, he was found drowned, an apparent suicide. To make matters worse, it was established at the inquest that he had spent his final hours wandering aimlessly along the seafront, his breath smelling strongly of alcohol.[18]

It was most convenient to ascribe the tragedy to Law's chronic illness, ' neurasthenia ', which – variously diagnosed – was something of an occupational disease among Edwardian churchmen. Others chose to mourn him as the victim of drink, which had ravaged his mind and induced him to anticipate his appointed day of death. But those most intimately associated with him in Council activities recognised him as, above all else, a martyr to an idea. Dr Robert Forman Horton, a past president and himself no stranger to melancholy, ambiguously eulogised Law as ' an abstemious and self-denying man seeking help from stimulants '. Clearly perceiving the link between Law's private and public anguish, he urged the National Council to turn to those purposes – evangelical instead of political – which Law had ' wished in his brightest and most inspired moments'. George Cadbury drew the same moral: the ' catastrophe ' was caused in no small measure by those who ' have driven the Council on to the stormy sea of politics '. For his own part, Cadbury devoutly hoped that

in the future . . . no resolutions of any kind will be passed at meetings of the Free Church Council. They are of no value, generally offend a minority, and where they verge on politics are made conspicuous in the secular Press and therefore large numbers of Free Churchmen look upon the movement as political and take no interest in it.

Not surprisingly, the *Methodist Recorder* applauded these sentiments: ' The Pope thinks that the welfare of the Church Catholic depends upon his possession of the Temporal Power, but Protestants see that he is mistaken.' Without necessarily coming to the same conclusions, most Radical divines suffered similar pangs of conscience. Perhaps the best proof of their distress was the National Council's difficulty in finding a successor to Law. The Rev J. H. Shakespeare declined nomination, and F. B. Meyer was eventually prevailed upon to accept an interim appointment as honorary secretary. The days of ' organising ' seemed to be over.[19]

This change of personnel and deflection of purpose was no less marked in the case of the Nonconformist Parliamentary Committee, which was reconstituted in the early weeks of the new session. The first order of business was to ascertain the number of Free Church M.P.s; the second was to decide whether to rechristen the body. 'Some are desirous that the appellation "Nonconformist" should be dropped, and that the committee should be a "Religious Equality" Committee.' But that, it was feared, would leave it virtually indistinguishable from the parliamentary Liberal Party. The question was then raised whether it was worth the effort to organise the Nonconformist members of a Parliament which was 'likely to be shortlived, and its operations confined to matters of Finance and the Lords' Veto'. These objections, however, were overruled. Sir George White was again elected chairman, and G. Hay Morgan assumed the duties of whip.

It is extremely interesting to observe the particular issues to which the committee, in its post-Perksian phase, addressed itself. Almost exclusively imperial in nature, they included the Congo question, with which White took special concern, and which Horne made the subject of his maiden speech ('If one might be allowed a suggestion, there is no need to address the House of Commons in a tone suitable to an audience of 5,000,' wrote 'A Baptist M.P.' in his denominational weekly), and the decision of the Colonial Office to endow an Anglican establishment at Lagos. With education and temperance questions temporarily (or so it was hoped) shelved, the committee was hard pressed to justify its existence. It was not until July, when the government proposed to alter the text of the King's Declaration, that the committee at last stood its proper ground. On the one hand, Free Church critics preferred the old phraseology by which the new monarch explicitly disavowed Roman Catholic doctrines; on the other, they keenly resented the modified wording, which committed the Crown 'to a distinct recognition of the principle of Establishment'. White notified the Liberal whip that 'he and his friends' could not support the second reading of the Bill, which was consequently amended, more or less to their satisfaction. No longer affiliated with the committee, Perks took up the attack in the columns of the *British Weekly*, where he waxed especially indignant on the subject of Lloyd George: 'Are his Protestantism and his attachment to Nonconformity things of the past, or re-

reserved for the hustings?' His denunciation of the government's compromise, which was carried with Horne's support, intensified the estrangement between political Nonconformity inside and outside Parliament.[20]

The gulf widened as the year progressed. The first bone of contention was whether the Liberal ministry, returned to power, should give priority to the Budget or to constitutional reform. Nonconformist divines – including Clifford, Meyer, and Shakespeare – strongly inclined to the latter course. Taking the seventeenth-century Puritan view that grievance ought to precede supply, they were eager to abolish the Lords' veto in order to clear the way for new education and licensing measures. Nonconformist M.P.s, however, overwhelmingly subscribed to the Prime Minister's view that the Budget had to take precedence. Or perhaps, by this point in time, one is no longer entitled to speak of 'Nonconformist M.P.s', who might be more properly designated 'M.P.s of Nonconformist background'. Although many of the younger, more articulate Liberal (and Labour) members continued to identify – and to be identified – as Free Churchmen, this fact had come to attain greater sociological than ideological significance. It was because they now conceived of themselves primarily as party politicians, and only incidentally as the proponents of distinctive religious views, that these parliamentarians were brought increasingly into conflict with their denominational elders: the two attributes no longer overlapped or coincided to the same extent as previously.

One possible reason why non-parliamentary Nonconformists may have wished to divert attention from the Budget was the middle-class antipathy to its allegedly socialist provisions. From all indications, Free Churchmen in the House had moved faster and further to the left than the preponderance of Free Churchmen in the country, and certainly than the overwhelming majority of Free Church divines. This dichotomy was most pronounced in late-Edwardian Wales, where, it has been observed, spiritual leaders were 'apathetic or hostile' to the doctrines of the so-called New Liberalism: 'In the main, the Nonconformist churches, so vocal on political themes like disestablishment, were conspicuously silent on social issues.' Their English counterparts, with less excuse for insularity, often revealed the same predisposition. In May 1910, a union of 'Non-Conformist Anti-Socialists' promulgated a 'Puritan Manifesto', which was no Leveller tract. It featured violent diatribes against Lloyd George and other 'Parliamentary Socialists who pose as Free Churchmen', including Horne, whose treachery was allegedly revealed by the absence of a Sunday school at Whitefield's Tabernacle. Thereafter, this group waged an insidious campaign to purge the pulpit of anything that smacked of collectivism.[21] Among parliamentary Nonconformists, who now took their cue from Lloyd George, countervailing forces were at work. On 6 October, Sir George White addressed the meetings of the Baptist Union at Glasgow and touched off a 'heated discussion' by his assessment of social problems: 'The Church of Christ would have to face the question of a more equitable distribution of the wealth produced by modern industrial conditions. Plutocrats and millionaires', he crudely insisted, 'were the greatest enemies of the nation and the greatest enemies of the Church.'[22] The rhetoric of class warfare had been heard before on Clydeside, but never from the platform of a Baptist assembly.

Free Church divines took scant notice of the autumn by-elections: John Simon, who still professed Congregational loyalties, could recruit no bigger gun than Principal Garvie to speak for him at Walthamstow. Elsewhere, they served notice of their intention either to remain neutral or to oppose the government. In his inaugural speech as president of the Sheffield Evangelical Free Church Council, the Rev C. Ensor Walters – who began as a protegé of Hugh Price Hughes – remonstrated that the movement 'did not exist, as some would have us believe, as the appendage, or the tail, of one of the political Parties. I know of no greater libel upon the ideal of the Free Church Councils' work than that.' At Newcastle-on-Tyne, the Rev A. T. Guttery repented of the support he had given to the Liberals at the previous election, and indicated that he would endorse Labour the next time around.[23] He did not have long to wait.

The constitutional deadlock precipitated a second appeal to the electorate at the close of 1910, this one as brief as the first had been protracted. Clifford was incensed: 'The will of the people is known', he protested, 'and it ought to be made to prevail without putting the country to the waste of time and damage to trade of another General Election.' Meyer, determined not to repeat Law's mistakes, responded guardedly to the challenge: 'He denied that the National Council is allied to any political party', but he conceded that

as a matter of fact at this moment their hopes lay with the
Liberal party. If that party failed them – which he did not
anticipate – and any other party, say the Labour party, were to
adopt their policy on the objects they had at heart, then they
would support that party. If it came to a choice between parties
and issues, the issues would have it.

Acknowledging that ' in many of our Councils . . . there is a
strong minority against entering the fight ', he recommended
that ' it will be wise for those Councils as such to abstain, leaving
individual members to take what part they like '. In point of
fact, the campaign passed too quickly for the parent body to do
much more than issue ' a quiet but firm manifesto in which they
declare[d] their steady adherence to the causes for which Nonconformity stands '. The contest merited no mention in the
minutes of the Council's organising committee, which had been
paralysed by Law's death. Nor did the general body of the Three
Denominations convene to pass its usual resolutions. From all
appearances, Nonconformist agencies were as relieved to be ex-
cused from direct intervention as were their secular allies by their
reticence.[24]

The *Daily News*, always a reliable index to Free Church
electoral activity, virtually ignored Nonconformity on either the
national or constituency level. From its pages, one may infer
that candidates who were Free Churchmen did not consider it
necessary or relevant to brandish the fact. There were, of course,
a few exceptions: Evan Spicer, who made a forlorn attempt
to win Dulwich; and the Rev R. H. Roberts, who sought with
temperance backing to displace the incorrigible Horatio Bottomley,
who carried official Liberal endorsement, at South Hackney.
Narrowly focused on the constitutional issue, the second 1910
election did not readily lend itself to Nonconformist purposes.
Not even the indefatigable Clifford, who peppered his speeches
with quotations from John Milton, could convincingly put the
case that religious interests were imperiled.

For Nonconformists as for everyone else, the December returns
only confirmed the verdict which had been delivered eleven
months earlier. Despite the usual quota of withdrawals and new
candidacies, the *Christian World* counted 170 Free Churchmen in the running, exaggerating the figure as ' almost identical
with the number who fought the last election '. According to its

calculations, 134 were successful, a slight improvement over the previous showing. More generously, the *Daily News* put the total of Free Church victors at 140, of whom 45 were Congregationalists, 27 Wesleyans, 23 Baptists, 11 Calvinistic Methodists, 9 Quakers, 7 Primitive Methodists, 7 Unitarians, 6 Presbyterians, and 5 United Methodists. Three of the Congregationalist M.P.s were divines: Horne, Charles Leach, and J. Hugh Edwards. Neither of these semi-official tallies took into account Presbyterians who sat for Scottish or Irish constituencies; nor, by the same token, did they include Nonconformists who defended the Unionist interest in England. Prominent among the latter were Col Sir C. R. Burn (who subsequently took the name of Forbes-Leith), a Presbyterian who scored at Torquay, and Sir George Doughty, the Wesleyan ' Demosthenes of Tariff Reform ', who recaptured Grimsby for the Opposition. Among the casualties was J. S. Randles, the senior Wesleyan on the Unionist side.

At least in part, the reluctance of religious spokesmen to join the fray reflected their preoccupation with internal problems, which had begun to be felt with new acuteness. At the time of polling, each denomination published statistics that attested to the fact of their continued decline. ' Last year the hope was expressed that the arrest in the progress of the churches in Great Britain had reached its limit,' the *Christian World* recalled on 29 December.

> The reaction from the Welsh revival seemed to have spent itself, and in other parts of the kingdom there was a small increase. This expectation has not been realised. There is again a considerable decline in the membership of the Welsh churches, accompanied this time by small decreases in England and Scotland also.

Statistics, of course, told only part of the story, and not necessarily the part that most worried contemporaries. The Wesleyan community, whose gradual politicisation had given numerical and financial strength to the Nonconformist cause, was suffering from a loss of spiritual and social dynamism to which Arnold Bennett, the son of a Wesleyan solicitor, gave literary expression in *The Old Wives' Tale* (1908), *Clayhanger* (1910), and other Edwardian novels. After 1910, Free Church leaders divided between two camps: either (like most Wesleyans and Presbyterians) they relapsed into a political quietism, or (like most Primitive Methodists and some Baptists) they exhibited a truculence that worked equally to the government's detriment.

The dominant fear was that, with the House of Lords stripped of its powers, Irish Catholicism would be the first (and perhaps the only) beneficiary. On 16 February 1911, the executive committee of the Liberation Society, at the initiative of Sir Halley Stewart, called for the legislation of Welsh disestablishment ' as soon as the Veto Bill has passed the House of Commons '.[25] On the subject of education, Nonconformists were no less impatient for results. On 16 March, Robertson Nicoll made a pilgrimage to Beachborough, where Lloyd George was recuperating from a throat ailment which he feared was cancer. The invalid showed his visitor ' a letter which seemed to annoy him very much, really a most foolish letter from Clifford threatening that Nonconformists would withdraw their support if an Education measure was not passed. It must be a strong Bill, and that sort of thing.' Nicoll assured him ' that he did not need to worry himself in the least ' about Clifford's ultimatum. But Lloyd George knew better. He scolded Nicoll for declining nomination as president of the National Council for the following year, when Nonconformists would require strong leadership to reconcile them to Home Rule.[26]

By 1912, however, Free Churchmen were jealous not only of the Irish, but also of each other. The management committee of the Liberation Society deputed Dr Massie to communicate to the Liberal whip ' the wisdom of some definite statement ' on education before proceeding with Welsh disestablishment, lest Welshmen lose the support of English Nonconformists.[27] The advice went unheeded, and, on 23 April, the government introduced a Welsh Church Bill that aroused little interest outside of Wales, except perhaps among militants who thought that the terms for disendowment were too generous. ' It seems like this ', Clifford told meetings around the country,

that the Irish can have their Home Rule and the Welsh their disestablishment, but we Free Churchmen are to have nothing but words. . . . For nine years we have been struggling, and I venture to say to the Liberal Government that if they think we are going in the year 1915 to work for their return with our ancient enthusiasm they are being misled.[28]

Finally, midway through 1913, word was received ' that the

Cabinet was seriously considering plans for carrying out the promises made by the Prime Minister to the National Council '.[29]

It remained to be seen whether the government would have the courage or even the opportunity to act. Horton was already resigned to the inevitability of ' a long Conservative Reaction ' that would preclude Nonconformist gains.[30] On 9 July, Nicoll dined at Sir George Riddell's house with Lloyd George and Masterman and came away with the

> impression . . . that their policy is to go through their work, finish Disestablishment and Home Rule, and then slide for a fall. I do not think they are anxious to get [in] at the next election. . . . They really have come to the dangerous conclusion that they had better let the Tories have a try at the problems.[31]

Given the government's Irish embarrassments, as well as the prevalence of Syndicalist and suffragette disorders, its capitulation was widely regarded as only a matter of time. In that case, Nonconformity would again be a hostage to fortune.

Reviewing Parliament's performance for 1913, Clifford summed up the Liberal record as one of betrayal: hope had ' flickered for a few moments as the session was ending, making the darkness more visible than ever '. The *Primitive Methodist Leader* shared his exasperation (' many amongst us have reached almost the verge of revolt ') and expected nothing to come from the negotiations that ' well-known and trusted representatives of Nonconformity ' were conducting with J. A. Pease, a Quaker who currently presided at the Board of Education. Pease's professed intention to promulgate a ' short ' Bill left his critics unmoved. The *British Congregationalist* was

> not prepared to express any great enthusiasm. . . . Nor are we prepared to advise Free Churchmen to abate their just minimum demands for the complete abolition of tests for teachers, and the setting up of popular control in all State-aided schools, whether urban or otherwise.

The *Baptist Times* calculated that ' the Parliamentary position is such that it would be impossible to get any measure of educational reform through even the House of Commons, to say nothing of the House of Lords.'[32]

Much of this indignation was directed inwards. Under the

new editorship of J. H. Shakespeare, the *Baptist Times* previewed the programme for the National Council's annual meetings, and tellingly asked whether that institution had lost its *raison d'être*: 'We believe that unless the Free Church Council can make some advance upon its past. . ., the usefulness of the Council is over, and the waste entailed by its elaborate machinery had better cease.'[33] It was under the cloud of such self-criticism that the Council gathered in March at Norwich. Nicoll, reporting the proceedings to Lloyd George, put the best possible construction on events:

> My distinct opinion was that the tide of Liberalism is rising. There is great anger at the idea of the Lords blocking the way & a determination not to be baffled in this way. It was evident that most of the men were disappointed that any concessions were made to Ulster, but I think the cooler headed saw the advisability of the step. At our Passive Resistance meeting we took the line of supporting the Government on condition that they gave us something to go to the country upon, that is a single school area Bill of a strong sort. Clifford said that if this were done he & the rest of us would take the platform at the next general election & fight as we did in 1906.
>
> . . . . .
>
> But the really notable feature of the meetings was that the subject which excites enthusiasm was your Land scheme. I mentioned Asquith's name & said that we fully trusted him. There was a mild response. But when I went on to speak of you & your scheme there was tremendous enthusiasm.[34]

Not everyone left Norwich with the same sense of optimism. The *Primitive Methodist Leader*, reflecting its own disillusionment, quoted Clifford in a darker mood: 'He said the patience of the Nonconformists over the education question was the wonder of the ages.' The *Christian World* concluded that ' " Good average " is the best that can be said of the . . . meetings at Norwich.' The Council heard some thoughtful papers, but there was precious little of ' the *élan* that marked its earlier years '.

Sir George White, who had had close ties with Norwich, died shortly before the Council met there. Silvester Horne died soon afterwards. The chairmanship of the Nonconformist Parliamentary Committee passed to Sir Albert Spicer, a genial but hardly an

authoritative figure. Presiding over the National Council was
the Rev F. Luke Wiseman, a Wesleyan who was determined to
occupy the middle ground. If not leaderless, as some contended,
organised Nonconformity was no longer strongly led. Those who
survived from the first generation were usually advanced in
years, and many had turned against the movement. Younger
talent was not to be found either in Parliament or, to any appreciable extent, on the nation's pulpits.

Dr John Scott Lidgett, who figured prominently among the
younger men, reported to the general committee of the National
Council on 12 June ' that the Education Question was being
watched '. He had had an interview with the Master of Elibank,
the chief whip, who provided ' an assurance that an Education
Bill will be included in the programme of the present session '.[35]
The committee had waited too long to feel gratitude, let alone
to accept yet another undated cheque. Ten days later, Primitive
Methodists gathered at Middlesbrough in Yorkshire, where ' the
arena became quite gladiatorial ' as a motion of censure was moved
against the government. The Congregational Union, invariably
more temperate in its responses, recorded its appreciation of the
government's good intentions, but deplored the time gone to
waste. Other denominational assemblies and journals expressed
various degrees of dissatisfaction. Their complaints grew increasingly vociferous until they were interrupted by news that a Haps-
burg archduke had been assassinated at Sarajevo. ' We have much
to give us shame ', the *Primitive Methodist Leader* declared on
9 July, ' but, happily, we are kept free from these upheavals.' It
was not much longer that this claim could be made.

6 The Impact of War

However much a commonplace, it is no exaggeration to say that war, when it came unexpectedly in August 1914, dealt a shattering blow to organised religion. The churches never recovered from the ordeal, either in terms of communicants or self-possession. Thereafter, men looked elsewhere, if anywhere, for their moral certainties. Yet one must remember that here, as in other social situations, wartime experience only hastened and intensified trends that were already underway.

Along with theologies, the institutions that had attempted to give secular currency to them lost relevance, if not repute. Charles Royle, who served briefly as Liberal M.P. for Stockport during the 'twenties, recalled the fate of the local chapter of the National Brotherhood movement: more than six hundred of its members had rallied to the colours, and ' although the big majority came back to the town only a small number resumed their membership of the Brotherhood. Is it to be wondered at ', he asked, ' after the devastating influences of such an experience, that men should have little room for things of a religious nature '?[1] The Free Church Council movement was no less afflicted. In an address to the Tottenham branch, the Rev C. Ensor Walters said that ' he would rather be an English Tommy lying in the trenches than President of the Federation of Free Churches in London ', a position he had been proud to occupy in happier times.[2]

Through a multiplicity of agencies, including Parliament itself, Nonconformists had striven to achieve disarmament and an accord with Germany. Determined to infuse international relations with a Christian spirit, they had participated more actively in the Edwardian peace campaign than their Anglican counterparts, who were bound by ecclesiastical restraints and sometimes Conservative allegiances. At the eleventh hour, success seemed to lay within reach. ' A new era is coming nearer and nearer ', Dr

Clifford trumpeted in his new year's message for 1914. ' Militarism belongs to the dark ages; it is not fit for our time. It must go. It is going.' The general body of the Three Denominations, encouraged by the drift of events, did not consider it necessary at its April meetings to renew its annual injunctions to the government. And the June number of the *Peacemaker*, the official organ of the Associated Councils of the Churches of the British and German Empires for Fostering Friendly Relations between the Two Peoples, found it ' almost difficult to realize that there are still unsolved problems affecting the relations of the two countries. The " new atmosphere " . . . is everywhere evident.'[3]

Like the statesmen of Europe, the spokesmen for British Nonconformity were caught offguard by the declaration of war. Several, including F. B. Meyer and Charles Brown, were across the Atlantic on lecture tours, which they terminated as quickly as possible. Others were stranded at Constance, where the World Council of Churches had summoned a conference to open on 1 August. More than 150 delegates from a dozen countries had been expected to attend, but many were unable to obtain transportation or had had misgivings about crossing international frontiers. An atmosphere of gloom hung over the proceedings, and only the most perfunctory resolutions were passed. The British deputation at Constance, headed by Clifford, had travelled via Cologne, Heidelberg, and Karlsruhe, against the tide of advancing German troops. Eventually, on 6 August, their return passage through enemy territory was arranged with the assistance of Dr Spiecker, who was said to be the Kaiser's favourite preacher. The Rev J. H. Rushbrooke, a Baptist fluent in German, refused to believe that civilisation had lost its sanity. From Constance, he proceeded as planned to visit friends in Berlin, where he was detained until October. ' Pray for me. I need your prayers,' he implored his congregation at the Hampstead Garden Suburb Free Church in a letter delivered by an American acquaintance:

> Perhaps the shock of this war has fallen on few as heavily as upon me, who had toiled for years on behalf of friendly relations between the two nearly-related nations. . . .
>
> My personal faith has almost reeled in the presence of the awful fact; and when I exhort you to believe still in the God of peace and love I am exhorting no less my own heart.[4]

Until 11 p.m. on the 4th, there were flickering hopes that

Britain might stand aside, lending her counsels to the negotiation of an early settlement. Seemingly overnight, Liberal opinion – of which Nonconformity was again representative – swung round to the view that intervention was not only morally justifiable but also strategically imperative. There were only two resignations from the Cabinet, neither by Free Churchmen. Lloyd George, to whom pacifists had mistakenly looked for leadership, kept his place and ultimately emerged as ' the man who won the war '. Sir John Simon, another who had threatened to resign, retained the attorney-generalship, supposedly to avert the dreaded prospect of a coalition. But it was J. A. Pease who performed the most daring feat of moral gymnastics; justly self-conscious, he reconciled his participation in a war ministry with his Quakerism and even with his continued chairmanship of the Peace Society.

As if to atone for their earlier pacifism and to compensate for centuries of outsidedness, leading Free Churchmen made a comparable *volte-face*. Apostles of peace, they were transformed into holy warriors, who often asserted their patriotism with calculated truculence. Take, for example, the case of the Rev A. T. Guttery. On Sunday evening, the 2nd, he addressed a crowded meeting at the Winter Gardens in Blackpool. ' The policy of war for Britain is the reign of madness,' he boldly proclaimed. ' The duty of the Church is plain. It must declare the will of God, which is brotherhood, the gospel of Bethlehem, which is peace, and the evangel of Calvary, which is the dominion of love.' Four days later, his text was blazoned across the front page of the *Primitive Methodist Leader*. By then, however, Guttery had found his inspiration in the Old Testament. ' I used to be an extremist ', he jested in 1918, at the time of his designation as president-elect of the National Council. ' Dr Meyer knows how to deal with extremists – move them to the Chair.'[5] Like Guttery, political Nonconformity was disarmed by the discovery of its own martial instincts.

It was Sir William Robertson Nicoll, a publicist who boasted a wider readership and more enviable contacts, who best typified the Nonconformist predicament. His leading article on 31 July won plaudits from Ramsay MacDonald, a vehement non-interventionist:

I am so glad that the *British Weekly* is taking up the line of strict neutrality. I never heard in all my life a more diabolical and wicked speech than Sir Edward Grey's war appeal yesterday afternoon in the House of Commons. Up to last Thursday he stood magnificently for peace and then suddenly he seemed to lose his nerve and his temper and swung round, outdoing Churchill in his demands that the Cabinet should agree to war. I shall get the B.W. this week & perhaps write you in view of the situation as it will be then.[6]

Instead of a contribution from MacDonald, the following week's issue of the *British Weekly* featured a leader, ' United We Stand ', which was tantamount to an editorial recantation. According to Sir George Riddell, the linchpin of Lloyd George's journalistic machine, the Chancellor affectionately cited Nicoll as an example of ' the amazing change which took place in public opinion between Friday July 31st and Friday August 7th '. Riddell recounted that, on 1 August, Lloyd George had

received a letter from you strongly protesting against the war and was very much impressed by what you said. He put the letter in his pocket, just as he was going out to dinner. He did not wear his dress clothes until the following Friday when he dined out to meet the Italian Ambassador. Meanwhile your remarkable leader of last week had appeared. During dinner, putting his hand in his pocket, he found your letter which he read to the Ambassador at the same time telling him of the contents of the leader.[7]

Beginning that week, Nicoll added to his weekly chores a column of ' War Notes ', in which he urged a vigorous prosecution of the struggle against Prussian despotism. Lloyd George, always generous in his tributes to Free Church friends, later eulogised him as the single most important influence in recruiting Nonconformist support for the war.[8]

Defensive by nature, Nicoll would admit to no discrepancy between his editorial position before and after the outbreak of hostilities. ' The Free Churches have worked for disarmament, and who can blame them?' he asked. Their attempt had been a noble one, but, having failed, left them no choice. George Cadbury was equally unrepentant. As proprietor of the *Daily News*, which had previously advocated the conciliation of Germany, he was particularly susceptible to charges of inconsistency. To these he offered no excuse save his good intentions. ' We have no need to be ashamed,

but to rejoice in the fact that we did what we could to prevent
war ', he assured A. G. Gardiner, his editor. ' Now that we have
entered into the war it is as impossible to stop it as to stop a
raging torrent. The anger of the people naturally has been
roused, and we must secure restitution to Belgium for the injuries
inflicted.'[9]

Convened by telegram, the general committee of the National
Council met on 5 August to deplore ' the crime and horror of a
universal war ' and to pledge its resources ' to foster those more
generous and humane sentiments which war so ruthlessly
destroys '.[10] As yet, it remained unclear how the Council proposed
to act. Its leaders, so far as one can tell, optimistically relied on
militarism to discredit itself, and without delay. Clifford, recuperating from his journey to Constance, prophesied that the
war would bring two results : ' (1) the setting aside in precept
and in practice of the axiom " to maintain peace, prepare for
war," and (2) the prohibition of private trading in armaments '.
By Sunday the 16th, he was sufficiently recovered to preach at
Westbourne Park, where he revealed that, on his way home, he
had ' actually drafted a letter to the Press in favour of . . . British
neutrality. . . . But when, arriving in England, he had become
acquainted with Germany's proposals and actions, he had [de-
cided] to keep that letter back.' Although he ' regretted un-
speakably that England should be embroiled in this Continental
strife ', his conscience was appeased by the knowledge ' that we
were forced into it '. The *Christian World* agreed that this was a
war with a difference, a ' War against War Lordism ', about which
Nonconformists ought to harbour no misgivings. Other Free
Church journals took the same line, with the *Baptist Times*
discerning welcome ' signs . . . that the sense of common peril
and common responsibility is kindling throughout all classes a
new feeling of brotherhood and mutual duty '.[11] If nothing else,
the war held out to Nonconformists the prospect of full acceptance into the community.

True to tradition, Nonconformity divided into ' hard ' and
' soft ' components : between a majority who sanctioned and a
small minority who utterly opposed the war effort. Of the so-called
absolutist minority, there is little that, for the purposes of the
present study, requires retelling : those who clung to their faith
withdrew from active politics, while those who remained active
no longer chose to emphasise their faith. Within the pro-war

I

majority, there was a subtle – but portentous – divergence between the super-militants like Dr Shakespeare, who led his congregation in prayer for Germany's destruction, and moderates like Dr Horton, who clung to the remnants of an abused liberalism. For the first time, these various distinctions openly owed less to denominational than to political allegiances.

In the autumn of 1914, broad agreement was still possible. A statement by German theologians, who asserted that their homeland had been the victim of 'a web of conspiracy', drew a swift riposte from British churchmen, including Clifford, Shakespeare, Campbell, Horton, Meyer, Scott Lidgett, and Nicoll. Identifying themselves with national policy, they replied: 'We have taken our stand for international good faith, for the safeguarding of smaller nationalities, and for the upholding of the essential conditions of brotherhood among the nations of the world.'[12] On 10 November, Free Churchmen had better occasion to demonstrate their solidarity with the government and with one another by participating in a conference called by the National Council at the City Temple. Nicoll, who took the chair, set the tone for the occasion. 'If we had not been Christians', he stridently insisted,

> we should not have been in this war. It is Christ who has taught us to fight for liberty, righteousness, and Peace. It is He who has taught us to care for small nations and to protect the rights of the weak, over whom He has flung His shield. The devil would have counselled neutrality, but Christ has put His Sword into our hands.

Campbell proposed a resolution, which Clifford seconded, pledging Nonconformity to the goal of victory. Lloyd George, who delivered the keynote speech, appealed to Free Churchmen 'to show their sympathy with the cause of justice and the small nationalities in the recruiting offices'. A reporter for the *Baptist Times* described the scene with greater poignancy than he perhaps realised: 'On the platform, upstairs and down, sat the recognised leaders of Nonconformist life.' Lady Robertson Nicoll patriotically 'brought her knitting, and was working away as unconsciously as if by her own fireside'. Her husband was obviously invigorated by the proceedings, and Shakespeare was 'taking his ease'. But Horton sat, 'chin in hand, and with eyes cast down, and thus he remained the evening through. If the war had not crushed him, at least it filled his sensitive soul with horror.' Nicoll, as yet oblivious to such nuances, privately communicated his relief and elation to J. St Loe Strachey, the High Anglican editor of the High Tory *Spectator*:

. . . The vast Nonconformist meetings held last night surprised everybody. They showed a far more militant spirit in English Nonconformity than I had dared to hope for. No name was cheered louder and longer than the name of Lord Kitchener. Dr Clifford, our Grand Old Man, who was a keen pro-Boer, appeared as a Cromwell Ironside, taunting the shirkers and urging that the War should be pursued with our whole force and brought to an end as soon as possible.[13]

As the war dragged on, taking its toll in men and principles, attitudes began to harden. Riddell, calling on Nicoll in early December, found him ' very broken by the war ', or, more precisely, by Nonconformity's increasingly contradictory responses to it. Nicoll complained ' that he had been at a Free Church meeting on Friday and that some of the dissenting ministers are still peace-at-any-price people. On the other hand, some are very militant.'[14] Though he dedicated the *British Weekly* to what he regarded as a middle course, Nicoll undoubtedly widened the breach by systematically boosting Lloyd George at the expense of Asquith. From the beginning, he had been convinced that the Prime Minister was an impediment to national organisation. ' The conscience and intelligence of the country have not yet been touched ', he had written to Riddell on the subject of recruiting, ' and I doubt whether Asquith's speeches will set the heather on fire. Lloyd George is our man for that.'[15] By the spring of 1915, Nicoll had become an avowed conscriptionist, who echoed the Northcliffe press in its clamour for the removal of Asquith and the substitution of Lloyd George.

J. D. Jones was among those moved to protest:

I know the feeling of our Church & the mind of our Congregational folk as well as anyone, & I think it right that you should know what I think. . . . There will be a complete shattering of our national unity, if the attempt to oust Mr Asquith succeeds. . . . We have been proud of Mr Lloyd George, but we dislike his present company & we resent his attempts to hustle the Prime Minister.

About conscription, Jones was even more adamant: 'I solemnly assure you that the Nonconformist people simply will not follow Mr Lloyd George on this tack.' Nicoll replied privately to Jones, defending Lloyd George's loyalty to the Prime Minister, but affirming his belief in Asquith's incapacity. Somewhat mollified, Jones wrote again, 'just to make my position quite clear'. He began by rejecting Nicoll's imputation that Nonconformists were tepid in their attitude towards the war. 'The so-called "Pacifist" group is negligible,' he remonstrated.

> Most of our ministers have given their sons quite freely. We have not taken a census as the Church of Scotland did, but I don't think we should come far behind. I have had to write to many manses to console with our ministers over sons who have fallen. My own son lies at this moment . . . wounded for the third time & this time rather badly. . . . We believe the war is just; we are ready to make our sacrifice to carry it on, & we want to see it pushed to a successful conclusion. . . .
>
> I can quite believe what you say about Mr Asquith. . . . I know too that mistakes have been made. . . . But all that does not affect my main contention which is this – that in the interests of national unity it is essential that Mr Asquith should retain the Premiership. I beg you to believe that I have no animus against Mr Lloyd George. On the contrary, I am on terms of friendship with him & greatly admire him. . . . I believe that some sort of compulsion will very likely have to come. But the country will only accept it from Mr Asquith. . . . But I only speak for my own people – quiet, steady, God-fearing people.[16]

Nicoll was not deflected from his purpose. Through Riddell, he received a constant flow of information 'for your private ear' from Lloyd George, 'our little friend', whom he adulated week after week.[17] The *British Weekly* greeted 1916 by recounting the parable of Simon, 'the victim of compulsion', whose burden was to shoulder the Saviour's cross. Nicoll was 'not disposed to press the parallel too hardly', but the implications were sufficiently obvious. He dismissed Asquith's Military Service Bill, introduced on 5 January, as 'a disappointment', too limited in its scope and self-defeating in its intentions. Sir John Simon's parliamentary defence of the voluntary principle was, in his opinion, 'a very disconcerting disappointment'. By the end of January, Nicoll had renewed his demand for a full-fledged conscriptionist government, with Lloyd George at its helm and a portfolio for Lord North-cliffe.

Unlike Nicoll, who castigated the Prime Minister for failing to go far enough, other Free Churchmen feared that Asquith had already gone too far. The previous spring, Dr Clifford had intimated his aversion to 'the idea of transplanting German institutions and especially the curse of military conscription'.[18] In his new year's sermon for 1916, he spoke out. 'Admit Conscription', he warned, 'and the Kaiser is not far behind. He will come, and you will be Prussianised by your own want of insight and faith in freedom.'[19] Instead of the reverence to which he was accustomed, Clifford was pilloried by 'Lorna' in the *British Weekly*, where numerous correspondents hastened either to applaud or disavow his statements. '. . . Our greatest single asset for victory is the unity of the nation', the Rev J. Ivory Cripps wrote from Southport. 'The imposing of compulsion will lose us that, and the balance will come out on the wrong side.' But the Rev J. Morgan Gibbon, preaching at Stamford, took his text from *Matt. v. 41*: 'And whosoever shall compel thee to go a mile, go with him twain.'

Simon, who resigned as Home Secretary, voted against the Bill along with some fifty Liberal and Labour members whose religious backgrounds were as diverse as their political motives. Clifford and J. Campbell-Morgan joined with various journalists and intellectuals – including G. D. H. Cole, Bertrand Russell, F. W. Hirst, J. A. Hobson, and H. W. Massingham – to send him a letter of 'wholehearted appreciation'. Horton expressed himself independently in a letter to the *Daily News*, which Simon read 'with great satisfaction and pleasure'.[20] The holy warriors were launched upon a civil war, more destructive than any battle they had fought against an external enemy.

The conflict cut clear across denominational lines. Walter Runciman, indisputably the most prominent parliamentary Wesleyan, had opposed the Bill, although he decided to remain in the government to salvage what was left of the *laissez-faire* tradition. His position, itself anomalous, stood in sharp contrast to that of official Methodism, as Arnold Rowntree discovered. Rowntree, an M.P. who took seriously his Quakerism, undertook to canvass the individual denominations to ascertain how they interpreted a clause in the Bill that exempted 'Ministers of Religion' from military service: would lay preachers, for example, fall into this category? ' At the Headquarters of Methodism ', Rowntree's assistant ' met with a curt reception: " We don't want to have anything to do with Mr Rowntree, or with you, or with any of your kind!" ' Rowntree was able to learn, however, that Methodist ministers of pacifist leanings ' had been placed on a black list '.[21] Presumably the first name on that list was that of the Rev S. E. Keeble, who, the following April, helped to draft a manifesto by which twenty-three Methodist divines proclaimed their ' uncompromising pacifism ' and announced the formation of a Peace League. Keeble further distinguished himself as a champion of conscientious objectors and as a sympathiser with the Union of Democratic Control.[22]

Principal Garvie, whose college was emptied of students and requisitioned for war use, reported the same intolerance towards dissentients – pacifists, enemy aliens, and antiwar journalists – on the part of some of his colleagues in the executive of the National Free Church Council. In particular, there was a want of sympathy with conscientious objectors, and an unwillingness ' to use the influence of the Council to protect them against the shameful treatment to which they were exposed '. In a parliamentary debate on the subject, Sir Joseph Compton-Rickett, a pillar of the Council, asserted the claims of state, and it was left to Lord Robert Cecil, the highest of High Anglicans, to put the case for supremacy of conscience. The Council proved more vigilant on behalf of Nonconformist recruits who, contrary to regulations, were often required to specify their denominational affiliations and who were rarely given an alternative to Anglican worship at the front. Sir Albert Spicer brought these grievances to the attention of the War Office, but to no avail. Shakespeare took up the issue, asserting that ' including the Wesleyans, the Free Churches have sent not fewer than 400,000 men to the war ', and deserved a due proportion of chaplains. With invaluable assistance from Lloyd George, he was able to obtain redress.[23]

Although Shakespeare and certain others were inclined to celebrate the appointment of Free Church chaplains as a major victory, as well as confirmation of Lloyd George's genius for getting things done, it could not be denied that most Nonconformist interests fell mortally victim to the war. The passive resistance movement, which had waned in ardour and in effect since 1906, finally perished. On 2 October 1914, Clifford appeared before the Paddington magistrates for the forty-second time and cited ' patriotic reasons ' for continuing the campaign; but the vast majority of his former associates regarded him as quixotic. With the outbreak of war, the Welsh Disestablishment Act, safely piloted through parliamentary shoals, was – like Irish Home Rule – placed in a state of ' suspended animation '; there were strong fears that it would be repealed before it was implemented.[24] Educational reform, of course, was a dead letter. And the ' King's Pledge' of total abstinence for the duration of the war was no substitute for effective liquor controls. For most of these disappointments, as well as for the stalemate along the front, more militant Free Churchmen blamed Asquith's lethargy .

Their prayers seemed to have been answered in early December 1916, when Lloyd George supplanted his longtime chief as head of a new coalition. Neither the machinations that attended his elevation to power nor the distinctly Tory hue of his administration perturbed enthusiasts like Nicoll and Shakespeare. Other Free Church leaders, who had looked askance at Lloyd George's recent activities, characteristically tried their best to see the brighter side. The *Christian World* proudly observed that he was ' the first Nonconformist, in actual membership with a Free Church, to be Prime Minister '. With more dubious logic, it also noted that the government contained a healthy leaven of Free Churchmen: among its Unionist members, Andrew Bonar Law was a Wee Free Presbyterian, F. E. Smith had been ' brought up as a Wesleyan ', and Austen Chamberlain came from Unitarian stock; on the progressive side, Christopher Addison was a Presbyterian, A. H. Illingworth was a Baptist, John Hodge and Arthur Henderson were Wesleyans, and George Barnes and Sir Richard Winfrey belonged to the Congregational Church, with which Sir Gordon Hewart had ' had some early associations '. Herbert Lewis, a Calvinistic Methodist, was named under-secretary at the Board of Education. But the most obvious sop to Nonconformist opinion was the appointment of Compton-Rickett to the paymaster-generalship. (His successor in October 1919 was Sir John Tudor Walters, cousin of the Rev C. Ensor Walters.)

Given to wishful thinking, some Free Churchmen fancied that the new premier would exercise a distinctly Nonconformist influence over Church of England patronage. Sir Albert Spicer, who drew up a memorandum on the subject, argued that Gladstone and Salisbury, both men of ' pronounced High Church sympathies ', had transformed the Establishment into a ' predominantly sacerdotal institution' by their appointments to the episcopacy. According to Spicer, Rosebery and Campbell-Bannerman had attempted to reverse this policy, which was 'largely resumed by Mr Asquith', who consequently 'immeasurably widened the breach between the Church of England and Nonconformist Christians'. It was hoped that Lloyd George, by availing himself of the authority vested in his office, would revolutionise the character of the Established Church. 'An unequalled opportunity is now before the first Nonconformist Prime Minister of promoting the two great causes of Religious and Educational peace.'[25]

Other expectations, while perhaps more reasonable, were equally doomed to disappointment. Under the constraints of the wartime 'party truce' the ebbing mainstream of political Nonconformity flowed into several tributaries, which in turn trickled into a number of divergent rivulets. By force of circumstance, prohibitionism was thrust into special prominence. Previously no more than one of the accoutrements of the Free Church cause, it now became a surrogate for it. The reasons are not difficult to ascertain. Here was a campaign, one of the very few available, by which Nonconformist activities might define and assert their position *vis-à-vis* the government at a time when it would have been considered unpatriotic to pursue more basic objectives. Secondly, here was the only 'Nonconformist' campaign which the war promised to spur to success, if only because of public concern with alleged drunkenness in munitions and other vital industries. That promise, however, was left unredeemed. Lloyd George, who had once trumpeted that 'Temperance men' constituted 'the best fighting men in the ranks of the Liberal army',[26] proceeded to alienate their support shortly after his elevation to a rival command.

On 17 April 1917, Nicoll was invited to luncheon at Downing Street, where he received a briefing on the government's measures to restrict and control the sale of alcoholic beverages. As his wife described it in a pencilled record of the day's events, he went with considerable trepidation, looking 'very neat in his new gray suit'. Before leaving home, 'he said his prayers as usual – when dressed – then went back & prayed again for quite 3 or 5 minutes'. Several hours later, he 'returned very silent & tired & serious'. Lady Robertson Nicoll 'asked no questions till he had drunk his tea, then very quietly he told me . . . what he could '. Lord Milner and Lord St Davids had been present. ' They discussed other things till 1/2 way thro' lunch ', when the conversation turned to a recommendation for State Purchase, against which Nicoll was firmly set. ' They were all very calm, knowing how intensely WRN feels on the subject, & his great constraint accounts for his being so tired now.' The Prime Minister told his guests that

> WRN was among his greatest friends. He had pledged himself to nothing yet. He thought that State Control would be a better management than the present control. But he saw when he got to Edinburgh that it could not be done. Finally he said he would do nothing without first consulting WRN.[27]

Nicoll was torn between his devotion to the Prime Minister and his natural aversion to a scheme by which the liquor trade would be bought out at generous terms with public funds. His distress was intensified by the extent to which others banked on him to press their cause. The Rev J. Hugh Edwards, the Congregationalist M.P. for Mid-Glamorgan, sent him a dossier of incriminating extracts from Lloyd George's recent speeches : ' . . . On every hand I hear expressions of warm gratitude for the splendid stand which the " British Weekly " is making against State purchase ', he wrote. ' If the project is defeated, it will be a great personal triumph for you.'[28] Arthur Mee, a Nonconformist journalist best known as editor of the *Children's Encyclopedia*, dedicated his Strength of Britain movement to ' the plain demand for War-Time Prohibition, that & nothing less '. He would accept State Purchase, he explained to Nicoll, only if the government intended it as the prelude to proscription of alcohol sales. ' If it is worth £4,000,000,000 to destroy the German Empire, is it not worth £4,000,000,000 to *destroy* the drink trade?' But Mee was ' opposed . . . determinedly ' to the idea of ' purchase pure & simple without that guarantee '. On this score, he was far less tractable than Angus Watson, his principal benefactor, a confirmed teetotaller who was nevertheless reportedly ' quite willing to accept ' the *Spectator's* proposals for ' Purchase in lieu of Prohibition '. Furious with Lloyd George, Mee and his friends threatened to organise ' a Covenant by which we hope to bind at least a million votes for Prohibition at the Demobilisation Election. The government will listen then, & not before.'[29] To Nicoll's relief, the Prime Minister soon reconsidered his policy, and eventually scrapped the controversial scheme. By his own telling, his decision owed far less to Nonconformist opposition than to the ' widespread discontent' among consumers in the munitions centres.[30]

Mortified to discover ' that the Trade have complete power over the present Government', Nicoll could at least console himself ' that L.G. has put a great deal more energy into everything, and that we are in a much better condition than we were a year ago '.[31] Other Free Churchmen, no less eager to win the war, were more critical of its conduct. In their opinion, for Britain to resort to ' Prussian' techniques would qualify as an implicit victory for the enemy. On 15 May, an ' emphatic protest' was lodged ' against the policy of Reprisal, represented in our recent bombing of Freiburg . . ., precisely that method of direct and indiscriminate attack upon non-combatants which we have been holding up to the condemnation of mankind '. The signatories included Clifford, Monro-Gibson, Horton, Scott Lidgett, Meyer, and Selbie, along with Lord Courtney, Mrs Fawcett, A. G. Gardiner, and Sidney Webb.[32] The National Council, in which most of these individuals remained active, maintained an embarrassed silence. In the wake of the 1916 political crisis, Meyer had proposed ' that the entire machinery of the Free Church Councils should be placed at the disposal of the Government '.[33] As a result the Council had absolved itself of any duty to censure official policy. When its organising committee next met in September, it moved only

> to re-affirm that its loyalty to those great and lofty ideals of liberty and justice, which compelled a reluctant Nation & its Allies to take up arms, makes it inevitable that they should continue the struggle till those aims have been achieved.[34]

The Liberation Society, likewise determined to preserve a consensus within its depleted ranks, was similarly committed ' to abstain from . . . public controversy '.[35]

These obsessive attempts to project an image of unimpaired unity conversely gave evidence of Nonconformity's growing discomfort and disability. ' The Churches are not at rest ', Clifford sadly acknowledged *à propos* of R. J. Campbell's ' succession to the Anglican Church '.[36] A further index to their debility was the promulgation of ecumenical schemes, always an indication of weakness. In his 1916 presidential address to the National Council at Bradford, Shakespeare advocated nothing less than the creation of a 'United Free Church of England', into which the various sects would merge. Sir Robert Perks, a pioneer for union among the Methodists, greeted the plan with enthusiasm:

> Purged by this terrible baptism of fire from materialist teaching, and preaching the old gospel of a full and free salvation through an omnipotent Redeemer, Nonconformity will renew her ancient glory and become once again a mighty power for good in our beloved land.[37]

Clifford saw no merit in the scheme, which ran the 'danger, as it seems to me, of sacrificing sincerity, liberty, and the truth of the Gospel, for the sake of obtaining an external and mechanical uniformity'. Yet he declined to publicise his objections out of consideration for Shakespeare, a fellow Baptist, who knew well enough 'my ineradicable hostility to clericalism in every shape and form'.[38]

Too grandiose to obtain requisite support, Shakespeare's blueprint was shelved in favour of a more tentative step to 'organic union', the creation of a Federal Council of the Evangelical Free Churches. Established in 1917, this body recognised the autonomy of its member churches, linking them together 'through their Conferences, Synods, or Unions'. Its executive was composed of a minimum of three representatives from each participating denomination, whose appointed task was to consider matters of common concern. The Federal Council held its first meetings in September 1919 at Christ Church in Westminster Bridge Road, London. From the start, it was expected to supersede or merge with the pre-existing National Council, but various obstacles, largely of a mechanical nature, delayed that inevitability until 1940. In the meantime, the Federal Council scrupulously avoided the partisan debate which, in the minds of its founders, had sapped the National Council of its strength. In 1927, for example, it considered a request from the League of Nations Union for a statement on disarmament. Although sympathetic, the Council replied that it 'prefer[red] to leave the duty of expressing opinions of this kind in formal resolutions to the National Free Church Council, which in such matters well represents the same constituency throughout England'.[39] This attitude reflected not so much a division of labour, but a tacit repudiation of the tradition of political Nonconformity.

While some Free Churchmen signalled their retreat from

political activism, others reaffirmed their loyalty to Asquith or indicated their support for an independent Labour opposition. Where did this leave Lloyd George? On 26 October, he attempted to reestablish his position by inviting Nonconformist leaders to a working breakfast at Downing Street. Ushering his guests into the room ' where William Pitt drank three bottles of wine ', he bantered ' that it never had so many Nonconformists in it before '. In the dialogue that followed, they professed confidence in the Prime Minister, but admitted their distrust of his Cabinet associates – specifically Curzon, Milner, and Carson – to whose baleful influence they conveniently ascribed the government's ' acceptance of the Scheme of Purchase of the Liquor Trade '. Scoffing at their fears, Lloyd George ' insisted that the majority of the War Council was Nonconformist, and he eulogised the service of Nonconformity in the war at great length '.[40] Several weeks later, Free Churchmen carried off a generous share of the New Year Honours, a commodity that Lloyd George always bartered to good effect. A knighthood was conferred on Kingsley Wood, the son of a Wesleyan divine and grandson of one of Wesley's preachers. Other recipients included George Lunn, the Lord Mayor of Newcastle-on-Tyne and a popular local preacher, and two brothers of the late Silvester Horne. The Rev Y. Y. Fullerton, in his capacity as president of the Baptist Union, reciprocated by sending the Prime Minister the ' hearty good wishes of your own people who honour you greatly for your constant loyalty to your Baptist principles '.[41]

Lloyd George's Liberal rivals were not inactive, though they lacked his resources and, more conspicuously, his gift for flattery. Asquith had too much integrity to exploit his own Congregational background and to deliver fulsome tributes. To Dr Horton, whose *Autobiography* he had just read, he wrote

that, although my thoughts about the things which I, like you, think the most important of all, have brought me to some conclusions with which you would be far from agreeing, I have a feeling of real reverence for that which you have been and done during the years of which this book is the record.[42]

Lloyd George, under the same circumstances, would not have dared to allude to his private doubts, but instead would have made a sanctimonious reference to his Welsh chapel or to his beloved Uncle Lloyd.[43]

Walter Runciman, Asquith's lieutenant, was better equipped than his leader to conciliate Nonconformist opinion. Expelled from office, he stepped up his participation in Wesleyan affairs and in the deliberations of the National Free Church Council. His articulation of ' The Radical Outlook ' in the January *Contemporary Review* won the commendation of the *Methodist Times*, which responded less cordially to Lloyd George's speeches on war aims. To the satisfaction of Scott Lidgett, who doubled as editor of the *Methodist Times* and co-editor of the *Contemporary*, there appeared to be no difference ' in principle, between Runciman and Arthur Henderson, the Labour chief and another Wesleyan.[44] Unfortunately, Runciman was prevented by illness from carrying the Asquithian banner to the City Temple in March, when the National Council held its twenty-third annual meeting. His replacement was T. McKinnon Wood, a Congregationalist who had served in the previous coalition as chancellor of the Duchy of Lancaster.

The National Council had been scheduled to convene for three days at Sheffield. Instead, its programme was abridged and the place shifted to London. Debate was spirited and, from all accounts, generally critical of the government.[45] Resolutions were passed condemning official attitudes to the drink question, to the encouragement of vice among fighting men in France, and to the League of Nations, about which the Prime Minister remained distressingly noncommittal. There was a ' lively scene ' concerning the treatment of conscientious objectors, with successive motions moved from the floor and voted down, including one that proposed nothing more than an acknowledgment of ' widely different views ' on the subject. The provisions of H. A. L. Fisher's Education Bill, concurrently receiving its second reading, received a ' luminous ' exposition from Herbert Lewis, who was able to allay most fears. Plans were laid to celebrate the tercentenary of the sailing of the *Mayflower*. But the *leit-motiv* of the proceedings was a determination to rehabilitate the Council, which had been accused of simultaneously preaching defeatism and practising warmongering. Principal Selbie, the outgoing president, undoubtedly compounded the confusion by putting forth the case that Free Churchmen were neither militarists nor pacifists ' according to ordinary terms '.

The climax came with the appearance of Lloyd George, who admittedly had been ' none too sure of his welcome '. Compton-

Rickett, anticipating the worst, foolishly lapsed into partisan rhetoric in an effort to persuade the delegates that ' the Prime Minister required not only the entire support but the prayers of the nation '. For this breach of etiquette, he was soundly rebuked. Lloyd George, introduced to the assembly as ' the husband of the President of the Women's Section of the Free Church Council ', measured his words more carefully:

> I have come here this afternoon not as the Chief Minister of the Crown, but as a humble member of the Free Churches, to talk to my fellow Free Churchmen in an hour of grave national emergency. . . . In the days of the great Civil War Nonconformists fought for individual liberty. They are now fighting for international right.

In defence of his government's record, he pointed to ' vast achievements that ought to be recognised by temperance reformers ', and promised support for a League of Nations at the appropriate time, namely when the war had been won. Interrupted by hecklers, who charged him with giving licence to drunkenness and vice, he replied with assurances that ' I resent no pressure and no criticism, except of one kind. I resent that kind of criticism that seems to imply that these evils began when I took office.' Thereupon, he completed his address and rushed off to an appointment with Clemenceau.

It was, by any standard, a masterly performance. ' Ben Ezra ', who kept ' A Londoner's Notebook ' for the *Methodist Times,* reported ' very divided opinions as to whether the speech was a success ', but conceded that ' it was a very clever one ' that accomplished its primary objective: ' Mr Lloyd George was well advised in attending the Free Church Council, for it is undeniable that opinion was hardening against him.' The Prime Minister obviously agreed, for he followed up his speech with appearances that spring at the assemblies of the Church of Scotland, the United Free Church of Scotland, and the Free Church of Scotland.

Those who went to the City Temple expecting an indictment of the government and its head came away bitterly disappointed. Arthur Mee put the blame on F. B. Meyer, who ' is not strong enough to deal with these intriguers, who dominate & overrule the whole body of the Council. In the interests of Nonconformity, not less than for Prohibition, they should be ruthlessly exposed.' To this end, Mee sent the *British Weekly* a stinging article, which Nicoll knew better than to publish. Being a professional journalist, Mee respected an editorial decision. Besides, he was in no mood to launch a new crusade. ' I am being pressed strongly to give a lead to those who would follow, but I am tired of the whole business,' he confessed :

> With the Government we are up against a mountain of lies about Drink; with the Free Church Council we are up against a craven crew, led by this Shakespeare who thinks he wrote ' Hamlet '. . . . I am going to give it all up.[46]

By giving Lloyd George a platform, and by failing to confront him with its full dissatisfaction, the National Council confirmed in many minds the view, advanced in the correspondence columns of the *Nation*, that it was ' a futile, timid, and somewhat discredited institution ', hopelessly in the grip of wirepullers : ' . . . The Free Church Federation is not Dr Meyer, but Dr Meyer plus Sir Joseph Compton-Rickett '.

The Prime Minister's intensified efforts to conciliate Nonconformist opinion presaged an early appeal to the electorate. During the spring and summer of 1918, the parties were busily adopting candidates, who took their stand for or against the Coalition. The House of Commons that sat at Westminster had been elected in the distant days of 1910 under vastly different circumstances. There had since occurred a drastic realignment of political forces which no one could have predicted, but which had to be taken into account. Eager to strengthen Lloyd George's hand, the *Baptist Times* likened the wartime Parliament to the Long Parliament, whose prolonged tenure had ' become intolerable '. The *Christian World*, backed by the *Methodist Times*, countered that a meaningful poll could not be conducted until peaceful conditions were restored. The armistice came on the morning of 11 November, and within hours, Lloyd George had called an election, which he appeared certain to win.

The Liberation Society had prepared for the eventuality by agreeing to Sir Halley Stewart's suggestion ' that no propaganda should take place at the Election and that candidates standing for re-election should not be approached by the Society directly or indirectly '. It was held permissible, however, for the Society to make discreet inquiry ' of new candidates and candidates in new constituencies on questions of religious equality '. The National Free Church Council showed even greater restraint. It adopted no policy beyond urging its affiliates 'to organise meetings . . . to support a League of Nations'. As the campaign heated up, there 'was fear in many quarters lest the Free Church Council should declare officially for the Coalition and follow the lead of some of its members in their personal fervour for the Prime Minister'. Contrary to expectation, the executive committee adhered to its self-denying ordinance, leaving its members free to take any side or none.[47]

On Saturday afternoon, 16 November, joined by members of the royal family, Free Churchmen of every sectarian and political persuasion gathered at the Royal Albert Hall for a special thanksgiving service which stole the limelight from Anglican observances at St Paul's and the votive mass at Westminster Cathedral. Nonconformity had paid a staggering price for its right to exult in the Allied victory. 'It had become too closely connected with a regime Conservative in complexion and nationalistic in outlook,' Trevor Wilson has cogently argued. 'Whereas the Church of England might survive, and even prosper from, identification with the nation in arms, such identification did violence to the genius of Nonconformity.'[48] The loss was revealed most immediately in the political sphere, where Free Churchmanship no longer operated as a tactical unit. Its disintegration mirrored that of the Liberal Party, to which it contributed in no small measure, and helped to foster a Labour alternative, which was as much the beneficiary of its mutual recriminations as of its undimmed idealism. In the welter of postwar electioneering, political Nonconformity proved unable to define its *raison d'être*, and consequently was denied one.

7 *Peace Restored*

It has been passionately disputed whether Lloyd George, by going to the country in November 1918 at the head of a preponderantly Conservative coalition, destroyed the historic Liberal Party. His apologists have suggested that, contrary to popular belief, the 'coupon' that he and Bonar Law jointly dispensed to their followers represented an astute manoeuvre to save as many Liberal lambs as possible from certain electoral slaughter; according to this revisionist view, it was the intractable Asquith who must bear the brunt of responsibility for perpetuating the split in party ranks. One fact, however, is incontestable: Lloyd George, by the hopes he first inspired and then dashed, ensured the calamitous fate of political Nonconformity.

The *Christian World,* never one of Lloyd George's favourite journals ('I find it totally unreadable', he told Robertson Nicoll in 1911[1]), heralded the approach of the Coupon Election with a repudiation of the Prime Minister: 'The truth is that he has been completely captured,' it wrote more in sorrow than in anger on 7 November, 'and we had better recognise the fact at once.' Five days later, Lloyd George moved to dispel that impression. In the oak-panelled dining room at 10 Downing Street, he outlined his policies and reaffirmed his loyalties to an invited audience of nearly two hundred Liberals, many of them Nonconformists, to whom nothing could have been better calculated to give gratification than his promise to seek a just and generous treaty with the defeated powers as a means 'to initiate the reign on earth of the Prince of Peace'.

J. H. Shakespeare, who attended the meeting in his capacity as editor of the *Baptist Times,* reported that the rousing address 'has left us even more determined and enthusiastic supporters of the Prime Minister than we were before'. In the weeks that followed, he lavished praise on his hero's programme, including

K

his handling of the vexing Welsh Church question. Here Lloyd George had supposedly

> shown his power as a conciliator. He has persuaded the Unionists to accept Disestablishment and Disendowment in return for a reconsideration of the financial arrangements of the Act now on the Statute-book. In any case it is worth a good deal to have Disestablishment carried out as an agreed measure, instead of reopening all the old bitter religious controversy.

Other Free Church spokesmen were not so sure, and reckoned the government's attempts to propitiate the Welsh bishops as part of the exorbitant price of coalition rule. Most of all, however, they faulted Lloyd George and his allies for declining to commit themselves on the question of temperance reform. Asquith, on behalf of the Independent Liberals, had endorsed the 'Nine Points of the Temperance Council of the Christian Churches'; and Arthur Henderson, overcoming opposition from Ben Tillett and other advocates of decontrol, had pledged Labour to a similar stand. 'On the general programme of reconstruction', the *Methodist Times* concluded,

> there is little difference between the Coalition, Liberal and Labour parties. But on the most vital concern of all – the temperance policy of the State – two of the parties have frankly declared their approval of the minimum requirements of the Christian Churches.[2]

The government's failure to tackle the subject of temperance might have rankled, but did not, as everyone knew, threaten to alienate a substantial body of Nonconformist support. Rather it was Lloyd George himself, by the postures he assumed and the policies he espoused, who turned most Free Church leaders against the Coalition. The process was gradual, as shown by the case of Dr Clifford. On Saturday morning, 16 November, Clifford 'occupied a prominent position on the platform' of the Central Hall, Westminster, where Lloyd George and Bonar Law launched their combined campaign. The Prime Minister's speech, while stinting in magnanimity towards his Liberal and Labour adversaries, was not objectionable. Ten days later, Lloyd George attended a private luncheon at the British Empire Club to commemorate Clifford's eighty-second birthday and ministerial diamond jubilee. Pointing to the guest of honour, he declared that there was ' no man in England upon whose conscience I would sooner ring a coin '. But, by then, Clifford's celebrated conscience was in the throes of crisis. He was outraged by the Prime Minister's demagogic appeals to chauvinism and Germanophobia, by his virulent attacks on former colleagues, and, not least of all, by the use of the coupon to secure the return of a rubber-stamp Parliament. As if to add insult to injury, the allocation of Coalition favours was entrusted to Sir George (later Viscount) Younger, Unionist Party manager and the heir to a well known brewery. In a letter published in the *British Weekly* on the 28th, Clifford enjoined passive resisters, whose number he was inclined to exaggerate, ' not [to] pay any regard to the " Coalition label " ', and to vote for candidates pledged to revoke ' the fraudulent Act of 1902 '. Within days, he issued a personal manifesto, addressed to all Nonconformists: ' We must not trust the Coalition label '.[3] Finally, on 11 December, he carried his opposition to its logical conclusion by taking the chair at a Free Church demonstration in support of the Labour programme.

To Clifford and numerous others, Asquithian Liberalism was a halfway house that afforded no shelter from the raging storm. Labour, with its principles of internationalism and its basic concern with human dignity, seemed a more promising alternative. Despite appearances to the contrary, Nonconformity and Labour had a natural affinity, which both sides were eager to exploit in the confusing circumstances of 1918. Imbued with the same evangelical fervour, each had previously functioned within the parliamentary structure as an adjunct of the great Liberal Party. No less than Free Churchmen, prewar Labour representatives had expected great things from Lloyd George, who betrayed them by joining with the enemy.

Broadly speaking, there was no fundamental conflict between Nonconformity, steeped in doctrines of egalitarianism, and socialism as it had distinctively evolved in the British context. In an 1897 Fabian Society tract, Clifford had underscored the parallels between *Socialism and the Teaching of Christ*, whom Free Church progressives unabashedly depicted as a humble artisan and ' the toilers' best friend '. With even less theological inhibition, social militants advanced the view, which would have astonished Marx no less than Matthew, that ' in its earliest form the religion of the Nazarene was a proletarian faith ', whose ' supreme exponent was put to death by the bourgeoisie of His time '.

Godfearing and teetotal ('Labour and liquor don't mix' was Keir Hardie's maxim), the founders of the Labour Party were eminently worthy of Nonconformist patronage, for which they were usually grateful. 'To the Christian Church', the Rev C. Ensor Walters wrote after the Labour breakthrough in the 1906 election,

> it is a matter of thankfulness that so many of the leaders of the Labour Movement are earnest disciples of Christ, whilst others, less emphatic in their religious beliefs, reverence His name and are inspired by His teaching. In this respect the English Labour Movement differs from the kindred movement on the Continent.

Shortly thereafter, Labour officials were genuinely distressed by imputations 'that we are atheists', and solicited a testimonial from Clifford 'that as a Christian you welcome the advent of the Labour Party'. After the war, when Labour had come into its own, its parliamentary leaders denied no less strenuously that they were rank materialists. In early September 1919, an international conference on the subject of religion in the labour movement was held at the Robert Browning Settlement in Walworth, London. British politicians in attendance included G. N. Barnes, Arthur Henderson, Thomas Cape, George Lansbury, and Tom Richards. F. H. Stead, the warden of Browning Hall and a former Congregational minister, paid tribute to 'the variety and vitality of the Free Churches', which had kept religion in England – as nowhere else – from becoming 'too largely the bulwark of the upper and official classes, a convenient department of state for the buttressing of the established order'.[4]

'Where religious feeling was still comparatively strong', an eminent scholar has suggested, 'Socialism took on most completely the guise of religion.'[5] This interpretation implies a disingenuousness that was doubtless present in certain cases, but that was hardly characteristic. To the contrary, one might argue that socialism found greatest acceptance in those areas where its ethic was reinforced by prevailing religious tradition. Surely it was no coincidence that so many of the Labour pioneers were Primitive Methodists, sent to Parliament from Durham and Northumberland where more than 25,000 of their co-denominationalists were clustered. Henderson was a Wesleyan lay preacher; but, his biographer informs us, his constituents at Barnard Castle were predominantly Primitive Methodists, and he ' had an understanding of their characteristic approach '.[6] In any event, Henderson identified with that undercurrent of Wesleyanism that emanated from the Wesleyan Methodist Union for Social Service, founded in 1903 by the Revs S. E. Keeble, J. E. Rattenbury and Henry Carter. These divines were probably more revolutionary in matters of social doctrine than most working-class M.P.s, though not necessarily more devout.

There were, of course, periodic altercations between Labour and Free Church officials, but none more rancorous than those that punctuated the relations of either group with the Liberal whip. On the one side, there were apocalyptic fears of godless socialism; on the other, exasperation with the way in which chapel-goers – as Aneurin Bevan, the son of a Baptist father and a Methodist mother, put it – ' could . . . sing themselves into a trance '.[7] At the 1914 Labour conference at Glasgow, one speaker made ' a rather ill-natured attack on ministers of religion '; but the *Primitive Methodist Leader*, turning the other cheek, reflected that Labour had suffered its share of ' supercilious sneering '.[8] In Wales, some Labour candidates had incurred resentment by ' devoting the sabbath to political propagandism, which has been openly hostile to the ministrations of the churches '. But, by the spring of 1918, they had seen the error of their ways, and even ' advanced Socialists ' were reported to be recruiting talent ' from the ranks of Nonconformist ministers '.[9]

Significantly, it was only after the National Council had disclaimed corporate activism that meaningful collaboration with Labour became possible. To be fair, the Council had attempted at various intervals to strengthen its links with trade unionism and working-class politicians, but without appreciable success. Ramsay MacDonald, invited in 1905 to take part in a ' free and frank expression of opinion ' at the Memorial Hall, demurred. ' Free Churchman as I am by all my prejudices and inclinations ', he tartly replied, he had ' almost given up hope ' that any good could be accomplished by an organisation whose notepaper was embossed with such names as Perks and Compton-Rickett.[10] The situation had changed by 1918: Perks had removed himself, and Compton-Rickett stood discredited as a lackey of Lloyd George. In its lay leadership, political Nonconformity had lurched to the left.

The *Christian World* counted 178 Free Church candidates in the 1918 general election, roughly the same total as in the previous polling, eight years before. There was, however, a dramatic up-surge in the proportion of Labour contenders. Primitive Methodists, it goes without saying, went solidly for Labour. Among Wesleyans in the field, the Unionists had doubled to six, and the Labourites had trebled to twelve. Nearly a fourth of Congregationalist candidates were Labour men, as were a third of Baptists in the field. No fewer than fourteen Free Church divines stood for election, eight of them (four Baptists, two Unitarians, one Primitive Methodist, and one Congregationalist) on the Labour ticket.

Among spiritual leaders, there was a corresponding shift, indicative not so much of a conversion to socialism, but rather of a disgust with Lloyd George's electoral tactics. Dr Horton went so far as to commend MacDonald to the electors of Leicester West, urging them to consider the candidate's ' splendid aims for workers ' and not his possible ' error of judgment' concerning the war. At Hampstead, where no Independent Liberal was standing, Horton and Garvie supported the Labour man against a couponed Tory. Dr Charles Brown, a former president of the Baptist Union, considered himself ' fortunate in having ' at North Islington ' a Liberal candidate who is not chosen by the Lloyd George caucus '. Otherwise, Brown announced,

> I should vote Labour, as I approve of its programme and I admire immensely men like Arthur Henderson (who has been shamefully treated) and J. H. Thomas. I wish from the bottom of my heart there could be a coalition of the forces of Liberalism and Labour.

The Rev Thomas Phillips, the Bloomsbury Baptist, declared his opposition to ' candidates being kennelled by a brewer whipper-in ', and helped to promote Labour candidacies. Scott Lidgett and the Rev George Hooper, both officers of the National Council, unofficially addressed anti-coalition meetings. Most interestingly, the Rev James Nicholas of the Castle Street Baptist Church, London, who was widely known as ' the Premier's pastor ', campaigned in the Neath Division for the Labour candidate, the Rev Herbert Morgan, against the Rev J. Hugh Edwards, a couponed Congregationalist.[11]

On 11 December, a bare three days before polling, Free Churchmen staged a pro-Labour rally at the Kingsway Hall, which was property of the Methodist Trust.[12] The *Methodist Times* called it ' one of the most exhilarating and amazing demonstrations ever held in London ', and was happily ' reminded . . . of the inspiring Nonconformist gatherings during the days of the Education crusade '. Hastily improvised and modestly budgeted, the event aroused such ' intense ' interest ' that the doors had to be opened three-quarters of an hour before the hour announced, and the great hall was packed to overflowing half-an-hour before the proceedings started '. Clifford, whose ' rousing sentences were received with ringing cheers ', presided and read letters of support from (among others) Brown, Horton, Phillips, and Hooper. In his opening speech, he asserted ' that the Labour manifesto was in every respect the programme of Christianity '. The Rev W. H. Armstrong, a Wesleyan who ' had the time of his life ' that evening, tellingly asked whether the *British Weekly,* a house organ of the Coalition, ' expected to get prohibition from Sir George Younger '. Dr W. E. Orchard, a theologically innovative Congregationalist, quoted scripture in reply to those who alleged that Labour was too revolutionary : ' He hath put down the mighty from their seat, and hath exalted the humble and meek. He hath filled the hungry with good things, and the rich He hath sent away empty.' ' No Labour programme ', Orchard concluded, ' ever went so far as that.'

While no one on the platform was heard to utter a ' disrespectful or sneering word ' against the Prime Minster, the mention of his name ' provoked some hooting ' from the floor. Throughout, the sense of the meeting was deeply antagonistic to him, with demands for the prompt abolition of conscription, for the establishment of ' a League of Free Nations ', for a peace conference with ' open doors ', and for non-intervention in Russian affairs. At the close, a statement was issued over the signatures of some of the best known spiritual leaders of Nonconformity : ' Not all of us commit ourselves to the full Labour programme ', they explained, ' but in a case where it is Labour opposing the Coalition ticket we unhesitatingly urge all progressives to support Labour.'

Polling, for the first time confined to a single day, took place on Saturday, the 14th. The results for Nonconformist candidates, of whom only a third carried the coupon, were disastrous. Eightyeight Free Churchmen were returned, the smallest number since 1880 : seven of them were Unionists, seven were Independent Liberals, twenty-two were Labour men, and the remaining fiftytwo were Coalition Liberals. The *Christian World* was cheered to report that ' almost all the Labour M.P.s returned unopposed for South Wales are well known Free Churchmen': William ('Mabon') Abraham was a Calvinistic Methodist lay preacher; William Brace was 'a prominent Baptist'; and Tom Richards was 'an active Congregationalist and an occasional speaker on denominational platforms'. Vernon Hartshorn, a newcomer to Parliament, was the son of a Primitive Methodist local preacher. Elsewhere in the area, seats were won for Labour by J. Winstone, a Baptist, and by Alfred Onions, Charles Edwards, and John Williams, all Congregationalists. It was further noted that 'the Primitive Methodist contribution to the new House of Commons is a solid block of Labour members, . . . all local preachers'.

The Independent Liberal forces were decimated, with Asquith heading the list of casualties. Fourteen Wesleyans failed to obtain re-election, among them Walter Runciman, T. R. Ferens, Sir Norval Helme, Sir George Toulmin, and Arthur Henderson, who was ousted from East Ham by Clem Edwards, a Congregationalist who stood as a Coalition Liberal. The trio of Nonconformist divines in the new house – T. T. Broad, J. Hugh Edwards, and Towyn Jones – were likewise Congregationalist Liberals to whom Lloyd George had given certification. Neither Sir John Simon nor Reginald McKenna were among the twenty-six successful Congregationalists, of whom eighteen were Coalition Liberals, one (George Barnes) was a Coalition Labourite, one was an Independent Liberal, and six were straight Labour. Twelve of the thirty Baptist candidates saw victory: six (one of them Lloyd George) as Coalition Liberals, three as Independent Liberals, and three as Labour. One of the losers was the anonymous 'Baptist M.P.' who, for nine years, had contributed weekly parliamentary reports to his denominational journal; denied the coupon, he had correctly prophesied that his 'chances of success are not very rosy under the remarkable circumstances of this Election'.[13]

A handful, at most, of Nonconformist candidates swam sucfully against the tide. Sir Donald Maclean, without benefit of the coupon, managed to retain his seat at Peebles by a thumping majority of 2,600. The only Presbyterian in the 1918 Parliament who did not attach to the Coalition, he was tapped to deputise for Asquith until the latter's return to Westminster in a 1920 by-election. At Wolverhampton East, G. L. Thorne, a Baptist, warded off an assault from the Rev J. A. Shaw, the couponed candidate of the British Workmen's League. Hayden

Jones (J. D.'s brother) and Major David Davies, both Calvinistic Methodists who were more or less identified with the Asquithian wing of the party, were relieved to be given a clear run in their respective Welsh constituencies. J. C. Thornborough, the Liberal contender at Morpeth, was a Wesleyan who unexpectedly received and promptly disavowed Coalition backing; he was defeated by J. Cairns, his Primitive Methodist Labour opponent. P. W. Raffan, the Congregationalist at Leigh, was another Liberal whom the Coalition refused to discountenance, however emphatically he discountenanced the Coalition. It was more usually the case that candidates vied for the coupon: Thomas Lough made an offer, which *The Times* thought ' to say the least, peculiar ' to support Lloyd George more loyally in the future than in the past; it was not accepted, and Lough lost the seat at West Islington which he had held since 1892.

Of the Free Church journals, only the *Baptist Times* and the *British Weekly* took a strong stand for the Coalition. Censured by the committee of the Yorkshire Association of Baptist Churches for its ' recent partisanship ', the former offered ' no apology. . . . We have never attempted to write vapid nothings. We are supporters of Mr Lloyd George and . . . we firmly believe that our view is that of the immense majority of the Baptist denomination.' Yet active cooperation between the editors of these two papers was precluded by their mutual antipathy on theological grounds. Robertson Nicoll, despite his Tory predilections, remained a radical in matters of church discipline. J. H. Shakespeare, on the other hand, had veered in the direction of clericalism. J. D. Jones applauded as ' admirable & . . . urgently needed ' Nicoll's critique (5 December) of Shakespeare's proposals for an elaborate ecclesiastical structure: ' A kind of " snobbery " has made its appearance in Free Church circles which needed stigmatizing as such you have done it.' In the same breath, he begged leave to ' add one other word not by way of criticism but by way of appeal. I am frankly terrified ', he revealed,

by the wholesale proscription of Independent Liberals. I don't know whether you realize how far it has gone. I have tried to keep our people sweet about the P.M. I have spoken up for him when it has been difficult. But what is one to say about this last performance? He has done his best to remove every independent Liberal out of Parliament. Frankly, I have no faith

in the reforming zeal of a Government which has so pre-
ponderating a Tory element. . . . And my suspicions are confirmed when I read that the Welsh Church Act is to be
amended & Protection is to be introduced. . . . They tried to
squeeze my brother out of Merioneth (& he has never given
a vote against the Government). They are trying to oust Ellis
Davies out of Carnarvon all because he will not give a pledge
of blind support. And alas for poor Scotland! The P.M.
could have squared the Reactionaries & swept the country without this miserable ' coupon ' business & he himself would have
been a free man.[14]

Although neither Nicoll nor Shakespeare wavered (to quote the
British Weekly) ' as ardent suporters of the Coalition, and
especially of its illustrious head ', they were both pained by the
disapprobation of old friends. On 6 December, the *Baptist
Times* reported that its editor was ' in a low and depressed
condition ' and forced to cancel all engagements.

By far the most momentous development in Nonconformist
journalism was the announcement of editorial changes at the
Methodist Times. At the close of 1918, Scott Lidgett retired
after a dozen years' service. Control was vested in a committee
of younger, left-wing Wesleyan divines among whom were Henry
Carter (who took charge), Benjamin Gregory, J. E. Rattenbury,
and C. Ensor Walters. Some had participated in the *Methodist
Weekly* venture at the birth of the century. Almost all had
taken part in the recent Kingsway Hall demonstration. Sir Robert
Perks, scandalised to learn that Hugh Price Hughes's newspaper
had fallen into the hands of the agents of ' Socialism and semi-
Bolshevism ', penned a letter of protest; he could not have been
placated by the flippant assurances he received ' that there would
be nothing " semi " about the *Methodist Times* '. More seriously,
the new regime took pains to make clear that the paper ' is not
an organ of Labour ', although its management were ' strong supporters of many Labour projects '. Along with Arthur Henderson,
the lay directorate included Walter Runciman and Gerald France,
a Coalition Liberal M.P. In its latest incarnation, the *Methodist
Times* treated Lloyd George with suspicion, if not hostility. The
coupon was denounced as a ' weapon against Temperance Reformers ', and the Prime Minister was said to threaten the country
with ' camouflaged autocracy. . . . If Mr Lloyd George combined

in his own person the genius of Shakespeare' – William, that is – 'and the character of John Wesley', the editors of the *Methodist Times* would still decline to 'trust him with a dictatorship'.[15]

But their most astringent criticism was directed at the custodians of the National Council, which was due to convene at Sheffield in mid-March. 'In past years', a leader recalled on the 6th, 'the Free Church Council did magnificent service for the Kingdom of God. It gave an instrument to the fervent and progressive members of the Free Churches.' And, not least of all, 'it made itself felt in the political sphere'. That, however, no longer held true.

To be perfectly frank, at the present time it represents nobody in particular. It is run to-day by a little oligarchy in Farringdon-street, which, to all intents and purposes, elects its own officials and poses as representative of the Free Churches, without gaining the authorisation either of their Conferences or of their people. In recent years it has been marked by a paralysing timidity of action and fails to carry with it any serious weight of opinion. It is high time that its methods were revised or that something better were put in its place.

The Federal Council scheme, which Shakespeare had propounded, had its merits, but it was no substitute ' for a Free Church Council like that of the 'nineties'. Nonconformists were asked to recognise that a new age was upon them: Russia had thrown off her yoke, and, at home, the Labour Party had emerged to prominence. Accordingly, the National Council would have to introduce democracy into its operations, and 'some form of dissension' into its discussions. 'Will the Sheffield Conference get a vision of the immense possibilities of these unparalleled times?'

The answer, delivered at Sheffield the following week, was decidedly negative. With Dame Margaret Lloyd George among those in attendance, and Guttery in the chair, the proceedings were singularly lacklustre. The one lively moment was provided by Thomas Phillips, who demanded to know how much longer conscientious objectors would languish in prison for having ' obeyed the Lord Jesus Christ'. His resolution, too forthright in its phraseology, was amended to read: '. . . because they think they have obeyed the Lord Jesus Christ'. By the same token, the twenty-fourth annual Free Church Council called its own inspiration into question.

The Liberation Society struggled even more pitiably ' to recover . . . some of its old prestige '.[16] As soon as the election returns were in, Clifford proposed to summon a meeting of those M.P.s ' in favour of the principles of the Society' to consider the question of re-endowing the Welsh Church. ' Members of the Government being excluded ', Clifford stipulated, making a pointed thrust at the Prime Minister, who continued as a vice-president of the Society while enacting legislation to which the Society was categorically opposed. John Steele, a member of the executive committee, resigned as a protest against Lloyd George's perfidy. Nevertheless, on 31 March 1920, the Welsh Church was officially disestablished, with ample revenues assured to its successor. ' . . . For more than a generation disestablishment had been the dividing question in Wales, not only in politics but also in religion and even in social life ', E. Morgan Humphreys wrote in *Y Genedl*, virtually the only Asquithian paper in the principality. ' Now it is gone, and there is sure to be a vacuum which may well be filled by – well, who knows?'[17]

Sir Robert Perks, always ready to recoup influence, offered ' to assist a movement' to organise ' Nonconformist opinion generally, especially in the House of Commons, in favour of the principles of the Society '. Besides extending hospitality at his house in Kensington Palace Gardens, it is difficult to see what he could have done. In any case, Joseph King, a Congregationalist who had sat as a Liberal in the last Parliament and then changed to Labour, was asked to canvass the views of his new associates concerning questions of religious equality. King promised to ' do what he could, but the Labour Party ', he cautioned, ' was very jealous of any action from outside '.[18] Sometimes obsessive, the party's fears of contravening alliances was altogether understandable, given its internal structure and the fluidity of the political situation. Arthur Henderson, whose own religious credentials were unimpeachable, held firmly to the view that the conflation of spiritual and secular loyalties was precisely the sort of thing that had worked to the detriment of Liberalism.[19] He and other party chiefs were insistent that a member of the parliamentary party owed unconditional allegiance to his whip. Such attitudes militated against extensive Labour involvement in the Liberation Society or other Free Church operations, including the 1935 Council of Action campaign.

Rebuffed by Labour, the Liberation Society fell back upon the

Independent Liberals. Planning their first triennial conference since the war, the management committee unanimously agreed to invite Asquith to deliver the major address, with Simon and Masterman proposed as alternates. As a calculated insult to Lloyd George, Asquith was also nominated as a vice-president of the Society. Out of office and temporarily out of Parliament, the former Premier enjoyed greater popularity among Free Church leaders than at any other time in his lengthy career. Lloyd George, by contrast, was slipping badly. The defeat of Coalition candidates in a string of by-elections shocked those who had come to think of him as invincible. Even Shakespeare, writing in the *Baptist Times* on 21 March 1919, was forced to conclude that the recent reverse at West Leyton had been ' a revolt against the Caucus system in politics ', and he called on Lloyd George to mend his ways. The following February, a by-election at Paisley brought Asquith triumphantly back to Westminster. Dr Horton tendered congratulations to the successful candidate, who assured his ' old & tried friend ' that ' I share your hopes, and shall do what I can; but the driving power must come from the inspiration and con- centration of a regenerated Liberalism.'[20] Lloyd George, ever more cynical, had already discounted the prospect of a Liberal renais- sance. Lunching at Downing Street with Nicoll and Riddell, he

> said that Labour had completely supplanted the old Liberalism, that the ' Wee Frees ' were hopeless in every way. George Riddell said there were two parties – one semi-Democratic, semi-Conservative, the other Labour. ' Yes,' said L.G., ' that is it. That is what it will be.'[21]

Restored to the leadership of the Liberal Opposition, Asquith failed dismally to impart the dynamism or even the credibility for which his supporters had hoped. During the spring of 1920, there was talk of bringing in Grey, perhaps partnered with Lord Robert Cecil, to head the party. Nicoll ingeniously offered his own solution: ' . . . We can see no reason why some who call them- selves Independent Liberals and some who call themselves Coali- tionists should not work together ' under Lloyd George.[22] But the Prime Minister was having problems of his own. Herbert Lewis alerted him to a ' very difficult ' situation that had developed in Wales, where Nonconformist opinion, already antagonised by the Church settlement, was further distressed by the Welsh Temper- ance Bill (with its provisions for financial compensation), and by the delay of the Place of Worship Enfranchisement Bill. On 22 October, Lloyd George gave breakfast to a deputation of Welsh Calvinistic Methodists, whom he attempted to mollify on these and related issues.[23]

His expenditure of time, eggs, and bacon, was not in vain. Early the following year, there was a bitterly contested by-election at Cardiganshire in which local Calvinistic Methodists took an active and, by some accounts, a decisive role. Goronwy Rees has vividly recalled how ' religious feeling only seemed to give added fury to political differences '.[24] The Asquithian candidate was W. Llewelyn Williams, a Congregationalist whose fierce denunciations of the Prime Minister had cost him his seat for Carmarthen at the general election. His opponent, a Coalition Liberal, was Ernest Evans, a young barrister whom Lloyd George wished to put into Parliament as his chief Welsh organiser. It has been calculated that Williams drew his support from among his fellow Independents, and from the local Baptist and Unitarian communities. With the exception of a few prominent laymen, chiefly highminded academics, the Calvinistic Methodists stood solidly behind Evans.

Rees's father, a Calvinistic Methodist minister at Aberystwyth, commanded a ' respect and influence . . . of not inconsiderable importance ' which, perhaps against his better judgment, he placed at the disposal of Evans, ' the son of a prosperous solicitor . . . who . . . was a pillar of my father's chapel, its largest single benefactor, and a close friend '. Along with Nicoll, who boomed Evan's praises in the *British Weekly*, and the Prime Minister's wife, who delivered more than sixty speeches in the constituency, the elder Rees

> flung himself into the electoral battle with an enthusiasm and effectiveness which surprised even his admirers, shocked others and convinced many that his talents were worthy of some larger arena than Cardiganshire and Calvinistic Methodism. . . . In so hard fought a struggle, the formidable qualities he had displayed might well have reversed the result if they had been exerted on the other side.

When the poll was declared on 19 February, Evans led by a margin of nearly 3,600 votes. But the outcome was less happy for his principal Nonconformist supporter. Some members of Rees's congregation ' regarded him, like Lloyd George himself, as a traitor to Liberalism, in Wales then a cause hardly less sacred than that of religion itself '. Worse, he was gnawed by ' his own feeling that . . . he had allowed personal considerations to get the better of what he himself knew to be right '. Shortly after the ' great by-election ', his calling took him away from Aberystwyth to Cardiff.

In Parliament, as in successive by-election campaigns, the Lloyd George Liberals functioned increasingly as an appendage to Unionist Party, at whose convenience they enjoyed office. Yet it was essentially as an antidote to official Unionism that they appealed for Nonconformist support. The situation, pregnant with irony, showed the Prime Minister at his most nimble. On the one hand, he hankered after a regularisation of the *ad hoc* arrangements with his Coalition allies; on the other, he sedulously wangled for the endorsement of Free Churchmen, whom he wished to carry along with him. But however much he may have prized Nonconformist backing, he was unwilling to abide Nonconformist criticism of specific Coalition policies. So far as he was concerned, ' the Irish Question is one of those in regard to which the churches are unfitted to pass an opinion '. The organising committee of the National Council, aghast at such a sentiment, unanimously retorted with a resolution affirming that it was the churches' ' unbounded duty to test the principles that govern the policy and methods that are pursued in the administration of the Government in this and all other questions by the spirit and teaching of the Christian religion '.[25] Subsequently, as we shall see, Lloyd George proved more receptive to the political instrusions of the Free Churches.

In January 1922, the Coalition Liberals sponsored a conference at the Westminster Central Hall, where Asquith and Grey had addressed a Wee Free rally a few weeks earlier. H. A. L. Fisher, one of the indisputable Liberals among Lloyd George's Cabinet colleagues, refuted charges by ' the venerable Dr Clifford ' that the Prime Minister had made ' pitiable concessions to Toryism '. Shakespeare, another speaker, fulsomely lauded Lloyd George as ' one of the most indomitable, gallant, wonderful figures in the history of the world '.[26] A few weeks later, on 24 February, the Prime Minister moved directly to renew old ties. To a special Free Church breakfast at Downing Street, he invited (among others) Clifford, Shakespeare, Garvie, Phillips, Scott Lidgett, Dinsdale T. Young, S. M. Berry, S. W. Hughes, and R. C. Gillie, who was due to preside in a fortnight's time at the

National Council's annual sessions in Liverpool. Before accepting his hospitality, the guests obtained Lloyd George's assurance that, contrary to press reports, he did not play golf on Sunday. Asked his impression of their host, one unidentified divine told the *British Weekly*:

> What I should like to know is his impression of us. What did he say about us to Birkenhead and Winston? None of us had come under false pretences, and some of us had been present at Sir John Simon's reception at the Wharncliffe Rooms the night before. Some of us found to our surprise that it was the same old Lloyd George, the passive resister whom we had followed. . . . We were glad to see that he knew why several of us had opposed him. . . . He is at present in the grip of circumstances, but when the call of a big moral challenge comes he will be once more Leader of the Progressives in a new world.

Ignored by the *Daily Chronicle*, which Lloyd George controlled, the gathering was described with gleeful malice the next day in the *Westminster Gazette*, where J. A. Spender's distinguished editorship was nearing an end. 'One Who Was Not There' began by recounting how, in an early novel by Ellen Thorneycroft Fowler (Sir Henry's daughter), a character had nonchalantly observed that no one with an income of over £200 a year makes love before lunch. 'But Mr Lloyd George', the article continued, 'has made the bleak hour of breakfast a time for the political love-feast.' Announced as 'quite informal and non-political', the meeting was ostensibly intended to acquaint the Prime Minister with 'the semi-political topics' that would come up for discussion at Liverpool. 'But was that all?', the *Westminster Gazette* asked incredulously. 'Behind the announcement, made with such a lingering air of wisdom, there is the lingering suspicion that the Prime Minister is turning to Nonconformity again in the hope of securing some political backing.' The *Methodist Times*, equally disdainful of the whole affair, heard it 'rumoured' that the object of the exercise had been to engineer Lloyd George's reinstatement to the executive of the National Council, from which he had been unceremoniously dropped two years before. Or perhaps, others speculated, he was seeking to bar the appearance at Liverpool of Sir Donald Maclean and Viscount (formerly Herbert) Gladstone, two prominent Asquithians who were scheduled to deliver non-partisan speeches.

Although Lloyd George's premiership survived into the autumn of 1922, the Unionist rank-and-file had long showed signs of restiveness. Days before Free Churchmen assembled around the breakfast table at Downing Street, the Prime Minister was ' furious ' to hear Sir George Younger call for ' a bill of divorcement' to dissolve the ' matrimonial alliance' between Tories and Coalition Liberals. The *Westminster Gazette* sardonically reasoned that there was nothing ' more natural' than for Lloyd George to turn to Nonconformity for ' spiritual consolation in a week when the cracks in the Coalition wall have grown wider and more threatening'. The day after the Free Church breakfast, the Coalition incurred its third by-election defeat within a week : Isaac Foot, a Wesleyan standing as an Independent Liberal, triumphed at Bodmin over a Coalition Unionist and thereby launched what was surely the last of the great Nonconformist parliamentary careers. Acknowledged by the *Daily Chronicle* as the most regrettable of recent government losses, the Bodmin result fueled the Conservative revolt against Lloyd George, gave a much needed fillip to the Asquithians, and induced Free Churchmen to keep their distance from the Coalition, whose break-up seemed imminent. Fearing the worst, the *British Weekly* issued dire warnings of ' the national and European dangers' that would attend Lloyd George's departure from office. Ignoring industrial strife and Irish disorders, Nicoll dwelled on the fact that Nonconformist leaders had received invitations to Buckingham Palace to celebrate the wedding of Princess Mary to Lord Lascelles. Were such fruits of national unity to be lightly tossed away?

Whether or not Lloyd George fought in harness with the Unionists, another general election could not be long deferred. To prepare for this eventuality, he strove to redeem his reputation among Free Churchmen. He could depend upon stout assistance from Nicoll, who systematically denigrated the Wee Frees (' Viscount Gladstone, who inherits nothing but a good name. . . .'), while he crammed the *British Weekly* with reports of Free Church bazaars opened by Dame Margaret Lloyd George, whose husband was prevented by illness from unveiling a memorial to Percy Illingworth, his fellow Baptist and ' old colleague'. The Liberation Society, also anticipating an early election, was in no position to take a stand ' on the present financial resources' at its disposal.[27] The National Council, almost as impecunious, was not nearly so defeatist. In mid-May, its executive passed a resolution that warmly supported the Prime Minister in his work at the Genoa economic conference ' to secure peace, security and prosperity for a divided and distressed Europe '. For standing up to the French on the reparations issue, Lloyd George was further commended by the general committee of the Primitive Methodist connexion, from whom he was not accustomed to receive praise on any score.[28]

The mood of political Nonconformity seemed to be shifting in his favour, and nowhere more markedly than among the Primitive Methodists. Although all of the members of the sect who sat in the 1918 Parliament were affiliated to Labour in one capacity or another, two of them – Barney Kenyon and T. W. Casey – had gravitated into his orbit. Already Albert Shaw, a Primitive Methodist alderman on the Staffordshire County Council, had proclaimed his intention to stand as a Lloyd George Liberal at Newcastle-under-Lyme against Josiah Wedgwood, the Labour incumbent. ' The day was when the vote of Primitive Methodist might be counted upon as solid for advanced Liberalism or Labour,' a denominational spokesman told the *Methodist Times* when the campaign had got under way.

> It is not so to-day. . . . It is true that nearly all the Primitive Methodist candidates in the field are either Labour or Free Liberal, but there are a number of Primitives who still follow Mr Lloyd George and who have never lost either their admiration for his gifts or their belief in his sincerity.

Basically, this reversion to Lloyd George reflected a rise in social status and a geographical dispersal within the Primitive Methodist community. At Newcastle-under-Lyme, which has been the subject of exhaustive sociological investigation, the executive of the Liberal association during the early 'twenties was almost solidly Methodist and constituted, ' broadly speaking, an alliance of the urban middle class and lower-middle class of Newcastle and Wolstanton (which mainly provided the leadership) and the miners in the outlying parts of the constituency '.[29] In other districts, too, there had been a corresponding drift of Primitive Methodist electors to the suburbs, where a vote for a Lloyd George Liberal was deemed the next best thing to a vote for a full-fledged Tory. The *British Weekly* welcomed this ' denominational move to the right, . . . with leanings toward or attachments in some quarters with the interests represented by . . . Mr Lloyd George '. But it is doubtful whether Lloyd George was as much the beneficiary as Nicoll liked to think. In the aftermath of polling, the *Methodist Times* calculated that ' more Primitive Methodists have voted Conservative in this election than in any of the five preceding elections put together '.[30]

The postwar Coalition, which had survived on borrowed time since its inception, fell on 19 October, when Conservative M.P.s met at the Carlton Club and voted to face the electorate under their own flag. Of the eight recognisable Free Churchmen who participated in the balloting, five supported the continuation of the Coalition, and three were opposed.[31] Later that day, Lloyd George tendered his resignation to the King, who presumed, like everyone else, that ' he will be Prime Minister again '.[32] But that was never to happen.

The following Sunday, J. H. Jowett, whom the *Daily Telegraph* had tipped as a likely parliamentary candidate, devoted his sermon at Westminster Church to the ' strange and bewildering events ' that had brought down the government. ' In the General Election may Thy will be made clear ', he prayed, ' and may it be carried out for the common good of mankind.' Lloyd George promptly volunteered to assist his friends in their efforts to realise and serve the divine will. On the 26th, he appeared at Whitefield's Tabernacle, where Sir Albert Spicer introduced him ' as a sincere Free Churchman, who has always, in foul weather and in fair, stood true to Free Church principles '. Finding it more convenient to conjure up the past than to commit himself on the future, Lloyd George delivered a tribute to the late Silvester Horne : ' He was a great friend of mine, and one of the most lovable characters it has ever been my privilege to be associated with.'[33]

All in all, Lloyd George conducted a curiously spiritless campaign. Not wishing to accept as final the Conservatives' declaration of independence from him, he exercised care to do nothing that might prejudice the chances for a *rapprochement*. Although liberated from ' the trammels of Toryism ', he kept silent on the question of temperance. At the same time, he was reluctant to hit out too hard at Labour, whom he might some day aspire to lead in an alliance of the left. The electorate, and Nonconformists in particular, were thrown into a hopeless confusion that was reflected in the returns.

The *Baptist Times*, whose editor ' still thinks that Mr Lloyd George is the greatest safeguard we have against reactionary and revolutionary legislation ', was the only denominational journal to bestow unequivocal support on the National Liberals, as Lloyd George and his followers now called themselves. The *Methodist Times,* taking a more representative view, put ' Temperance Before Party ', and, on that ground, endorsed the Unionist candidacy of Lady Astor in the Sutton division of Plymouth. The *British Weekly* stood by Lloyd George to the extent that Nicoll refused to publish a pair of highly critical articles which he had rashly commissioned from A. G. Gardiner over a glass of wine at the Reform Club. But, between the lines, one could perceive greater caution than in the past.

There were approximately 220 Free Churchmen in the field, of whom a quarter were Congregationalists, another quarter Methodists of one variety or another, and twenty-nine Baptists. They represented, in differing proportions, all parties, and sometimes opposed one another, as in the Wansbeck division of Northumberland, where John Neal (a Wesleyan and National Liberal) fought M. Davies (a Primitive Methodist local preacher and an Independent Liberal). There were seven Congregational divines in the running (two as National Liberals, one Liberal, three Labour, and one Independent), none of whom obtained election. The Rev R. H. Dunnico, a Baptist, fared better in the Consett division of Durham, though his Labour candidacy received ' amazingly little support from Baptists and Free Churchmen ', to whose temperance questionnaire he had not replied ' entirely satisfactorily '.

Less than a third of the Nonconformist candidates – a mere seventy-eight – were successful, and they, for the most part, were veterans of the previous Parliament. There were only a handful of newcomers, of whom none was more notable than Geoffrey Shakespeare, J. H.'s son and Lloyd George's private secretary, who stood (obviously) as a National Liberal, and who trounced the sitting Labour member at Wellingborough. Fourteen other Baptists were returned, and fourteen were defeated. Among the Wesleyans, eighteen either lost seats or had declined to defend them, and the same number won majorities. Primitive Methodists did poorly, losing in eleven of their eighteen contests. Only nineteen out of fifty-six Congregationalist contenders won seats. They were accompanied by three Presbyterians, eight Calvinistic Methodists, and one Independent Methodist.

Thirty-two of the Nonconformist members in the 1922 Parliament were Liberals, of whom fourteen used the prefix ' Independent' and eighteen classified themselves as ' National '. Combined, the two factions exactly equalled the total of Nonconformist Labour M.P.s. In addition, at least twelve Nonconformists sat on the Unionist benches; and one Wesleyan, Edwin (' Ned ') Scrymgeour at Dundee, was elected on the Prohibitionist ticket. Winston Churchill, whom Scrymgeour at last outpolled in his fifth attempt, had once put him down as a politician who ' pleaded for the Kingdom of God upon earth with special reference to the evils of alcohol '.[34]

Had Lloyd George and Asquith joined forces, an inevitability which each resisted, they would have been able to boast – with independent support – a one-seat lead over the Labour Party, which now formed the official opposition at Westminster. But, even so, they would still not have commanded a majority of Nonconformist parliamentary votes, which had been lost to Liberalism. This divergence of interests was reflected, among other places, in Lloyd George's own bailiwick: R. T. Jones, a Calvinistic Methodist who stood for Labour, captured Carnarvon District from C. E. Breese, a National Liberal of Anglican background.

On 7 December, Lloyd George joined Austen Chamberlain, his trusty Coalition ally, at the Victoria Hotel, where Sir George Hayter Chubb hosted a lunch in honour of newly-elected Wesleyan M.P.s. His presence pointed not only to his lingering ambition for reunion with the Conservatives, but also to his vague intention somehow to use Nonconformity, with its broadened political base, as a bridge to transcend party differences and accomplish his return to power. In the next decade, when all else had failed, he tried to implement precisely such a design. In the short run, however, his interest lay in achieving a reconciliation with Asquith, who, at seventy years of age, could not long stand in the way between him and the Liberal Party leadership. After another year had passed and another election had been called, the feuding Liberal chiefs at last reached a tentative accord. It came too late and too grudgingly either to save their afflicted party or to retrieve the support of those who, more out of habit than out of logic, continued to conceive of themselves as political Nonconformists.

8 *Beyond Liberalism*

The demolition of the Lloyd George Coalition left a vacuum in British political life. Three general elections followed in rapid succession; new – or at any rate, untried – men were thrust forward at Westminster; party labels seemed to have lost their relevance; and national voting patterns were drastically altered by what Maurice Cowling has described as a ' psephological earthquake '. In Parliament and outside, Free Churchmen reflected the general uneasiness and disarray. Bitterly divided among themselves, they turned self-consciously to those essentially non-partisan issues – unemployment, international conciliation, sabbatarianism – on which broad agreement was still possible. Or they turned all the more fervently to temperance, an issue which had lost its partisan connotation precisely when they had lost their capacity to command serious political attention.

The times were made more difficult for Nonconformists by the loss of two of their most authoritative spokesmen. In May 1923, after decades of infirmity, Sir William Robertson Nicoll took to his bed and died. ' The nation has lost a great literary figure ', Lloyd George wired to Nicoll's widow, ' nonconformity its most brilliant and experienced publicist, and I personally a devoted and loyal friend.'[1] Then, six months later, Dr John Clifford was struck down in mid-sentence during a Baptist Union debate on evangelism. Depite the vast differences between the two men in background and temperament, both had believed passionately in the destiny of political Nonconformity, which they had sometimes seemed almost to have willed into existence. Each had been a reassuring link with a more vital past. On the evening of 7 July, a commemorative service for Clifford was held at the Westminster Chapel. Asquith and Lloyd George, dutifully accompanied by their wives, shared the platform. In an attempt to quash recurrent rumours of a rupture between them, they glowingly recalled the dawn of the century, when they had cooperated with Clifford and with each other to achieve a spectacular Liberal revival. Unfortunately for their cause, Clifford's memory proved a more dubious asset than had his active electoral assistance.

On 28 August 1923, the ultra-Tory *Morning Post* took delight in featuring a polemic on ' The Nonconformist Conscience : A Fading Phenomenon '. Written by ' A Dissident Dissenter ', it was intended more as an epitaph than as an analysis. The National Council of Evangelical Free Churches, the anonymous author intoned, had died ' from chronic anaemia '. Its demise, however, was not to be mourned, but celebrated. Year after year, its executive had passed resolutions on the sanctity of the Lord's Day, while its parliamentary accomplices had spent their Sundays at the National Liberal Club, where they indulged in card-playing and billiards.

It is doubtless this yawning contrast between precept and example that led Mrs Asquith recently to declare : ' At one time the Nonconformist Conscience was the backbone of the country, but the men I know who claim to have it to-day are maidenly, mulish, and misled.'

The article further noted that Free Church elders did not dare to condemn Lloyd George's sabbath ritual on the golf links as they did Balfour's. That was because Lloyd George had worked feverishly to win their confidence.

He knows that there is no such efficient election-room as the vestry of a Nonconformist chapel, and no such zealous electioneer as the Nonconformist minister, and for that reason he has now set himself to capture so valuable a piece of machinery in the furtherance of his own political interests.

It did not go unnoticed that,

since his departure from Downing Street, he has addressed the annual assemblies of the Baptist, the Congregational, and the Wesleyan Methodist bodies. He has paid eloquent tribute to the memory of John Wesley and pronounced a panegyric on the memorable ministry of Spurgeon. He has even travelled so far as Scotland to address the General Assemblies of the Scottish Churches. . . . Indeed, so successful has Mr Lloyd George been in his pilgrimages that the organisers at the Wee

Free Headquarters have recently become alarmed, and steps have now been taken to emulate his example.

The author of the piece took pains to specify that his barbs were directed not at Nonconformity *per se*, but at those who presumed to speak in its name through such organisations as the National Council, which had become 'no more than the last refuge of Mr Lloyd George, withdrawn to the native fortresses from which he first emerged'.

Not surprisingly, controversy flared. 'It is a clever article, but too clever to be taken seriously,' protested the Rev Thomas Nightingale, general secretary of the National Council, who saw no reason to deny allegations that his organisation was political:

> It is impossible to avoid it being so, since progressive or retrograde measures find their way to the Statute Book. Hence its support or opposition. We are bound to rush into the political arena when moral issues are bound up with a given political situation, as, for example, Irish reprisals.

According to Nightingale's jaundiced rendering of events, it was only after Sir Hamar Greenwood, the Irish chief secretary in the late government, had been threatened with 'the full weight of the Free Church forces', that the Black and Tans were ordered to curtail their campaign of terror. Similarly, Nonconformist outrage, actual or anticipated, was said to have 'scotched the Fisher proposals and killed Premium Bonds'. The Rev F. C. Spurr, president of the National Council, replied less defensively in a letter to the editor of the *Morning Post* on the 31st: 'The malice and spleen of the writer are so obvious that none, save those who desire to be deceived, can do other than express disgust with the article.' Other correspondents, many identifying themselves as Wesleyans, wrote not in anger, but in accord with the 'Dissident Dissenter'. Among them was Sir Robert Perks, who thought that the article had contained 'some elements of truth. At all events', he concluded, 'it will please the people who used to worship Mr Lloyd George, and [who] will be ready to do so again if he comes to power.'

Neither Perks nor the 'Dissident Disenter', whose identity was never publicly revealed, exaggerated the extent to which the hopes of Free Churchmen were pinned to Lloyd George, especially after Asquith's death in 1928. Indeed, Perks himself was soon extolling Lloyd George as ' the only man who can deal with the Communists' at home and abroad.[2] Possessed of a vast following, an undiminished vitality, and a vaulting ambition, the 'Welsh Wizard' continued to cast a potent spell throughout the interwar period. Only in retrospect did it become evident that he had fallen irretrievably in 1922, that all avenues were thereafter closed to him, and that his long dominance over public affairs had been broken once and for all.

Who could possibly rival him for Nonconformist adulation? Simon, Runciman, and Maclean made the circuit of denominational assemblies, but each suffered from social scruples and perhaps from theological doubts. (When Simon eventually died in 1954, he was cremated in his Oxford robes without religious ceremony.) Instead it was Isaac Foot, a newcomer on the parliamentary scene, who quickly emerged as Lloyd George's counterpart among the Asquithians, and all the more inveterate an opponent for that. His standing among West Countrymen, to whom he was known as ' Our Isaac', was comparable to Lloyd George's among Welshmen. A Plymouth solicitor, Foot was the son of a Wesleyan lay preacher who professed to be prouder of him as a temperance reformer than as M.P. for Bodmin. An active participant in various anti-drink and anti-betting crusades, Foot also figured prominently in evangelical movements. Not least to his credit, he was the founder in 1937 of the Cromwell Association, dedicated to the memory of the Lord Protector (' the dictator with a difference') and implicitly to the propagation of Puritan values. It was from the seventeenth-century struggle that Foot, who described himself as ' one of John Milton's " common people " ', drew his political as well as his religious inspiration: as he put it in his Ramsay Muir Lecture in 1947, ' the Liberal Party, as a party, began when Hampden and Pym made their preparation before the summoning of the Long Parliament of 1640.' Foot, who had entered Parliament in a by-election in February 1922, successfully defended his seat in the general election nine months later and again in December 1923.

In the latter contest, a reunified Liberal Party returned 158 members, with Free Church candidates sharing in the revival. As no single party commanded a parliamentary majority, Labour was allowed its first taste of the fruits of office. Under the circumstances, there was no possibility that it would bare its teeth. Still, many Nonconformists expressed apprehension at the prospect of a Labour administration, even one that survived on Liberal sufferance. The *British Weekly* declined to extend a welcome to Ramsay MacDonald and his comrades until it had obtained some indication of the 'Christian' content of socialism, and specifically of Labour's intentions toward the 'irreligious' Soviet Union. Arthur Henderson brusquely replied that he was 'by no means inclined to admit the right of those who speak for organised religion to apply to the Labour Party on the eve of entering office a test which it has not thought necessary to impose upon the Liberal or Conservative Party'. Nevertheless, he proffered assurances that 'the advent of a Labour Government will not mean the dethronement of Christian ideals'. J. R. Clynes, George Lansbury, the Rev Herbert Dunnico, and Hamilton Fyfe, editor of the *Daily Herald*, likewise attempted to allay Nonconformist fears.[3]

The *Christian World*, which made a speciality of such tallies, was pleased to report that the 1924 Labour Government 'includes a very large proportion of Free Churchmen, and has perhaps a more definite religious complexion than any Cabinet in recent years': MacDonald was a Scottish Presbyterian; J. H. Thomas and William Adamson were Baptists; Henderson, a Wesleyan; Clynes, a Congregationalist; Lord Parmoor, 'a very comprehensive Churchman with Quaker sympathies'; Noel Buxton, a full-fledged Quaker; Vernon Hartshorn, a Primitive Methodist; and Lord Haldane was the product of 'Baptist forbears'. Many of the junior appointments went to Wesleyans. The Rev Thomas Nightingale recounted how, during a recent excursion on the London underground, he had chanced to meet MacDonald, with whom he engaged in a spirited conversation until the premier-designate alighted at Belsize Park. 'Whether we agree with his political dreams or ideas or not', Nightingale told the readers of the *British Weekly* on 31 January, 'the present Prime Minister is a Christian, and brings to the great task a Christian outlook and spirit which he believes to be the expression of his faith.' For his own part, Nightingale looked forward to an intimate collaboration between the new government and the National Council.

His hopes were not fulfilled. The parliamentary Labour Party, anxiously rejected the patronage of those who tried – as John Burns used to say – to 'governess' it. A degree of antagonism

was unavoidable, given the libertarian views of some members
of the socialist left and the proverbial puritanism of Nonconformity: Fenner (later Lord) Brockway has recalled, from his
days as organising secretary of the I.L.P. information department,
the outcry among Free Churchmen when young John Strachey
wrote a column for the *New Leader* in which he implied an
advocacy of free love.[4] On the question of drink, Labour seemed no
less guilty of moral laxity. The government's weak performance
on the Welsh Local Option Bill brought a stinging indictment
from temperance reformers, who agreed with Lady Astor that
MacDonald was afraid to take action against the workingmen's
clubs from which he drew electoral support. ' In our judgment ',
the editors of the *Methodist Times* ruefully declared on 21
February, ' Labour has not only lost a great opportunity of justify-
ing its claim to moral independence ', but also ' it has taken a
serious step towards the alienation of its friends '.

MacDonald, mindful of these developments, went to Brighton
in March to address the annual meetings of the National Council
on ' the social implications of Christianity '. He shared billing
with Foot, Viscount (formerly Lord Robert) Cecil, and Lloyd
George, who, as one might have predicted, stole the show.
Although it was only recently and reluctantly that he had parted
company with Sir George Younger, he had the temerity to attack
Labour's record on temperance. ' Which country got the most out
of the war?' he asked his audience. ' It was the United States ',
he answered. ' The United States got Prohibition out of the war.'
He thereupon proceded to contrast ' the altruism of the nation
when it was pouring out its blood ' – and when, incidentally, he
had been its leader – to ' the present parsimony ' of spirit. The
Welsh Local Veto Bill was cited as an example. The *Methodist
Times* conceded that ' Mr Lloyd George had made many great
speeches, but none ', it thought, ' greater or more timely than
this.'[5]

A mood of uncertainty hung over the 1924 National Council
sessions, where the chair was taken by Dame Elizabeth (Mrs
George) Cadbury, the first woman president. It was regretfully
noted that, except for invited speakers, not one Free Church
M.P. had bothered to make the brief journey from Westminster to
Brighton. There was considerable discussion regarding the propriety and, for that matter, the utility of clergymen sitting in
the Commons. With a Bill before the House to remove disabilities

from Roman Catholic and Anglican clerics, the Primitive Methodist Conference had ruled that its ministers could not stand
for Parliament without first resigning their pastorates. The Rev
J. H. Jowett, who had had second thoughts in the fourteen years
since he had encouraged Silvester Horne to embark on a public
career, served notice that ' I would not willingly give my vote
for any minister or clergyman who was a candidate for Parliamentary services '. Nevertheless, eleven divines were adopted to
stand in the next general election: eight in the Labour interest,
two as Liberals, and one (at County Down) as a Conservative.
From all indications, none were particularly eager to hasten the
day of judgment.

For a quarter of a century, Radical Nonconformists had posited
a confluence of interests between the two progressive parties,
whose relations at Westminster, if not always in the constituencies,
were held to be governed by laws of political mutualism. Mac-
Donald, in the course of his nine-month premiership, deliberately
gave the lie to this comfortable assumption. Gratuitously offensive to those who sustained him in power, he made it clear that
he would sooner surrender office to the Conservatives than submit to Liberal tutelage. The editors of the *British Weekly*,
shocked by his base ingratitude, denounced him in a leader that
encapsulated the attitude against which he was doubtless reacting:
' We are willing to give the idea of Liberalism a broad and
inclusive interpretation', they wrote self-righteously on 16
October. ' For this reason we have avoided all factious or partisan
criticism of the Labour Government so long as it was working
along essentially Liberal lines.' But, now that MacDonald had
thrown down the gauntlet, there was no choice. ' We do not for
a moment subscribe to the pessimistic forecasts which are at
present fashionable as to the Liberal Party.'

That political Nonconformity remained overwhelmingly wed-
ded to historic Liberalism was evidenced by the *Christian World's*
roster of Free Church candidates: out of a bumper crop of 218
nominees, 122 were Liberals, 84 Labour, and twelve Conservatives. The Liberal Party, largely by process of elimination, received
the goodwill, but no longer the active assistance, of Free Church
agencies. The National Council hastily issued a manifesto in
which non-partisanship was carried to the point of self-abnega-
tion: ' The dissolution of Parliament has been brought about
and the General Election precipitated by issues political and inter-

national in respect of which the Churches, as such, have no particular title to speak.' Temperance societies, also determined to maintain neutrality, pointed out that ' electors will find in every party, in differing proportions, candidates sound on the temperance issue '. Baldwin and the Tories, it had to be said, were less forthcoming than one might have wished. Labour, on the other hand, invited censure by scheduling at least seven campaign rallies, each addressed by a Cabinet minister, for the Sunday that preceded polling. ' Labour can never make a successful appeal to the Nonconformist electors of this country ', the *Methodist Times* professed icily, ' so long as it flagrantly disregards the obligations of the Lord's Day.'[6]

Baldwin easily shrugged off any criticism from Nonconformists, who did not as such constitute a significant element in the Conservative rank and file. But MacDonald, if not some of the Marxist fundamentalists in his camp, was less ready to dispense with Free Church support, which was all the more attractive to him as a means of superseding his Liberal rivals. In a major speech at Sheffield on Tuesday, the 21st, he made an explicit bid for Nonconformist votes. ' In the Labour Party ', he boasted, ' we have the spirit that used to animate your souls, widened, brightened, and heightened '. The *Westminster Gazette* begged to differ. ' Nonconformity shared with the rest of the nation the political confusion wrought by the war,' it maintained:

> The advent of the Labour Party drew many Nonconformists into sentimental attachment. . . . It was the last straw at which many half-submerged idealists clutched. . . . With the third election in two years there is another opportunity to reflect upon the results attained, and unless a sentimental idealism has lost the power of thought, the depressing contrast between promise and performance must be felt to the full.

The *Christian World* found itself in agreement: ' Nonconformist Liberals are standing firmer and more unitedly for Liberalism today than they have ever done since the war,' it declaimed on the 23rd:

> It may be true that the bitter disillusionment after the war caused younger members of the party, eager for quick and decisive reforms, to veer in sympathy towards the Labour Party. But another disillusionment has followed. The sentimental

idealism and rosy promises of the Labour Party, when they took office, have produced nothing real or effective. . . . Whatever has been solid in their achievement in legislation or administration has been Liberal in spirit and form. The younger generation of the old Liberal families, we believe, recognise this and will act accordingly.

As correspondents to the *Westminster Gazette* were quick to remonstrate, many more questions had been raised than answered. Lacking sufficient time, candidates, and especially capital, Liberal headquarters decided to run only 340 candidates, 113 fewer than in the 1923 election. Lloyd George, while holding tight to the purse-strings of his private fund, suggested that the party might ease its penury by co-opting ' one or two Nonconformists, experienced in raising money'. He proposed the names of Perks and Nightingale, both of whom declined to serve.[7] Ultimately, the Liberals had no choice but to submit to a policy of retrenchment that cost them credibility and gave rise to unfortunate rumours of collusion with the Conservatives. In nearly half the constituencies, no Liberal stood. In those cases, were Liberal Nonconformists to vote Labour or Conservative? Sometimes the temperance issue provided the criterion for a moral choice; but what was one to do in a place like Deptford, where the Labour incumbent and his Tory challenger were equally dismissive of the perils of drink? A Nonconformist in such a situation could either refrain from voting or put his political preference on another basis, usually class orientation. Nonconformist voters, who may have wished to continue as Liberals, were therefore often denied the opportunity. By the same token, it had become impossible in many constituencies for Liberals to persist as Nonconformist voters.

A landslide victory for Baldwin and the Conservatives, the 1924 general election all but obliterated the parliamentary Liberal Party, whose representation plummeted to 43 seats. Of these, 21 were held by Nonconformists: eight Congregationalists (counting William Wedgwood Benn, who soon defected to Labour), six Calvinistic Methodists (counting David Davies, who soon proclaimed himself an independent), three Baptists, two Primitive Methodists, and two Wesleyans. Forty-five Free Churchmen sat upon the Labour benches, eleven secured places on the government side, and three triumphed as self-styled independents, bringing the total of Nonconformist members to an unprepossessing 80.

For the first time, no denomination gave a majority of its M.P.s to the Liberals. The percentage of Liberal victors was highest among the Congregationalists, and low among the Wesleyans, the Presbyterians, and, most surprisingly, the Baptists. Four divines found their way to Westminster, none following the Liberal route. Methodists, who were busily engaged in negotiations for union, suffered a particularly heavy toll. With 61 members, they had constituted a tenth of the previous House of Commons; now, they returned only 35 out of 108 candidates. Of the 16 Wesleyan Liberals who had entered Parliament in 1923, not one survived the onslaught; within their ranks was Norman Birkett, the eminent jurist, who was to play a peripheral role in Nonconformist politics during the next decade. The Primitive Methodist contingent fell from ten to six, leaving two Liberal and four Labour M.P.s. 'Vigilant', who submitted a weekly column to the *Primitive Methodist Leader*, upbraided his many co-religionists who had 'contributed to Mr Baldwin's huge majority by supporting members of his party' and had thereby killed any hope for local option or Sunday closing. ' I wonder how they feel about it?' he queried rhetorically.

With remarkably few exceptions, Liberal candidates polled poorly in the traditional Nonconformist strongholds, which went either to Labour or, in a few cases, to Wesleyan Conservatives. In the northern districts, including Lancashire, nine Liberals were elected as compared to 48 the previous time. In the southwest, the results were equally calamitous, with Free Church Liberals evicted at Bodmin, Barnstaple, Chippenham, Taunton, Bath, North Cornwall, and Weston-super-Mare. In 36 Welsh contests, only 16 Nonconformists were returned. They divided evenly between the Liberal and Labour parties. By far the most startling feature of the Welsh results was the upsurge in the Tory vote, with a corresponding jump from four to nine seats, none of which was held by a Nonconformist. With *de facto* Conservative support, Liberals had managed reasonably well to hold their own in Welsh constituencies, where they secured eleven seats, one less than the previous year. Five of the six Calvinistic Methodist M.P.s from Wales were elected as Liberals, but only two of the five Welsh Congregationalists. Among the five Baptists sent by the principality to the 1924 Parliament, only Lloyd George had defended the Liberal interest. His son, Gwilym, who worshipped as a Calvinistic Methodist, was rejected by the electors of Pembrokeshire.

Sir Richard Winfrey, a sturdy Congregationalist who had held a junior appointment in the Lloyd George Coalition, was turned out at Gainsborough in Lincolnshire. But, as a rule, the Lloyd Georgians fared distinctly better at the polls than the former Wee Frees. Asquith, himself beaten at Paisley and without an alternative, went to the House of Lords as the Earl of Oxford and Asquith. Among his lieutenants, Runciman held Swansea, but Maclean, Foot, Simon, and W. M. R. Pringle (all Free Churchmen) went down to defeat. Lloyd George seized the opportunity to consolidate his authority over the parliamentary rump. With the Rev J. D. Jones as a willing intermediary, he tried to patch over his differences with H. Hayden Jones, J.D.'s brother, who had sat for Merionethshire since 1910. 'Unfortunately Hayden never came to see me', he told J. D., who had rendered him useful assistance in the past and could be expected to do so again: 'That may have been due to a natural shyness about pressing his claims. . . . I have always regretted our misunderstanding, and I have never been quite able to fathom the cause. What matters, however, is that it should be forgotten.'[8] Apparently, the breach was quickly healed, for Hayden Jones supported Lloyd George's election in December to the vacant party chairmanship. Nearly a quarter of the parliamentary Liberal forces balked at accepting Lloyd George's wayward leadership and allegedly tainted money. Banding together as a 'Radical Group' under Runciman, they tried in vain to impede their enemy's gradual ascent to the party command.

Adversity brought to the surface all of the antipathies and resentments which Liberal chieftains had previously tried to conceal from public view. 'Liberal Reunion', Asquith candidly admitted in October 1926, had 'turned out to be a fiction, if not a farce'.[9] The spectacle of renewed internecine warfare was a particular affront to the sensibilities of highminded Nonconformists, and accelerated their drift to other parties, where they expected to find sanctuary from incessant wrangling and petty jealousies. The *British Weekly*, in the wake of the electoral disaster, ran a lengthy correspondence on the 'Christian' nature of socialism, always a sure sign that Liberalism was being given up for lost. 'R' (who identified himself as a third-generation

deacon of a large Baptist church, and, for 23 years, the super-
intendent of a Sunday school) volunteered his ' truthful testimony :
I have been as conscious of the presence of God in Labour meetings as I have been in any church '. Here was a telling example
of the continued reciprocity between spiritual and political enthusiasms, but with effects markedly dissimilar from those a
generation earlier.

Others, including the editors of the *British Weekly* themselves,
were more inclined to regard Baldwinian Conservatism as the
logical successor to Liberal idealism. The Prime Minister, who
laid claim to ' nonconformist ancestors ' advertised his party as
' a natural haven of rest ' for ' the independent and sturdy individualism ' of Free Churchmen. Prominent among his colleagues
was Sir William Joynson-Hicks, who was recognised as a Tory
die-hard, but also respected as a teetotal sabbatarian, who had
' maintained the best relations with Free Churchmen ', and who
had defended the sacred principles of the Reformation by his
resolute stand against the revised Prayer Book. Although practising Nonconformists were at a premium in Baldwin's successive
administrations, he compensated by surrounding himself with the
likes of Joynson-Hicks (later Lord Brentford), W. C. (later Lord)
Bridgeman, Sir Samuel Hoare (later Lord Templewood), Edward
Wood (later Lord Irwin, and, still later, Lord Halifax), and the
5th Marquess of Salisbury, who collectively qualified – as one
historian has pungently put it – as ' the only body of leading
politicians in English public life for whom prayer was a reality '.
The *British Weekly,* if it could not have a Cabinet of non-
socialist Free Churchmen, was willing to settle for a Cabinet
of true believers. Its open-mindedness was commended by Bernard
Alderson, a city-councillor at Birmingham, who, ' having seen the
error of my ways, . . . joined the Unionist Party '. Inviting other
readers to follow his example, he assured them that, ' although
a Nonconformist, a democrat, a keen social reformer, a believer
in the League of Nations, I am more convinced a Unionist than
ever '. It required only a glance at the electoral map to see that
Alderson was no rare specimen and that his breed was no longer
restricted to the environs of Birmingham, where Free Church
Unionism had a long history. Austen Chamberlain, himself such
a hybrid, addressed 170 guests at Sir George Hayter Chubb's
usual post-election luncheon. The Foreign Secretary ' said that
he knew he spoke the mind of the Prime Minister and of his

M

colleagues when he said that they recognised that to the formation of their majority at the recent election went the votes of many who by tradition were not within their ranks.'[10]

The circumstances and outcome of the 1924 general election, followed by five unedifying years of internal conflict, sealed the fate of the Liberal Party, at least as it was then known. Much the same can be said about political Nonconformity. Torn by leadership quarrels, it suffered from a fatal inability to devise a strategy consonant with past principles and present needs, and, simultaneously, from a steady diminution of support among its regular constituents. During Baldwin's second premiership, which lasted until May 1929, the situation went from bad to worse.

The postwar decade witnessed a precipitous decline in Christian piety which, if impossible to quantify, was everywhere evident. The lowering of moral standards was doubtless more apparent than real; not so, however, the retreat from religious devotion, which, as contemporaries often failed to perceive, was a quite separate phenomenon. The evangelical Free Churches, with their Puritan ethos, were most conspicuously out of touch with the times. Denominational statistics can only hint at the malaise, to which they provide an imperfect index. Although some sects, most notably the Wesleyans, recorded a modest gain in absolute numbers before 1929, their membership was slipping relative to the national population. In other cases, subsidence began earlier and proceeded further. The Primitive Methodists, for example, estimated 200,000 adherents – fewer than they had had in 1908 – when they amalgamated in 1932 with the Wesleyan and United Methodist connexions. Compared with the Anglican establishment, whose membership in the British Isles has declined by seven per cent since 1925, the total of Methodist communicants had dropped by fifteen per cent. Since the time of the Edwardian revival, Baptist and Congregationalist memberships had been nearly halved. The Presbyterian Church of England reported 87,000 members in 1911, 84,000 in 1922, and 70,000 in 1965. Church affiliation does not, of course, imply attendance at church services, which, from all indications, fell even more sharply.[11]

The patriarchs of Nonconformity were appalled by the moral bankruptcy of the age, which they tended to measure in terms of increased alcohol consumption, a declining birth rate, Sunday newspaper sales, and, not least of all, empty pews at divine worship. Unfashionable and censorious, they were dismissed alternately as Quixotes and Malvolios. In response, they groped for an issue with which they might stir the popular conscience and perhaps restore their public influence as they imagined it to have existed before the war. ' Is there not a cause?' Isaac Foot asked plaintively in the title of his 1949 Ernest Winterton Lecture, in which he reviewed two thankless decades of temperance reform activity. Others flogged at the dead horse of the 1902 Education Act: ' We protested against its passing; we protest still ', J. D. Jones harangued the delegates at the 1928 Congregational Union assembly. Did he notice how few joined in his nostalgic ritual?

Like temperance and education, disestablishment was no longer capable of rousing more than a perfunctory interest. The nexus between Church and State had ceased to agitate anyone save certain High Anglicans, like Hensley Henson, Bishop of Durham, and Lord Hugh Cecil. In the light of the 1927–28 Prayer Book controversy, they sought to strike off Erastian shackles. Augustine Birrell, writing in the *Nation* on 9 February 1929, was amused by the paradox of ' the boot . . . on the other leg '. The Liberation Society, while it continued to exist, was as inactive as ' the Giants Pope and Pagan in Bunyan's Allegory ', and its cry had been taken up by its former adversaries. ' The horror of prelacy, once the " soul-animating " strain of historical Nonconformity, must have died down ', Birrell sneered, ' for when the other day the new Archbishop of Canterbury was enthroned in his Cathedral, there were to be seen, comfortably seated, representatives of all the Free Churches.' Aside from this growing intimacy among churchmen in the House would be moved to take collective action :
there were other factors that demanded consideration. Why should Nonconformist M.P.s, out of devotion either to constitutional or religious principles, assist Anglicans to escape from parliamentary surveillance? In any case, Birrell doubted whether Free Churchmen in the House would be moved to take collective action :

. . . The Nonconformist vote will, so we suspect, be divided. The old cry ' a Free Church in a Free State ' still has life in it, but the Nonconformist vote is not so large as it once was, and cannot now be regarded, if it ever could, as a vote *en masse*.

Sir Henry Lunn, a Wesleyan old-timer who had belonged to the Hugh Price Hughes brigade, took the same view for essentially different reasons. Surveying the scene in April 1929 for *The Review of the Churches*, an inter-denominational journal which he edited from 1891 to 1896 and again from 1924 to 1930, Lunn agreed with Bishop Henson (and implicitly with Birrell) that Nonconformity had become ' politically negligible '. Far from lamenting the fact, he celebrated it as the prerequisite to the attainment of Christian unity.[12]

' Politically negligible ' was a description applied increasingly often to Nonconformity, and not only by supercilious laymen. Dr Charles Brown provoked a storm of controversy by writing off the Baptist community in Bradford as a ' negligible and diminishing quantity '. The label struck the Yorkshire correspondent for the *Christian World* ' as being somewhat hasty, and the result of a rather cursory knowledge of the actual facts of the case '. After all, it was argued, not only the Lord Mayor of Bradford, but also the Stipendiary Magistrate and the City Treasurer were all Baptists.[13] Brown was vindicated, however, by the atrophy of the local Free Church council, and by the absence of Baptists from among the parliamentary candidates in the city's four divisions. Bradford's Baptists were typical of Nonconformists throughout the West Riding; previously a vital electoral force, they now languished.

Nevertheless, the leaders of all three national parties avidly sought to recruit Nonconformist support when the country next went to the polls in May 1929. In successive issues, the *Christian World* published open letters from Baldwin, MacDonald, and Lloyd George, the last of whom invoked the memories of Clifford, Horne, Hugh Price Hughes, and the prophet Elijah. There were as many as 262 Free Churchmen nominated, 156 by the Liberals, 87 by Labour, 13 by Conservatives, and six by various splinter parties. Among them were 73 Wesleyans, 64 Congregationalists, 27 Primitive Methodists, 26 Quakers, 20 Baptists, 15 Unitarians, 12 Welsh Calvinistic Methodists, ten United Methodists, ten Presbyterians, and three fringe sectarians. Of the 69 women candidates, eight were identified as ' daughters of the manse ', and two of the others were Lloyd George's daughter Megan (who stood successfully at Anglesey), and the wife of Walter Runciman (who lost at Tavistock).

The Anglican *Church Times* peevishly complained that its readers were being denied the attention due to them as members of the establishment: the Conservatives ' show themselves far more eager to gain sympathy from Nonconformists than from Church-people '; Labour was ' generally saturated with Protestant prejudices '; and the Liberals constituted ' more than ever a party of political Dissenters '. The reason was not difficult to surmise. There was a widespread belief that this election would hinge on the Nonconformist vote, which was expected to increase as a result of the previous year's Equal Franchise Act, which had lowered the voting age for women to 21. ' The serious young women who attend Nonconformist chapels are almost certain to make use of their new privilege,' the *Church Times* postulated :

Until the war, probably eighty percent of Nonconformists voted Liberal, and the Liberal *debacle* of 1924 is to be directly traced to the secession of the Nonconformists, for a variety of reasons, to Labour and the Conservatives. The younger ministers and that section of the working class that the chapel still contrives to hold voted Labour, but perhaps an even larger number of the better-to-do voted for the Conservatives. There is little chance of Liberalism winning back the votes that, five years ago, went to the Left. But it is almost certain that many Nonconformists who wandered away to the right will return to the Liberal fold. How the chances of a Liberal revival, due to the return of Nonconformists prodigals, will be affected by three-cornered contests has yet to be seen.[14]

The National Free Church Council, buoyed by generous estimates of Nonconformity's importance, issued a barrage of resolutions on topical issues, all drafted by Dr John Scott Lidgett, its general secretary since 1914, with sufficient skill and verbiage to avoid the taint of partisanship. In March, its thirty-fourth annual assembly called for the election to the next Parliament of those candidates – ostensibly regardless of party – pledged to such diverse goals as compulsory arbitration treaties, a naval pact with the United States, ' an early and complete evacuation of the occupied territory of Germany ', industrial peace, ' a comprehensive programme ' to combat slum conditions, the alleviation of unemployment, temperance, and control over ' such sports and amusements as subsist chiefly for their appeal to the betting and gambling instincts that are so deplorably widespread at the present time '. Beginning in the same year, the National Council installed a slate of vice-presidents, who tended to be laymen of national stature and advanced age. According to the amended constitution, they were to be ' elected annually by the Assembly on the Nomination of the Executive Committee ', but the election was a mere formality and the usual tenure was life. Lloyd George was among the earliest vice-presidents, along with Perks, Henderson, and Sir Albert Spicer. In 1929, but not before, his name also appeared in the list of subscribers to Council funds. His gift of £100 was among the largest recorded. Significantly, his name did not again appear among the Council's benefactors until 1934, when another general election was in the offing and when he contributed the modest sum of £20. He gave the same amount in 1935, and nothing thereafter.[15]

The 1929 returns left no doubt that political Nonconformity continued to exist chiefly as a figment of men's imaginations. If the Free Church factor had any bearing on the outcome, which is problematical, it was reflected in the Liberal Party's popular vote (which rose to 23.4 per cent) and not in terms of parliamentary representation. With 513 candidates in the field, and after a strenuous campaign, the Liberals netted only 59 seats, a slender improvement in their dismal 1924 showing. Free Churchmen took some consolation in the return, after five years' absence from the House, of Foot, Maclean, Simon, Leif Jones, and Geoffrey Shakespeare. In all, 103 Nonconformist M.P.s were elected: 32 on the Liberal ticket, 63 for Labour, five as Conservatives, and three as independents. According to denomination, there were 19 Congregationalists, 29 Wesleyans, ten Baptists, ten Quakers, ten Primitive Methodists, nine Calvinistic Methodists, eight Unitarians, four Presbyterians, two United Methodists, two Independent Methodists, and a member of the Brotherhood Movement. The newcomers included A. E. (' Alec ') Glassey, who was known to his constituents at East Dorset as one of the West of England commissioners for the Congregational Half Million Fund, Dr Somerville Hastings, who was active at Whitefield's Mission, Holford Knight, the brother-in-law of Dr Sidney Berry, Geoffrey Mander, a prominent Wolverhampton Congregationalist, R. J. Russell, a Wesleyan who doubled as Liberal M.P. for Eddisbury and president of the Birkenhead Free Church Council, and P. J. Noel Baker, son of the late J. Allen Baker, ' the fighting Quaker '. Not that Nonconformist credentials carried any infallible guarantee of success. Arthur Mortimer, a Primitive Methodist lay preacher, who carried the endorsement of the Revs J. D.

Jones and Thomas Yates, made a vainglorious bid to reclaim Bournemouth for the Liberals. Dingle Foot, Isaac's eldest son, was defeated on home ground at Tiverton, as was Thomas Magnay, a Wesleyan local preacher at Blaydon; both launched their parliamentary careers elsewhere two years later. And the Rev G. J. Jenkins, a Welsh Baptist whose campaign focused on religious themes, lost a Liberal seat at Oldham. Five divines were returned to the new Parliament, four Labour men and one Liberal; among those rejected was Dr F. W. Norwood of the City Temple, chairman-elect of the Congregational Union, who contested Stoke Newington as a Liberal.

For the second time, Ramsay MacDonald took office as the head of a minority Labour government. Again, the *Christian World* gave him high marks for packing his administration with Free Churchmen: the Prime Minister himself was a ' Presbyterian, steeped in the traditions of John Knox '; Philip Snowden at the Exchequer ' come of Wesleyan Methodist stock, and at heart is an austere Cromwellian Puritan '; Arthur Henderson was a Wesleyan ' of long standing '; J. H. Thomas had taught in a Baptist Sunday school at Swindon, and shared his background with A. V. Alexander and William Adamson; while Margaret Bondfield, William Graham, H. Lees-Smith, Lord Arnold, and Captain Wedgwood Benn were all Congregationalists. One would not wish to suggest that MacDonald selected his colleagues with the intention of squaring Nonconformist opinion. More out of instinct than opportunism, he made appointments and pursued policies that gave evidence of Labour's moral purpose. The successive honours lists during his premiership, by taking special cognisance of temperance reformers, attested to his ' sympathy with Christian work in many spheres '. And, in 1930, when Dr Robert Forman Horton celebrated his golden anniversary as minister at London's Lyndhurst Road Congregational Church, MacDonald's warm congratulations anticipated Lloyd George's by three days.[16] The pupil had surpassed the master.

Unlike the first Labour government, the second had not been put into office with the connivance of Liberals, who were above reproach on that score. But the parliamentary Liberal Party was fretfully divided in its response to Labour's ministerial performance, especially after the impact of the international financial crisis and the growth of mass unemployment. Free Churchmen, who occupied over half the places on the Liberal benches, diverged in every conceivable direction, with scant reference to denominational affiliation or to previous secular loyalties: Lloyd George and his immediate followers were basically willing to give Labour a chance; Foot and Maclean, who nursed an Asquithian mistrust of their nominal leader, were typical of those who tried to steer a middle course; Simon, accompanied by Shakespeare, Magnay, and Ernest Brown, veered towards the Conservatives; and Runciman held aloof to the point of contemplating his retirement from the Commons.

Given the depletion in Liberal ranks, it was understandable that traditionally Nonconformist interest groups should seek their allies beyond Liberalism, which stood further discredited by its contradictory impulses. The parliamentary temperance group, once a Liberal domain, was now dominated by Labour members: on its executive, Foot was outflanked by James H. Hudson, the Quaker M.P. for Huddersfield, and Ernest Winterton, the Baptist who sat for Loughborough. The Peace Society, too, found its parliamentary mainstays on the Labour side. More often than not, the M.P.s to whom the individual denominational conferences looked for leadership and advice were Labour or, to an unprecedented extent, Conservatives. Sir Kingsley Wood commanded as much respect among Wesleyans as Foot or Runciman or Henderson.

In August 1931, the situation was further complicated by MacDonald's decision to exchange his Labour administration for a coalition in which Liberal and Conservative leaders were invited to serve. The formation of a National Government made a mockery of Nonconformist political allegiances. Simon and his friends, who had recently renounced the Liberal whip, did not qualify for inclusion at this juncture. Lloyd George was then recovering from a serious illness that fortuitously relieved MacDonald and Baldwin of the obligation to accommodate him in their arrangements. The top-ranking Liberals in the new ministry were, therefore, Sir Herbert Samuel and Lord Reading, both Jews. Among the Liberal Free Churchmen assigned to places were Maclean, who took the presidency of the Board of Education, Sir John Tudor Walters, who was restored to the paymaster-generalship which he had held in the postwar Lloyd George Coalition, and Gwilym Lloyd George, who accepted a junior office with his father's concurrence. Alec Glassey and Foot were also soon accommodated. The endemic disruptions within the

Liberal Party were momentarily overshadowed by the economic emergency and by MacDonald's over-reaction to it.

At the instigation of its Conservative principals, who stood to profit most, the National Government proceeded to call a general election shortly after its formation. The Liberals, who had joined precisely to avert such a likelihood, went to the country in a hopelessly stricken state and emerged from the ordeal with their divisions formalised. The Simonite wing of the party, under the label of Liberal Nationals, won in 35 of the 41 contests they entered, largely with the support of Conservatives from whom they were virtually indistinguishable. The Samuelite centre, rallying to the National Government as Free Traders, returned 33 out of 112 candidates. Finally, the Lloyd Georgians, who opposed the official party line of cooperation with MacDonald, sent four M.P.s – all members of the Lloyd George family – to Westminster. Now it was Lloyd George who, so to speak, was the victim of a snap ' coupon ' election, who styled himself an Independent Liberal, and who had become – as Asquith's son gloated – ' a sort of Wee Free '.[17]

There were 23 lay preachers in the 1931 Parliament, a dozen fewer than in the last, but ' more evenly divided among the political parties '. They, like other Free Churchmen in the House, were also indiscriminately distributed among the discordant Liberal factions. The parliamentary representatives of Nonconformity, while still numerically impressive, had been completely atomised and diffused. In the electoral convolutions of the early 'thirties, one Free Churchman was pitted against another, much to the embarrassment of the extra-mural bodies in which they often continued to serve together. Isaac Foot, for example, was soon at loggerheads with Runciman, and (less acrimoniously) Lloyd George with Geoffrey Shakespeare. One may obtain some sense of the dislocation when one considers the emergence on the one hand of an alliance of Simon, Wood, Neville Chamberlain, Shakespeare, Runciman, and Ernest Brown, and, on the other, one of Lloyd George, Foot, Norman Birkett, and Philip Snowden.

Never before had there been greater estrangement between the National Council and the politicians, or, for that matter, between it and its local affiliates. The Rev E. Griffith Jones, who served as president in 1932, acknowledged the sorry state of affairs:

If the F.C.C. has fallen on comparatively evil times, and is

functioning with slacker impulse and lessened efficiency as compared with its palmy days of thirty years ago, so have the Free
Churches generally, which form the constituent members of
the local councils; and can it be expected that the liaison institution should be more prosperous than the churches themselves?

His argument was substantiated by annual membership reports,
which sometimes showed impressive gains in foreign mission
fields, but which, without exception, showed increased losses at
home.[18]

The Liberal Party was a shambles, and the Free Church Council
movement was, to all intents and purposes, inoperative. It was
natural, but not wholly logical, to posit a mutual causality. In any
case, there were some incurable optimists who wondered whether
the National Council, cut adrift from its partisan moorings, might
somehow set sail under its own steam. In the 1931 general
election, Griffith Jones had reminded Nonconformist electors of
the Council's resolutions, which were to be brought ' effectively
to the attention of the Parliamentary candidates in your constituency '. The Rev S. W. Hughes, in his subsequent report as
general secretary, observed with qualified satisfaction that the local
councils and federations had shown themselves ' increasingly
aware . . . that in any action they may contemplate they have
behind them the force of a great national body '.[19] Others were
similarly persuaded either by wishful thinking or by the sincere
conviction that the deteriorating international and domestic situations demanded the sort of moral leadership which they prided
themselves in having helped to impart during earlier decades.

Doubtless Free Church officials overestimated their potential
strength, and Lloyd George encouraged them to do so. Under his
personal banner, they regrouped for a final electoral offensive:
the 1935 Council of Action campaign. To a surprising extent, they
proved capable of closing ranks, but to no avail. Their last rally
pointed up the contradictions that had plagued political Nonconformity from the start and that had grown more pronounced
as society had become more secularised. The reality was one that
Free Church activists were slow to perceive, either because of
tribal self-delusion, or because, like Lloyd George, they were
without other alternatives in public life.

9 *The Last Rally*

For four years after the political crisis of 1931, Lloyd George stood apart from official Liberalism; thereafter, he returned to the fold, but never resumed the party leadership, which passed from Sir Herbert Samuel to Sir Archibald Sinclair. As companions in the wilderness, he had the leaders of evangelical Protestantism, who, even if they continued to vote as Liberals, had by then ceased to regard the Liberal Party as their accredited agency. They and Lloyd George, having no one else to whom they could turn, once again made common cause. The result was the launching of the Council of Action, surely one of the most hopelessly misconceived of modern political enterprises. A non-starter, it was nevertheless significant for the hopes invested in it and for the fears it aroused. Not least of all, it provides a commentary on the aims and methods of political Nonconformity and those of its foremost parliamentary champion, both past their prime.

This observation holds true in a literal as well as a figurative sense. In 1933, Lloyd George turned seventy. Like him, the Free Church dignitaries who joined in this curious crusade were usually men of advanced age, who sought to restore the link between political and religious radicalism that had existed in the early years of the century. Veterans of the agitation against the 1902 Education Act, which many of them had passively resisted, they were stirred by undimmed memories of their electoral victory in 1906. Old men in a hurry, they grasped at the chance, however remote, to revive and give effect to the celebrated Nonconformist Conscience. To be sure, some Nonconformist leaders kept their distance from the movement or gave it only nominal support either because they feared renewed intimacy with Lloyd George or because they had come to reconsider their part in the Edwardian education controversy. But, overwhelmingly, spiritual and lay elders reverted to type, taking up anew the cudgels that had been blunted by decades of disuse.

It is not difficult to see what attracted Free Church activists to Lloyd George. Still the most dynamic of public figures, he was unquestionably the most eminent to worship as a Nonconformist and to espouse Nonconformist causes. Perhaps less obvious is what Lloyd George saw in the Free Churches, and particularly in the National Council of Evangelical Free Churches, which was in the doldrums.

Compared to the Liberal Party, which lay shattered and demoralised, the National Council seemed to have much to offer. There were an estimated 10,000 chapels in the country, of which nearly 7,000 received and distributed literature from the Council's Church Publicity and Service Centre. In 1934–35, there were slightly fewer than 500 local councils throughout England and Wales; in addition, 22 regional federations coordinated activity. Closely linked was a National Free Church Women's Council, of which Dame Margaret Lloyd George was a past president. While the Council's financial resources were limited – contributions for 1934–35 totalled £1,760 1s. 3d. – it counted among its supporters a number of very rich men who might be expected to endow an attempt to evangelise public life. The Council published its own monthly news-letter, the *Free Church Chronicle*; more important, it had links with a network of denominational and inter-denominational weeklies, which, if less numerous and prosperous than in former times, continued to claim an impressive collective readership. But the movement's greatest asset was its moral fervour, the quality the Liberal Party had once boasted and now most sorely lacked.

The National Council took its colour less from its presidents, who served one-year terms, than from its secretaries and treasurers, who were more or less permanent fixtures. Dr John Scott Lidgett was honorary secretary and secretary for public questions from 1914 to 1940. The Rev S. W. ('Sammy') Hughes, a more avuncular personality, was general secretary from 1932 to 1940. The Council's treasurers, of whom there were usually two and sometimes three, were laymen whose chief qualification for office tended to be their benificence. Of the four who served during the 'thirties, the most influential and by far the most generous was R. Wilson Black, a Baptist property-developer, whose gifts to the Council included its handsome headquarters in Tavistock Square.

Increasingly, the National Council had made it a practice to invite public figures to address its annual assemblies. No one put this platform to better use than Lloyd George, a Baptist lay preacher. It was during the mid-'thirties that his lifelong collaboration with the agents of political Nonconformity was transformed into an active electoral alliance. At whose initiative, and to what purpose? Free Church spokesmen, confronted by critics in their own ranks and outside, strenuously insisted that they served only their consciences and no political master, that their objectives were moral and not partisan, and that it was they who exploited Lloyd George's reputation and knowhow rather than he who exploited their numerical and institutional strength. The Prodigal Son, as they half-facetiously depicted him, had resumed the crusade from which office had diverted him three decades earlier. Patently sincere, these explanations failed to satisfy many Nonconformist regulars, who knew the limitations of Free Church unity, and more seasoned political observers, who knew too well the workings of Lloyd George.

So far as one can tell, it was not against his private life that Lloyd George's antagonists reacted.[2] Most, one can be quite certain, did not suspect his relationship with Frances Stevenson, his private secretary and later his second wife. Nonconformist patriarchs did not move in those circles where they might have heard gossip, and furthermore distrusted those who did. A few must have had suspicions – Angus Watson, the Newcastle Congregationalist businessman, through his publishing contacts, and perhaps J. D. Jones, who spent weekends at Churt – but they were the sort of men who either put aside the idea as too repugnant, or, for the sake of a higher cause, willingly suspended any disbelief in their hero. The situation, as one can imagine, was not without a certain amount of piquancy: these Puritan saints wrote to Lloyd George, deploring the decline in national morals, only to receive a commiserative reply through Miss Stevenson.

Apologists for the Free Churches have stressed the importance of Lloyd George's appearance in 1933 at the thirty-eighth annual gathering of the National Council.[3] There, at Sheffield's city hall, he enjoined the churches to take ' speedy action ' to deal with unemployment, ' a great moral issue '. His speech also touched upon foreign affairs: Englishmen, he declared, should be less hasty in condemning the Germans, whose treaty obligations ' had been carried out in the letter and the spirit, until those who enforced the Treaty broke it '. In a sense, Lloyd George's Sheffield speech adumbrated the themes of his subsequent Peace and Reconstruction campaign. But it is a mistake to interpret these vague injunctions as a ' Call to Action '.

Deeply concerned with social questions, particularly on the local level, the Free Church Council was eager to explore ways in which it could bring an influence to bear. Hughes arranged a meeting of concerned individuals at the Memorial Hall, and Lloyd George, ' as a Nonconformist ', was invited to open the discussion. He made a good impression, winning the confidence even of Arthur Porritt, from whom he had been estranged for more than a quarter of a century. Further sessions followed, resulting in the establishment of a small standing committee to advise the Council executive.

During these months, Lloyd George was widely regarded as semi-retired from public life. He seldom appeared in the House of Commons, and divided the greater part of his time between the writing of his *War Memoirs* and the tending of his prize orchards at Churt, fell fertilised by the abundant supply of manure from nearby Aldershot. His staff at Westminster, larger than one would normally expect an elder statesman to maintain, assisted in his literary work, provided the data with which he occasionally embarrassed the government, and kept him informed of developments, including those in the religious world. Preoccupied at this time with prescribing a remedy for the country's manifold economic ills, he was given impetus by an urgent appeal in August 1934 from representatives of the business community in Wales, where the effects of the depression were particularly acute. The public works programmes instituted by Roosevelt and Mussolini, confirmed his view that something could be done, and incidentally pointed to new ways of influencing opinion.

His Free Church friends, although sympathetic, were more concerned with the menacing international situation. They ranged in attitude from the Rev J. Ivory Cripps, chairman of the Baptist Ministers' Pacifist Fellowship, to Scott Lidgett, who gave each Christian leave to decide for himself whether ' defensive warfare, or . . . warfare in the fulfilment of trust ' was compatible with Christ's teaching.[4] While all of them championed the League of Nations, many feared the possible consequences of League commitments. They were particularly anxious to achieve an understanding with Germany in order to ensure peace, and, if possible, to obtain concessions for persecuted Protestants and Jews. Economic recovery, they reasoned simplistically, would follow automatically from increased cooperation among nations and from a halt to wasteful expenditure on armaments. With allies such as these, Lloyd George was deflected, much against his inclinations and perhaps against his better judgment, into a movement that tenuously linked peace and reconstruction, with emphasis decidedly on the former.

The Nonconformist leaders had in mind an international crusade for peace that would begin in Britain and fulfill the promise of the World Alliance for Promoting International Friendship. ' It seemed a practical idea ', reflected Miss Stevenson, until things started to go wrong:

The first discordant note was sounded by one of the Free Church leaders who said he refused to take part in anything with which D. was associated; as the fact that he was connected with it would taint any movement from the outset. Next came a blow from the Roman Catholics.

Undeterred, Lloyd George delivered an Armistice Day address in which he warned of the danger of war ' unless peace is organized; and unless those errors of policy are avoided which, in the past, have led to war '. With the prolonged threat of Italian aggression against Abyssinia, and Britain's response by no means certain, he summoned seven prominent Free Churchmen to an emergency meeting at lunch on 7 December ' for consultation regarding necessary action by all religious forces to preserve peace '. The seven were Hughes, Scott Lidgett, J. D. Jones, Charles Brown, S. M. Berry, Carnegie Simpson, and James Lockhart, all except the last two of whom signed the Council of Action manifesto the following June.[5]

At the same time that he was consulting with clergymen on foreign affairs, Lloyd George was communicating ' with all sorts of lay experts ' on the question of unemployment.[6] Without taking the slightest trouble to conceal his operations, which would have defeated his purpose, he drafted a lengthy memorandum which he circulated for ' suggestions and criticisms '.[7] Among other things, he advocated a drastic reconstruction of the Cabinet on the model of his own wartime administration to make for greater flexibility. When it became apparent that the government would not respond, he took the next step. On 17 January 1935, his seventy-second birthday, he promulgated his New Deal proposals in a speech at Bangor.

Was it his programme or his claims to office that Lloyd George was most determined to advance? Did he aspire to membership in a reconstituted National Government, or did he hope to patch together an alternative ministry with the support of Opposition Liberals, Labourites, and renegade Tories? Despite the fact that he scrupulously prefaced his Bangor speech with a vow that he had not come ' to launch a party campaign ', his ambitions continued to arouse greater interest than his guidelines for reconstruction. The *Baptist Times,* fresh from celebrating its eightieth anniversary, was jubilant:

> Mr Lloyd George is still the greatest Parliamentarian of the day. He is perhaps the only one of our statesmen with the sacred spark of genius and it is a great misfortune for the country that he was not included in the National Government. He is not a spent force, though an incalculable one, and we must remember that he is now at the age at which Mr Gladstone was almost at his best. It is by no means impossible that Mr Lloyd George may return to power as the leader of a new National Party.

The *Methodist Recorder,* however, took a more critical view. The National Government could perhaps use ' an infusion of new energy . . .; but if changes are to be made, it would be better to look towards the younger rather than the ageing generation '.[8]

With only his small ' family group ' to support him in Parliament, Lloyd George nonetheless commanded a vast following in the country. Could the custodians of the National Government, given the weaknesses of their respective positions, afford to ignore his challenge? During February, there seemed a good chance that Baldwin and, more surprisingly perhaps, MacDonald, were willing to accept Lloyd George and his general recommendations. But Neville Chamberlain, who had old scores to settle, persuaded a majority of his Cabinet colleagues to resist any such accommodation. Instead, Lloyd George was invited to submit his proposals to a Cabinet committee, before which he would have the opportunity to testify. The result was a foregone conclusion, but he could not refuse without calling into question his own motives.[9]

While the Cabinet committee deliberated, Lloyd George cast about for allies. His first important recruit was Lord (formerly Philip) Snowden, who had been chancellor of the exchequer at the inception of the National Government, and who welcomed all the New Deal proposals save the 'reform' of the Bank of England. Negotiations were opened with Harold Macmillan and the other charter members of the 'Next Five Years' Group, several of whom affiliated with Lloyd George on an individual basis. But Lloyd George leaned most heavily on Lord Lothian, once (as Philip Kerr) his private secretary, who had since acquired a reputation – never quite justified – as an authority on international relations. Not the least among Lothian's virtues was that he provided his old chief with a link to the Astors, on the one hand, and to the official Liberal leadership, on the other. On 10 March, he received from Lloyd George a memorandum – 'Organising Prosperity: a Scheme of National Reconstruction' – that was intended to lay half the foundation for a national movement for peace and reconstruction. A few days later, Lothian accepted Lloyd George's commission to draft a companion memorandum on 'foreign affairs and peace'.[10]

Lothian had five colleagues to assist him: Eleanor Rathbone, a Unitarian who sat as an independent M.P. for the combined English universities; Sir Walter Layton, the economist and director of the *News Chronicle*; Lady Layton; Mrs (later Dame) Margery Corbett Ashby, who had recently resigned in protest from the British delegation at the Disarmament Conference; and Dr F. W. Norwood, minister at London's City Temple, chairman of the Churches' Advisory Committee, chairman of the New Commonwealth ('a Society for the Promotion of International Law and Order through the creation of a Tribunal in Equity and an International Police Force'), and, most importantly, president-elect of the National Council of Evangelical Free Churches.

Norwood, a Baptist who considered himself a Congregationalist during his tenure at the City Temple, was in many ways typical of the Nonconformists who clustered around Lloyd George. With equal fervour, he alternated between secular campaigns and bouts of intense revivalism. Like many men of his stamp, he was deeply shaken in March by the announcement of German plans for rearmament and conscription. The following month, he presided at the National Council assembly at Lland-

N

rindod Wells, where Baldwin opened the proceedings with a bland recitation of homilies. By contrast, Norwood's presidential address – ' The Free Churches and the Military State ' – was all fire and brimstone. With more ardour than logic, he first proclaimed ' that the duty of the churches was a complete repudiation of war ', and then ' proceeded to uphold the right of self-defence. . . . We will support ', he proclaimed, ' every effort towards the pacification of the world, even the putting of armed forces behind a just and equal law, but we will not agree to the riveting of the war system upon us, or the amassing of armaments as an attempted guarantee of security.' Norwood had to admit that, ' of late years ', the concept of a Nonconformist Conscience had ' become rather a joke '. But his presidential tour, which he undertook with the zeal of a Clifford, gave him hope that an awakening was imminent : ' It is not only that the meetings are crowded and enthusiastic; their more valuable sign is in their moral restlessness and in their longing for courageous leadership.' There were similarities to the mood that had prevailed among Nonconformists before 1906, when an evangelical revival had heralded a new political order. Being a man of faith, Norwood expected history to repeat itself, this time with more perfect results.[11]

Lloyd George, too, was a veteran of the Edwardian evangelical and Liberal revivals; but did he expect a Second Coming? More probably, he simply realised how few options were open to him, and he acted accordingly. In April, the Scottish Liberal Federation rebuffed him by passing a massive vote of confidence in Samuel as leader of the party. If he were to impress either the government or the electorate, he would have to find a base of support elsewhere, and preferably one he would not be forced to share.

Although he maintained that he wished only to impress upon the National Government the wide appeal that his New Deal proposals commanded in the country, it was clear that Lloyd George was engaged in attempts to strengthen his bargaining position for the Cabinet reshuffle that was due when Baldwin would inherit the premiership from MacDonald. During May, rumours abounded that Lloyd George would soon be given office, possibly in the company of that other pariah, Winston Churchill. The ' supreme thing ', according to J. L. Garvin, the well-informed editor of the *Observer,* was for Baldwin ' to avoid Ll.G. in opposition at the General Election ', which could not be long postponed. On the 15th, at Baldwin's behest, Thomas ('Tom') Jones lunched at the Chinese room of the Metropole with Lloyd George, who revealed that

> he was of course in touch with his electoral experts. He had arranged to meet in the week after next privately twenty or thirty leaders of nonconformist opinion. He mentioned the names of Dr Berry and J. D. Jones. They were for his Programme and would arrange a big demonstration in its favour presently if required.

While Lloyd George 'stressed repeatedly that his primary concern was for the adoption of his Programme, not for office', he did let slip his desire to see Simon evicted from the Foreign Office, where he would himself consent to go if he could 'be of some use in placating Germany'. Professing no great ambition to be saddled with departmental responsibilities, he pointedly recalled 'how much Joseph Chamberlain was able to do when outside'.[12] Implicit was a threat that Baldwin could not have mistaken.

The day after Lloyd George tipped his hand to Jones, he sent Lord Lothian an invitation to a 'Free Church lunch on the 27th'. Yet it remained likely, even at this stage, that a gesture from Baldwin would have left the movement stillborn. Hearing nothing, Lloyd George grew 'extremely impatient and somewhat irritable'. The lunch was held as planned, but, for the time being, received no publicity. The showdown came in the early days of June. On Tuesday, the 4th, Lloyd George met for the ninth time with the Cabinet committee that was considering his proposals. The atmosphere was 'most polite and studiously pleasant', but he came away with the feeling that his hosts 'knew in their hearts they were going to knife me'. He was not perturbed, however, and assured Miss Stevenson 'that I too had a dagger in my sheath for them', by which he meant his Council of Action.[13]

Without waiting for the tenth and final meeting of the Cabinet committee on the 6th or the official announcement of Baldwin's Cabinet the next day, he released to the press a report (which *The Times* buried at the foot of page 9) that, at the instigation of 'a number of well-known Nonconformists', he was planning a nationwide campaign 'to rouse public opinion on issues of peace and unemployment'. At the same time, he wrote confidentially to a select group of public figures, whose signatures he solicited for a ' Call to Action ' which he had held in readiness for such an eventuality. The manifesto was to announce a national convention early in July, which, in turn, would launch a movement to secure the return of particular parliamentary candidates. The idea, he explained, ' originated with a group of leading Ministers of Religion and social workers representative of all creeds and differing political allegiances. They were good enough to invite me to become a Member of the provisional Committee.' The object, he went on, was to set ' in motion a movement which may alter the history of England and the destinies of the world at large '. There could be no doubt that the British public was overwhelmingly in favour of peace and employment, but ' unless all this sentiment is organized and focused, we shall have a reactionary Parliament, where the pressure would be entirely in favour of re-armament, and where we should be consigned to another period of enforced idleness for millions of our people.'[14] Such elaborate preparations amused *The Times*, which cynically concluded on the 8th that it was just as well that Lloyd George had not been invited to take office, as he probably could not have been induced to ' forego the delicious dream of leading a Nonconformist rally for Peace and Public Expenditure '.

Thirty-two names (one was unintentionally omitted) accompanied Lloyd George's on the ' Call to Action '. The best known were Snowden, Lothian, Professor Gilbert Murray, and H. A. L. Fisher. Other laymen included Norman Birkett, Miss Rathbone, Mrs Corbett Ashby, and Sir Basil Blackett, the Conservative M.P. and financier. Sir Walter Layton's adherence assured sympathetic coverage in the *News Chronicle*; and the religious press was represented by the editors of the *Baptist Times*, the *Methodist Times*, the *British Weekly*, and the *Christian World*. Angus Watson, a Tyneside businessman, owned a controlling interest in the *Spectator*, was a partner in the firm that published Lloyd George's and Snowden's memoirs, and had the rare honour as a layman to be elected chairman of the Congregational Union. Sir Richard Winfrey, a passive resister who had been carried into Parliament by the Liberal floodtide of 1906, boasted important press connections in Lincolnshire and the east Midlands. Milner Gray, a Wesleyan, had previously sat for Mid-Bedfordshire, where he was again standing. From the National Council, the movement drew Norwood, Scott Lidgett, Hughes, Black, and J. E.

Rattenbury, the president-elect. Among the other spiritual leaders were S. M. Berry, secretary of the Congregational Union and moderator of the Federal Council, Charles Brown, formerly president of the Baptist Union, J. D. Jones, honorary secretary of the Congregational Union, and F. Luke Wiseman, general secretary of the Methodist Union who had attended the birth of the National Council and had served as its president in 1914. Walter Ashley, who served his apprenticeship on the Peace Ballot, was appointed chief organiser, and Victor H. Finney was general secretary.

The manifesto was issued on the evening of 12 June, just in time to meet the deadlines for the week's religious journals, all of which published on the 13th. While the weeklies scarcely had time to offer editorial opinion, the dailies responded along the lines that one could have predicted. The *Manchester Guardian* gave the document its qualified approval: ' Its effects must necessarily be indirect, but they will almost certainly be great.' *The Times* branded it ' rhetorical ' and found it ' suggestive . . . rather of politics than of Christianity '. And the *News Chronicle* applauded the Free Churches for taking ' a definite stand in the political arena '. Splashed across its front page was a banner headline that broadcast the ' Free Churches Call to the Nation '. The remaining columns were divided between a paraphrasing of the manifesto and the report of a visit to Britain of Walt Disney and Mickey Mouse.

The manifesto provoked fierce controversy by its insistence that the Council of Action was to be ' non-political ' in character. ' How can the pursuit of peace and the remedies for unemployment be separated from politics?' a sceptical Lord Reading asked Sir Herbert Samuel.[15] Strictly speaking, it would have been more correct to describe the movement as non-party, if only because past experience had shown the impossibility of containing Lloyd George within party bounds. Clergymen who had signed the manifesto rushed to defend their action in sermons, interviews, and letters to the press. They vehemently denied that the Council was designed to become a new party, that it planned to put forth its own candidates at the general election, or that it was conceived out of hostility to the National Government. Most of all, they played down Lloyd George's role and attested to his good intentions. Had not Baldwin, in his recent speech at Llandrindod Wells, reminded Free Churchmen of their social obligations?

Professing their loyalty to the National Government ideal, several signatories asserted that their ambition was to elect the kind of Parliament that would strengthen and sustain Baldwin, if necessary against his own party. While not disingenuous, some of these disclaimers were a trifle less than candid. The editor of the *British Weekly* described how deeply certain allegations had wounded one signatory, whom he 'happen[ed] to know . . . with the utmost intimacy, in fact I have known him for as long as I remember'. He neglected to add, however, that the individual in question was himself.[16]

One would have to have been terribly naïve, as indeed many were, to mistake Lloyd George's strategy. As Tom Jones knowingly put it, the enterprise 'was a fresh attempt by Lloyd George to get his hands on the levers of power at the next election by means of an organization under his control'.[17] But why this particular organisation at this particular time? His antipathy to Baldwin and MacDonald cannot be discounted, but it was only one of several factors. Although his energies were as yet unflagging, he had reached the age when delay was no longer an option. His 'Lloyd George Fund' had been augmented by shrewd investment: according to a report in the *Evening Standard* on 6 July, 'a large part' had been 'invested in a company whose First Cumulative Preference shares stood at 3s. 8½d. in 1932, and are now quoted at 20s.'. This money could not be left to go to waste. The Free Churches, if not the perfect vehicle for a comeback, were probably the best available to him. But were they capable of delivering the support which he seems to have anticipated? John Rowland, another Welsh crony, 'respectfully' advised him that, while there was no harm in making 'every possible use of the Free Church Council people', it was well to remember that they no longer counted a 'Dr Clifford or Evan Jones (Caernarvon) amongst them. What the Chief wants', Rowland told Miss Stevenson,

is a political fighting Party in the country and in the House of Commons. The Free Churches will not provide him with this machinery. They can give him the background but their support may be shadowy at times. Mr Baldwin has addressed their high gatherings! . . . The Wesleyan element (which is a strong one) is Tory. I say again make every use of them but not as members of a 'Council of Action'. I should not like to go 'tiger hunting' with them. They expect awards which only a political party *in power* can give.[18]

Lloyd George did not heed Rowland's sage advice. Out of faith or desperation – who can say which? – he clutched at the straws of political Nonconformity.

Although no representative of the Salvation Army had signed the 'Call to Action', its officers pledged informal cooperation. So, too, did Ramsay Muir, president of the National Liberal Federation, and George Lansbury, the embattled leader of the parliamentary Labour Party. Lansbury welcomed the Free Churches' intervention, but pointed out, tactlessly perhaps, the impossibility of running 'a great movement for social reform plus disarmament and peace without going into politics'. The Archbishop of Canterbury, who reached the same conclusion, discouraged 'certain bishops' from taking part, though he himself did not hesitate to support the Peace Ballot.[19] On 25 June, 21 Nonconformist M.P.s, the vast majority of them Conservatives, joined to express the view 'that the work of the Churches is not assisted by the manifesto's methods of electioneering'.[20]

A far more crippling blow was soon delivered, much as Rowland had prophesied, by the Methodists. Despite Scott Lidgett's platform exhortations and frenetic efforts behind the scenes, the Methodist Conference at Bristol failed to come out on behalf of the Council of Action. Indeed, the Methodists wondered aloud whether it might not be 'a profound mistake to try to identify Christianity, as such, with any one political party'. It was proudly noted that two of the mainstays of the National Government – Walter Runciman and Sir Kingsley Wood – were Methodists; was it to be said by their co-religionists that these statesmen were less devoted to peace and social welfare than other Nonconformists? Then, on the eve of the Council's national convention, three of the five Methodists who had signed the 'Call to Action' (the Revs Henry Carter, Robert Bond, and Benjamin Gregory) withdrew, taking with them Dr P. T. R. Kirk, secretary of the Industrial Christian Fellowship and a stray Anglican.[21]

Not that any one denomination had a monopoly on second thoughts. While local Baptist associations declared their adherence to the Council and its programme, the general secretary of the Baptist Union resigned from the Free Church Council executive in protest against its link to the Council of Action. 'The Manifesto makes upon me the impression ', M. E. Aubrey confessed, ' that the politicians have swallowed up the Christians '. He recalled how strenuously the Free Churches had campaigned to elect a Liberal Parliament in 1906, and how disappointed they had been thereafter. That precedent ' might have raised some doubts of the value of this method of seeking the Kingdom of God '. J. C. C. Carlile, the editor of the *Baptist Times*, remembered with no less remorse how the Free Churches had been ' sidetracked ' in the early years of the century, and how they had been reduced to ' an adjunct of the Liberal Party '. Yet, in an article appropriately titled ' A Confusion of Issues ', he defended his signing of the manifesto as consistent with support for the National Government. His arguments could not have given much comfort to Lloyd George; nor, for that matter, could they have carried weight with most Baptists, who saw themselves represented within the National Government by Geoffrey Shakespeare and Ernest Brown, whose elevation to the ministry of health, which came unexpectedly and over the claims of more obvious contenders, may be seen as a deliberate attempt by Baldwin to undercut Lloyd George's Baptist support.[22]

Four of the thirty-four charter members had been frightened away and others were doubtless disturbed by reports on 28 June that the Council of Action was prepared to sponsor its own candidates – as many as 350 if necessary – in those constituencies where the established parties offered no acceptable alternative. Had Lloyd George been misquoted or, reverting to old tricks, was he flying a kite? He tried to retrieve the situation by calling an emergency meeting at his Thames House headquarters, but his disclaimers came too late and too grudgingly to restore a semblance of unity. The master seemed to have lost his touch, and those closest to him were worried. According to Miss Stevenson, he proclaimed ' alternately (1) . . . that he never wanted to work with the Government and that he will smash them ultimately; and (2) that he and Baldwin will probably be able to come to terms after the election '. In either case, she was sorry to see him waste himself on ' this somewhat comic convention [that] . . . forces itself upon a somewhat inhospitable world tomorrow '. He had given his word ' that if he sees that the Free Churches won't fight, he will throw up the whole thing. But ', she admitted, ' I know him too well to believe that he will give up any idea once he has started on it, & the more opposition he receives the more determined he will be to force the thing through.'[23]

For all Miss Stevenson's apprehension, the convention did not go off too badly. The Central Hall, Westminster, was packed with 2,500 delegates, of whom more than 400 were clergymen. Some 90 Free Church councils and nearly twice as many other religious groups were represented. At the first day's sessions on 1 July, the subject was peace, and the speakers included Lord Cecil, who made clear that he was a guest of the movement and not one of its sponsors. Macmillan and Lansbury were others who gave the council the benefit of their presence, but not their allegiance, while Snowden and Lothian attended as full-fledged supporters. The chair was taken by Scott Lidgett, who complained that for years the National Council of Evangelical Free Churches had passed thoughtful resolutions, which were forwarded to the appropriate authorities, politely acknowledged, and then ' pigeon-holed '. This year, he vowed, the National Council's resolutions were going to be followed up and acted upon.

Lloyd George saved his appearance for the second of the two days, when the subject before the convention was reconstruction. He professed that it had been his ' thorough disinclination to leave the fragrance of my orchards and return to the acrid and arid atmosphere of political controversy ', but that conscience had compelled him to answer the appeal that came ' from two men connected with the Free Church movement '. More explicitly critical of the National Government than previous speakers, he pulled out all the stops. A. H. E. Molson, one of an estimated 80 M.P.s who attended out of either devotion or curiosity, took *The Times* to task for failing to report the effrontery of ' Mr Lloyd George's peroration in which he explained that his cause was that of the Prince of Peace, and that authority for undertaking public works was to be found in the Parable of the Vineyard '.

Yet, despite the rhetoric and cheering crowds, something was missing. The correspondent for the *Methodist Recorder* went to the convention ' wondering if it would reproduce the moral passion of the Free Church movement thirty years ago ', and he came away oddly dissatisfied :

Such a revival may now be impossible, because issues are not so simple and audiences are more sophisticated. Where emotion at that time ran to ends, now it rather centres in means and parties. These meetings were non-religious in form and intensely religious in spirit. The movement would be stronger as a purely religious force.

In the *Baptist Times*, Carlile returned wearily to ' the old question of the relation of religion to the State ', and Aubrey rebuked his contemporaries for ' placing too much reliance on what men can do and leaving God out '. From the sidelines, Neville Chamberlain taunted that the primary effect of the Council of Action had been ' to create consternation and dissension in the ranks of the Free Churches ', whose gullible leaders ' reminded him of that Young Lady of Riga '.[24]

By mid-July, when the government officially announced its rejection of Lloyd George's New Deal package, the Council of Action had mapped its campaign. There were to be nine area conventions, each to be addressed for 30 minutes by Lloyd George, at which ' organisers ' were to be appointed to establish local Councils of Action in each constituency within the area. After considerable juggling of places and dates, it was decided to hold the first convention at Plymouth on 12 September, with others to follow at Llandrindod Wells, Manchester, Nottingham, Bradford, Bristol, Birmingham, Newcastle-on-Tyne, and London. Each area was to have a council of 200 members, with direct representation on a national council of the same size. The structure was patterned on that of the Free Church councils, which it duplicated to the greatest extent possible. Consequently, where Free Church councils were entrenched, Councils of Action flourished. Often they shared the same officers and premises, always the same mailing lists. At a special meeting on 12 July, the executive committee of the National Free Church Council resolved to encourage this collaboration, ' provided always ' that local Councils of Action adopted programmes that conformed to National Council resolutions, that the movement did not embroil the Free Church councils in party politics, and that action did not divide and debilitate the Free Church councils.[25] It was more easily said than done.

The executive committee's qualifications were hardly sufficient to reassure those Nonconformists who resented the impropriety of electioneering, and, still more, of trafficking with Lloyd George. But, if the denominational press provides any index, opinion seemed slowly to be changing in favour of the movement. On 25 July, the *Baptist Times* published a long letter from Black, who had first obtained clearance from Lloyd George, in which the aims and origins of the Council of Action were again explained. 'An attitude of inaction and complacency on the part of the Churches at critical times is a betrayal of a sacred trust', he thundered, and he warned that such an attitude would 'aggravate still further the decline in Church membership and . . . give colour to the fallacious arguments of those political extremists who link social revolution with anti-religious propaganda.'[26] In the same number, the Rev Charles Brown identified himself as an 'unrepentant signatory of the Manifesto', and likened the arguments against political involvement to those which had once been used to deter Baptist opposition to slavery. Elsewhere on the same page, spokesmen for the Bradford Baptist Ministers' Fraternal communicated their 'fullest sympathy'. By the week's end, Lloyd George was professing 'much optimism about his election prospects. Thinks Labour may get 275 seats and that he will have enough supporters to reduce S.B. to impotence and to force S.B. to come to terms with him (L.G.) as Labour won't take office unless it has effective powers.'[27]

While he remained 'confident that he is going to smash the power of the National Gov. at the election', Miss Stevenson was shaken on 30 July by 'a string of "regrets" in tonight's bag from people who had promised to support D.'s Council of Action but who are now crying off and do not want to attend a wedding feast that looks like being a frost.'[28] Particularly disappointing was the failure to recruit Harold Macmillan and other progressive Tories. Although the Council shared principles and indeed personnel with Macmillan's 'Next Five Years' Group, the latter's officers – most categorically Lord Allen of Hurtwood, chairman of the executive committee – refused to affiliate with Lloyd George, or even to invite him to sign their manifesto. Macmillan, a match for Lloyd George in cunning and dexterity, managed to get what he wanted from the Council of Action without providing anything tangible in return. At the other end of the spectrum, Lansbury launched his 'Truce of God' mission, which, if anything, competed with Lloyd George's movement.

Leslie Hore-Belisha, who had got his start in Liberal politics as a Lloyd Georgian and then went over to the Simonites,

' thought that Ll G had made a mistake in trying to work his campaign through the Free Churches'. In an interview with W. P. Crozier, editor of the *Manchester Guardian*, he

> gave an account of a visit that he had paid to Churt some time before the Council of Action business had been announced, and he said it was apparent then from Ll G's conversation that he was assuming the existence of a ' Nonconformist vote' of the old kind. He had talked a great deal of what had happened in the days of Gladstone . . . and seemed to think things had not changed.

Crozier confirmed that Lloyd George had subsequently spoken to him in the same vein.[29] How could someone who boasted such a reputation as an astute tactician go chasing after phantoms?

But the professional politicians, by their incredulity, were not the only ones to cause Miss Stevenson distress. The last days of August brought evidence that ' D.'s Nonconformist friends are running away again from the Council of Action'. On the 27th, Lloyd George arrived at Churt after conferring in Wales the previous day with Hughes and Scott Lidgett. Within hours, he received an anxious telephone call from Hughes, who

> said he *must* see D. that night. D. was furious, knowing that it meant that Hughes had gone back *again* on his agreement of the previous day. When Hughes came, bringing Wilson Black with him, D. turned on them. . . . ' Gideon knew how to distinguish between the funks and the brave men', he said. ' I wish someone would give me that power.' ' He only had 300 left at the finish', said Hughes. ' *But he won*', retorted D. The interview was extremely unpleasant, and D. was considerably upset by it.

Once again, Miss Stevenson was moved to ' *wish* he had not embarked upon this enterprise', or should she say ' folly'? It seemed to her ' to be the most complete muddle, and scarcely anyone believing in it'. There was some consolation to be taken from the ' keen interest' showed by Lothian, but even his ' excellent' memorandum – ' The Peace Aspect of Reconstruction' – only made one ' realise how hopeless it seems to be '.[30]

Lothian's memorandum afforded considerably less satisfaction to the lay members of his sub-committee, who found it ' unduly defeatist in temper', and, in effect, dismissive of the League of

Nations. That Dr Norwood failed to join in their complaint was indicative not necessarily of his approval, but more probably of Lloyd George's success in keeping the clergymen in the movement at a safe distance from their 'political' colleagues. Miss Rathbone, determined to have Lothian alter the text before publication, threatened 'to sound a warning in the ears of the Free Church members who may not realise the full implications of the policy set forth in your memorandum'. One suspects that, like many public figures, she exaggerated the willingness of churchmen to give substance to their pro-League sentiments. Sir Francis Acland, preparing to defend the seat at North Cornwall which he had won in a 1932 by-election, informed Lloyd George that he had 'been doing a good many unreported open-air meetings lately', at which he had 'followed fairly nearly the lines of Lothian's paper about an active peace policy' in order to 'appeal to the Nonconformist minister type of man whom I have been trying to get hold of'. Acland revealed that, 'while strongly approving the present action of the Government in acting under the Covenant of the League', he had argued that members of the League, collectively and individually, had ignored for so long 'Abyssinia's appeals' that there was now little to be done. Lloyd George was soon to take much the same line, which allowed his followers to assert the righteousness of their past positions without being required to come to terms with the present predicament.[31]

Acland was among those on the platform on 12 September, when Lloyd George launched his Peace and Reconstruction campaign at the Stonehouse Town Hall, Plymouth. They were joined by other prospective parliamentary candidates from the area, including Isaac and John Foot, A. L. Rowse, and J. J. Moses. The Rev J. Colliver Williams, president of the Plymouth Free Church Council, took part, as did the president and vice-president of the Devon and Cornwall Baptist Association, the secretary of the National Congregational Union, and the chairman-elect of the Devon Congregational Union. Two days later, Lloyd George carried his standard to Llandrindod Wells, where his presentation took special account of Welsh problems. He was attended by the moderator of the Welsh Presbyterian (Calvinistic Methodist) church, the chairman of the Welsh Congregational Union, and the presidents of the Welsh Methodist and Baptist Unions, as well as by a complement of 'leading preachers'. At

Nottingham on the 18th, the speakers included Norwood and the Rev G. Hartley Holloway, who ' discerned in the Council of Action the rebirth of the Nonconformist Conscience', and who scoffed at allegations that political activity would split the Free Churches. 'But', he added, ' I would rather see the Free Churches split by movement and life than rot within from stagnation.'[32]

At each stop in his tour, Lloyd George was greeted by a massive turnout. ' Plymouth was crammed to the doors, Delegates with tickets packed the passages', his secretary minuted. ' The Llandrindod Hall, holding 800, was packed to suffocation, with an overflow meeting of 300. Bradford with its 800 Delegates could not possibly take more ' – a fact that did not prevent the *News Chronicle* from putting attendance there at a thousand – and there was a ' similar report' from Nottingham. At Bristol, the demand for tickets ran so high that a second hall was engaged; then, at the last moment, the entire proceedings were shifted to the more capacious Grand Hotel. Local Free Church ministers helped to distribute more than 700 advance tickets, 420 of which went to official delegates. On this occasion, the sponsors thought it best not to rely exclusively upon the Free Church councils in the area, which did not ' represent the whole of Nonconformity', and which sent only 36 delegates to the convention. There were 120 other Nonconformist divines, 54 laymen representing individual congregations, 40 members of the Society of Friends, and small delegations from such groups as the Salvation Army, the British Temperance Association, the Democratic Front, and the Co-operative Guilds. The Lord Mayor came to cheer, strictly in an unofficial capacity, and heard Lloyd George (in a speech that lasted an hour and ten minutes) declare that the Abyssinian crisis was ' just as much a dispute as when Jezebel demanded Naboth's vineyard '. Others on the Bristol programme were the Revs S. W. Hughes and Thomas Davies, president of the Bristol Free Church Council.[33]

Tactical considerations, not fatigue, led Lloyd George to cancel his appearance at Birmingham on the 26th, and to send his son Gwilym instead. ' It would appear ', the *Manchester Guardian* wrote with classic understatement, ' that the Free Churchmen in the West Midlands are not so completely agreed about the wisdom or propriety of the movement as in other areas where conventions have been held.' The chair was taken by Dr J.

Vincent Shaw, the mayor of Hereford, who admitted that he had been unable to persuade his fellow members of the Hereford Free Church Council to send delegates. A procession of speakers, including the Revs J. Ivory Cripps and F. C. Spurr, emphasised that they represented only themselves and none of the groups to which they belonged. Unlike preceding conventions, the one at Birmingham did not implement plans to set up a regional Council of Action. Two days later, at Manchester's Milton Hall, the situation was better, but not by much. There, Lothian gave the featured address, and the Rev R. W. Weeks announced that the movement had the backing of the Manchester and Salford Free Church Council, subject ' of course ' to ' certain safeguards ' which he did not specify.[34]

At a tense meeting on 19 September, the executive of the National Free Church Council, by unanimous agreement, cautiously reaffirmed its instructions to local councils to render ' service . . . in the causes which called the Council of Action into being '. (The devious phrasing was Norwood's.) At the same time, members of the executive appeased the consciences of certain colleagues by joining deputations that waited upon the Prime Minister, who did not disguise from Tom Jones his disdain for these ' Men of God '.[35] But the real tug-of-war began in mid-October, when the country was plunged into an election campaign. On the 17th, Lloyd George assembled his team to devise strategy and prepare a questionnaire for candidates. The Free Churchmen among them ' announced . . . that they were taking special steps to ensure that the Council's policy is emphasised in connection with the various Free Church organizations '. Scott Lidgett, Berry, Hughes, and Norwood composed a public letter in which they recalled and defended their activities, and expressed confidence ' that the Council of Action will play an honourable part in the forthcoming General Election by giving effect on non-party lines to a policy of peace and reconstruction '.[36]

Exactly as Baldwin had intended, the Council of Action – like the Liberal and Labour Opposition – was caught off guard. Its manifestos were drafted, but its constituency organisations were in an embryonic state. The situation was sufficiently critical to bring together Lloyd George and Samuel, an inevitability each of them had resisted. Samuel, although initially ' sticky ', eventually agreed to advise ' Liberal voters, in constituencies where there is no Liberal candidate, to vote for whichever candidate supports the policy of the Peace and Reconstruction movement'. Snowden, in a pre-election broadcast, savagely echoed these sentiments.[37]

With no time to spare, the Council scheduled a one-day convention in London on the 29th: Lothian held forth in the morning at the Essex Hall, and Lloyd George in the afternoon at the Kingsway Hall. No part of Lloyd George's address gave greater satisfaction than his

assurance that he [had] received over 4,000 favourable answers from local preachers and ministers, who had been approached as to their willingness to speak during the next fortnight on behalf of the Council's programme. . . .

Yet the Council's attempt to recruit clergymen for electioneering often aroused more antagonism than enthusiasm. The ' president of a fairly influential Free Church Council on the outskirts of London' complained to *The Times* that he and his associates ' resented very much ' the pressures which were brought to bear:

I was asked by a Methodist minister to send my Circuit plan to the Council, so that all my lay preachers might receive notes of speeches which they could give on behalf of the Council's programme. I never sent my plan, since I regard this as an unwarrantable intrusion on the real purpose of a preacher's duty.

Elsewhere, too, there were indignant charges that local Free Church councils were bullied by Council of Action organisers.[38]

But the Council directed its main thrust at parliamentary candidates, each of whom received a questionnaire on general subjects of peace and reconstruction. By 2 November, approximately 700 of the 1,300 candidates in the field had sent in their replies, and 300 qualified for Council approval. Four days later, a supplementary list brought the number of endorsements to 354. There were 55 contests in which both Liberal and Labour candidates were supported, and a few in which the Liberal shared the Council's commendation with his Tory opponent. Eventually, a total of 362 candidates was approved: all 161 Liberals in the running, 183 of the 552 Labour contenders, 16 supporters of the National Government (Conservatives or Liberal Nationals), and two independents.[39]

In several constituencies, the Council threatened to mount an independent campaign until a satisfactory reply was extracted from one or another of the official candidates: such was the case in the Tavistock division of Devon. In a few places, it ran its own candidates, usually on the Liberal ticket: such was the case at Bristol South, where J. O. M. Skelton stood as 'a New Deal Liberal'. There were many contests in which the Council and its questionnaire were ignored with impunity either because a particular candidate (like Geoffrey Shakespeare at Norwich) boasted impeccable Nonconformist credentials, or because the Nonconformist vote was negligible. But it was more frequently the case that candidates were anxious to have the Council on their side. Mrs G. E. G. Catlin (better known as Vera Brittain) invited Lord Lothian to speak on behalf of her husband, one of two Labour candidates for Sunderland. Professor Catlin, she assured him, had 'replied favourably to the Council of Action questionnaire', and was rewarded by an appearance from Angus Watson, chairman of the Council, and a promise that some 'eminent Nonconformist member', Dr Norwood perhaps, would speak at Sunderland on Armistice Day.[40]

The choice between candidates was not always so straightforward. There was a good deal of wirepulling behind the scenes, and candidates were sometimes supported – or, at any rate, not opposed – who hardly merited the Council's consideration. It would be impossible to provide a complete catalogue of these infractions, but several stand out as particularly egregious: 1. J. J. Moses and G. Ward, Labour candidates for the Drake and Sutton divisions of Plymouth, were both Free Churchmen who identified themselves as early supporters of the peace and reconstruction movement, to the extent that Moses had appeared on the platform at the Plymouth area convention. Neither stood against a Liberal, but both had the misfortune to oppose Conservatives (F. E. Guest and Lady Astor) whom Lloyd George and Lothian did not wish to affront. Consequently, their names were omitted from the final list of approved candidates. 2. At West Woolwich, George Wansborough made a bid to unseat Sir Kingsley Wood, and the *News Chronicle* believed that his 'message of peace and reconstruction is certain of intensive circulation despite the prevailing apathy'. But the Council of Action did not see fit to support an upstart Labour candidate against one of the nation's most prominent Methodist statesmen. 3. At Stockton-on-Tees, where Harold Macmillan was engaged in a three-cornered fight, attempts were made to get the Liberal candidate (who shared with Macmillan the Council's approval) to stand down. Although the Council was officially pledged to neutrality in such circumstances, Lloyd George 'went out of his way' to secure Macmillan's return, and Scott Lidgett journeyed to Stockton to give 'considerable support'. 4. Occasionally, key participants in the Council of Action movement either gave testimonials to candidates who were denied Council support, or else declined to back approved candidates. Professor Gilbert Murray, for example, made statements on behalf of Anthony Eden, Sir Samuel Hoare, and Philip Noel-Baker. Angus Watson, more perversely, withheld his endorsement from Sir Nicholas Grattan-Doyle, the National Conservative candidate at Newcastle North, whom the Council found eminently suitable. 5. Although her reply failed to give complete satisfaction, the Council bestowed its blessing on Ellen Wilkinson, the Labour challenger at Jarrow, who had a brother in the Methodist ministry, and who was personally commended by the Rev F. Maclachlan, chairman of the local council. Miss Wilkinson's speeches during the campaign induced the Council to strike her name from the roster. 6. At Bodmin, H. Falconer insisted that he had answered the questionnaire affirmatively, but that the Council had bypassed him in favour of Isaac Foot; at Torquay, F. Scardifield, another Labour man, was said to have suffered a similar fate, and here at some sacrifice to Nonconformist interests.[41]

It was only when the campaign was well underway that it became clear to what extent the Free Church effort hinged on one man, Dr John Scott Lidgett. Norwood was always on hand for a ranting supplication, and Hughes for a prolix speech or newspaper article; but it was Scott Lidgett, the senior member of the Free Church Council triumvirate, who occupied the pivotal position. Age and tenure of office had conspired to make him authoritarian and sometimes impetuous. Worse, he failed to appreciate the complexities of the situations in which he found himself, and, especially, the subtleties of the personalities with whom he dealt. At the outset, he issued each Free Church Council in England and Wales a portfolio of documents, accompanied by instructions to 'be assisted and guided by the [12 July] Resolution of the Executive Committee'.[42] How did he himself interpret that ambiguous resolution?

Like many Nonconformists of the older generation, Wesleyans particularly, Scott Lidgett prayed for divine intervention to halt the seemingly inexorable march of socialism. To his consternation, nearly a third of the Labour candidates in 1935 accepted with enthusiasm the Peace and Reconstruction proposals, which they found in no way incompatible with the fundamentals of party doctrine. The stumbling block to greater socialist acceptance of the questionnaire was, in most cases, not ideological, but procedural: did it constitute a commitment, if elected, to follow Lloyd George's lead, and thereby a defiance of the Labour whip? Scott Lidgett, faced with the unwelcome prospect of large scale Labour support for the Council, hedged on his initial ' commitment to accept any and every candidate who might accept the policy of the Council of Action. As you are aware ', he protested to Lloyd George, ' the basis upon which you and I co-operated in formulating our policy was that there was no likelihood of the Socialist Party accepting it.'[43]

Had Scott Lidgett been hoodwinked, or had he failed to grasp the essentials of electoral politics? In either case, his treachery was worse than anything of which he might accuse Lloyd George. On 8 November, only six days before polling, Sir John Simon brandished a letter addressed to him by Scott Lidgett, ' vice-president of the Council of Action '. Describing himself as ' a non-party man of Liberal antecedents ', Scott Lidgett embraced the National Government as a bulwark against socialism, and urged the return of its supporters over any and all Labour candidates. This was taken, not unreasonably, to include those Labour candidates approved by the Council of Action. Three days later, he clarified his position in a letter to *The Times,* in which he asserted that, while Baldwin's administration had made ' declarations which go far on the road to meet our demands and raise hopes of still further progress ', Labour had offered ' proposals which, in my judgment, would bring about such a crisis as would disable them from giving effect to the policy of the council, however well-disposed their followers might be '. With laudable restraint, Lloyd George replied to his lieutenant in an interview at Tenby. Of the more than 350 candidates who had thus far replied satisfactorily to the Council's questionnaire, there were 182 Labour men and women, but only twenty who sported the ' National ' label. He would have been prepared, he averred, to support loyally all 202 of them even had the proportions been reversed. Chastened, Scott Lidgett joined Norwood and Hughes in issuing an election eve statement that renewed the injunctions of the previous July. But there was no denying that irreparable damage had been done.[44]

It is possible, although with less precision, to evaluate the Council's support on denominational as well as party lines. The total number of Nonconformist candidates in 1935 was put by various sources at about 140. Whereas, three decades earlier, Nonconformist candidates were almost exclusively Liberal, there was now a preponderance of Labourites and a phalanx of Conservatives among them. The Methodists were by far the most numerous, with 63 candidates of whom 24 enjoyed Council backing. Not surprisingly, the Methodists included the largest contingent of government supporters (11 Liberal Nationals and 7 Conservatives), only one of whom was endorsed. All 15 Methodists who stood as Liberals had Council approval, but only eight of the 30 Labour contenders.

The same held true on a lesser scale with the Baptists, Quakers, and Unitarians: each produced a greater number of candidates for Labour – a majority of whom failed to satisfy Council requirements – than for either of the older parties. Approval was given to three of the ten Unitarian hopefuls, four of the eight Baptists, and eleven of the 23 Friends. The pattern was broken only by the Congregationalists, who, alone among the major sects, maintained their historic commitment to the Radical tradition. Twenty-four Congregationalists stood for Parliament, of whom 17 won Council support, including two of the four Liberal Nationals, and, more significantly, eight of the twelve Labour candidates. The same tendencies can be discerned among the eight clergymen who contested seats (a ninth, a minister of the Protestant Reformers Church, fought Kirkdale as a self-styled 'Protestant candidate'): the Council of Action approved a Methodist minister (Liberal), rejected a Baptist (Liberal National), rejected a Quaker and a minister of the United Free Church of Scotland (both Labour), approved one Unitarian and rejected another (both Labour), and approved two Congregational divines (both Labour).

Polling took place on 14 November, and Baldwin scored decisively. How much, if anything, did the Council's exertions affect the outcome? Of 362 approved candidates, 67 were returned: 21 Liberals (including all four members of Lloyd

George's ' family group '), 34 Labourites, eleven supporters of the National Government, and one independent. Obviously, the Council's endorsement afforded considerably less guarantee of electoral success than either its sponsors had anticipated or its critics had feared. The Liberal Nationals held their ground, usually without Council assistance, but the Opposition Liberals were routed. Sir Herbert Samuel and Isaac Foot were among those who left the Commons, never to return. Milner Gray, whose name appeared on the June manifesto, failed in his bid to re-capture Mid-Bedford. Mrs Corbett Ashby, another signatory, was rejected at Hemel Hempstead. But Ellen Wilkinson triumphed at Jarrow, notwithstanding the Council's repudiation of her candidacy.

The Rev J. Nicholson Balmer's confident prediction of success in the West Riding, where he was area organiser, proved mistaken. Although ' enormous ' supplies of literature had been distributed on behalf of the 20 approved candidates in the area, there was no appreciable effect. Six seats in the West Riding changed hands from one party to another, but only at Penistone did the victor bear the imprimatur of the Council of Action, and he was not a Nonconformist. At Colne Valley, an unapproved Labour challenger, again not a Nonconformist, dislodged the approved Liberal incumbent, who was.

Of the 20 Free Church M.P.s who had spurned the Council at the time of its birth, only one suffered retribution. Sir George Gillett, who had sat for Finsbury since 1923, was defeated by the Rev G. S. Woods, a Unitarian. It is doubtful, however, whether the Council's endorsement of Woods affected the Finsbury result half as much as the fact that Gillett was a follower of Ramsay MacDonald. Two others lost their seats, but neither to an approved candidate; one had retired at the dissolution; and one had died before the election. The remaining 15 were returned without difficulty.

The Council had entertained high hopes of helping to defeat L. S. Amery, a notorious sabre-rattler, at Sparkbrook, where 17,000 signatures had been collected for the Peace Ballot; but Amery held on by a margin of more than two-to-one. At Altrincham, Sir Edward Grigg, who was viewed as another hardliner, retained his seat by a comfortable majority against a Labour opponent with strong Council backing. Macmillan, a Conservative of quite another stripe, warded off a strong Labour assault at

Stockton; but the Council's assistance could not have contributed significantly to his 4,000-vote plurality, and certainly failed to help the Liberal, who lost his deposit. Sir Francis Acland scraped by in North Cornwall, as did his son Richard at nearby Barnstaple, and it is conceivable that in each case a few votes were swayed by the Council's intervention. Looking back, the younger Acland was inclined to give more credit to the financial assistance – something on the order of £100 – that the Council provided, and to conclude that, if any of his constituents had been open to the Council's influence, ' they must have been such as could be counted on your fingers. I can't actually recall the name of a Free Church minister who spoke for me,' Sir Richard continued:

> But it would be very strange if many were not using their influence quite openly for me. But this they would do because of the whole background relationship between Liberalism and Non-conformity; and their enthusiasm would not be increased as much as 1 per cent by any declaration from the Council of Action.[45]

In other words, the Council proved largely irrelevant, securing Nonconformist support – itself of questionable worth – for candidates who, for the most part, would have had it anyway. And all at a cost of £400,000 from Lloyd George's funds alone.

Tom Jones surveyed the wreckage with detached amusement, purveying to his correspondents other people's attempted witticisms. ' L.G. has been captious and bad-mannered ', he wrote to Dr Abraham Flexner at Princeton University, ' and his Councils of Action have justified the quip Councils of Faction '. And to Lady Grigg, who was in India with Sir James, Jones described ' L.G.'s campaign ' as ' a big and expensive bluff. . . . The " old men " have not improved their reputations in this fight. Snowden and L.G. have been left with only their spleen, some one observed, after their operations on the prostate gland.'[46] But Jones was manifestly unfair in putting all the blame on a few stooped shoulders. ' The wind was taken out of the sails of the movement ', Lord Lothian declared more thoughtfully, by a combination of factors and events: Hitler's proclamation of rearmament, the Silver Jubilee (which some resentfully regarded as a sideshow improvised by Baldwin to divert attention from social problems), the Abyssinian crisis and Sir Samuel Hoare's much acclaimed speech at Geneva in September, a perceptible upturn in the economy, ' and the sudden election capitalising [on] these things '.[47] But, about all else, the Council of Action had foundered because, although its aims and leadership were essentially secular, it relied for organisation and support on religious bodies which were shown to command limited resources and a still more limited perception of political reality. In the improbable event that the Council had made an impact at the polls, its Free Church enthusiasts would have expected it to deliver peace on earth, legislation for temperance and Sunday observance, economic recovery, and moral regeneration. Electoral defeat was by far the lesser disappointment.

10 *Lazarus Unraised*

' Eventually ', two eminent sociologists have explained with crisp logic, ' all organized movements begin to flag, and means are sought to revitalize them.'[1] On the face of things, the 1935 Council of Action campaign was such a means, and a not un-promising one. In a more profound sense, however, it was fore-doomed to failure, coming long after political Nonconformity had ceased to function as an organized movement. Resuscitative tech-niques, inherited from a bygone age, proved inapposite: patterns of religious behaviour, no less than the structure of politics, had changed too irrevocably. Thereafter, the Free Churches never again ventured corporately into the electoral arena. Like prominent Anglicans before them, their leaders have since resigned them-selves to Burke's dictum that ' Politics and the pulpit are terms that have little agreement '.

True to form, some stalwarts mistook defeat for qualified success. The *British Weekly* was pleased to count 63 Noncon-formists in the 1935 Parliament, the last elected before the war, whom it could classify by denomination. By some undisclosed arithmetical process, it calculated that ' almost a hundred Free Church Members are pledged to the programme of the Council of Peace and Reconstruction '. Dr John Scott Lidgett, with his penchant for self-deception, found at least ' two things ' on which

> we may congratulate ourselves. In the first place, Mr Baldwin and his leading colleagues have given very substantial pledges in regard to Peace, the League of Nations, the Raising of the School Age, and the Depressed Areas. . . . In the next place, the increased number of the Opposition, and the fact that most of the Socialist leaders have been returned to Parliament, is all to the good.

He vowed that the National Free Church Council and its local affiliates would exert ' continuous influence on non-Party lines in support of the Council's policy of Peace and Reconstruction '. On 6 December, the executive held a ' lengthy discussion ' on its past and future relations with the Council of Action, and Dr F. W. Norwood ' stated his earnest conviction that . . . great work . . . had [been] accomplished . . . in a short time '.[2]

Lloyd George appears to have been rather less certain that the Council of Action, and particularly its Free Church component, had served any useful purpose. In the aftermath of the election, he dropped strong hints that he was contemplating the creation of yet another agency to succeed where the last had failed: Lord Lothian, whom he sought to enlist, declined to ' accept [the] Chairmanship of the new body you spoke about '.[3] But the Council survived to intervene, not without effect, in a number of prewar by-elections. Walter Ashley, its chief organiser, worked diligently to broaden its base of support. ' In several cases ', he reported early in 1936, ' a number of leading Anglicans are already rendering useful assistance; and in one Area, the chief Rabbi of the district is one of the most active members of the Committee.' Ashley's subsequent memoranda tacitly acknowledged the extent to which the Council remained a Nonconformist proposition, and, as such, a losing one. Its national membership steadily declined, although at a slower rate in those parts of the country where the Free Church councils were strong: Yorkshire, the East Midlands, Lancashire, and Wales. Finally, in the early weeks of the war, the Council of Action put its services and facilities at the disposal of the All-Party Parliamentary Action Group.[4]

Soon after the 1935 election, Norwood resigned his pulpit at the City Temple. One of his last sermons there was an apology for Hitler's remilitarisation of the Rhineland: ' I think for the first time in my life I wanted to say today " Heil Hitler!" '[5] Thereupon, he embarked on an evangelical tour that took him up and down the kingdom and eventually to Canada, where he spent the wartime years and died. Like him, the National Council of Evangelical Free Churches turned abruptly from political agitation to revivalism. Even its revised roster of vice-presidents gave evidence of a determination to straddle political fences: the appointment of Megan Lloyd George was carefully balanced by Runciman and Isaac Foot. Norwood's successors in the presidency were the Revs J. E. Rattenbury (a Methodist), James Colville (a Presbyterian), and J. D. Jones (a Congregationalist), each of whom held aloof from secular controversy during his term of office. For the remaining years of the decade, until he retired as honorary secretary in 1940, Scott Lidgett submitted annual reports on 'Public Questions' that scrupulously ignored the Council of Action, and, except in the most general sense, other topical issues.

Within Parliament, where its numerical strength had dwindled, Nonconformity was more than ever a negligible quantity. Those who professed to speak in its name tended to lack political stature and, increasingly, moral authority. The Rev G. S. Woods, a Unitarian whose Labour candidacy at Finsbury had carried the Council of Action imprimatur, made occasional allusion to the Free Churches' indignation at conditions of poverty and unemployment;[6] but he drew his inspiration and support from his secular rather than from his religious background. More by default than by ordination, the responsibility of speaking for Nonconformity at Westminster devolved upon men like Thomas Magnay, a Wesleyan lay preacher who practised as an accountant at Gateshead, and who believed that 'all our political institutions are outward and visible signs of inward and spiritual convictions.' Having stood unsuccessfully at Blaydon as a straightforward Liberal in 1929, Magnay was returned at Gateshead two years later as a Liberal National who enjoyed enthusiastic Conservative backing. Under any label, he qualified as one of the last of a breed. But it is significant that the breed, which was once defined by its inveterate antagonism to Toryism, now depended upon Tory compliance to obtain a voice in public affairs.

Magnay's association with Liberalism, in one or another of its varieties, antedated the first world war. In 1911, he delivered a rousing address to a Young Liberal conference at London, and he was informally asked whether he might like to offer himself as a parliamentary candidate. 'He had very little money, & a young family,' his son has recalled.

He did what was to him a normal thing. He went into the nearest church, which happened to be St Paul's, to pray for guidance. It so happened that it was Evensong. The text of the sermon was 'Go Home'. He had no doubt then what to do. He caught the next train home, and thus it was that he entered Parliament in 1931, instead perhaps in 1911, and he never doubted that he had made the right decision.

Magnay had little confidence in Lloyd George, from whom he had diverged at the time of the 1926 General Strike, and whose Council of Action he regarded as a disreputable stunt. When Magnay nominated those who deserved to occupy pedestals in a pantheon of immortal British statesmen, one name was pointedly omitted: 'Gladstone, Disraeli, Campbell-Bannerman, Asquith . . . and Baldwin and Chamberlain in no lesser degree '.[7]

It is not without interest that Magnay promulgated his list in a lecture at Heidelberg University in 1936. It was over the totalitarian threat from abroad and the pusilanimity of the National Government at home that Free Churchmen divided most bitterly. Runciman, raised to the peerage in 1937, was dispatched to Prague in July 1938 as the accredited agent of appeasement. Simon, who had to wait three years longer for his viscountcy, was tarred by the same brush. Among the other M.P.s prominently identified with Nonconformity, Sir Kingsley Wood was one of Chamberlain's most intimate friends and advisors, and Ernest Brown and Geoffrey Shakespeare were otherwise attached to the government.

Isaac Foot, from outside the House, battled against the prevailing ethic. Defeated at Bodmin in 1935, he nursed a bitter resentment against Runciman, ' a brother Methodist', who had backed his 'National' opponent.[8] Two years later, Foot unsuccessfully attempted a comeback at St Ives, where a by-election was occasioned by Runciman's elevation to the peerage. His candidacy was supported by the Rev Henry Carter, with whom he had been at school, as well as by A. L. Rowse and other advocates of a Liberal-Labour pact against the appeasers. Lady Violet Bonham Carter, Asquith's daughter, agreed to speak for him, but reconsidered when she heard that Lloyd George also planned an appearance at St Ives: 'Without going back into past history,' she protested, ' his boom of Hitlerism & description of Hitler as " the greatest man in Europe " as lately as last autumn must I think have come as a shock to most Liberals (even those Cerebresces the Free Church Ministers!).'[9]

As usual, Lloyd George's attitudes defy simple classification. On the one hand, he took an emphatic stand against Italian aggression in Abyssinia, to the extent that Lord Lothian resigned in protest from the executive of the Council of Action, which seemed to him to be awash in a ' morass of flapdoodle and pro-French timidity '.[10] On the other hand, Lloyd George returned from his celebrated visit to Germany in September 1936 with a profound admiration for Hitler, if not necessarily for the Nazi order. His response to foreign affairs was, to say the least, confused. Yet it faithfully mirrored the response of the Nonconformist public.

The Munich settlement of September 1938 brought the discrepancy between sentiment and policy into full relief. On 26 October, Lloyd George addressed a luncheon at the City Temple on the subject of ' The Free Churches and the World Situation '. In preparation, he had commissioned Malcolm Thomson, his accomplished ' devil ' and future biographer, to provide him with ' a note on the achievements of the Free Churches in social reform ' which was, in effect, a review of English history with special emphasis on the Nonconformist contribution :

> In periods when the Evangelical Free Churches have failed to play any notable and active part in the struggle for social reform and for international justice and freedom, they have been weak and negligible. Which of these two symptoms was cause, and which was effect may be debatable. But it seems not unfair to assume that they become strongest when they are fired with enthusiasm for some living cause which vitally affects the practice of Christianity in human life.[11]

His speech was introduced by Wickham Steed, who had been displaced as editor of *The Times* by the arch-appeaser Geoffrey Dawson, and it was broadcast to America. But Lloyd George, who decried the betrayal of Czechoslovakia (' We had lost honour, but we had not gained tranquility '), was primarily concerned with opinion nearer at hand. 'In all that welter of broken pacts and covenants, where was the traditional voice of the Free Churches?' he demanded to know.

> It seemed to him that Nonconformity through its leadership had sounded a broken, intermittent, and muffled tocsin. The call which had come from them had lost its sustained power and resonance, and he was afraid that, even if the metal had not deteriorated in quality, it had been corroded very largely by the patronage of the ecclesiastical and official hierarchy.

Needless to say, his strictures gave umbrage to many ' men of God ', who welcomed Munich as the triumph of Christian precepts.

Henry Carter, who had recently joined him in endorsing Isaac Foot at St Ives, deplored his ' ferocious and irresponsible speech ', and called upon ' Free Churchmen everywhere to affirm, over against this vengeful utterance, their willingness to work with rulers and citizens of any State, so as to lessen tension and to build peace and social justice.' Sir Henry Lunn, another Wesleyan old-timer, was similarly aggrieved by what he considered the tendency of Lloyd George and other parliamentary Liberals to indulge in factious partisanship; in retaliation, he announced his resignation from the Liberal Party, 'convinced . . . that there was no room ' in its depleted ranks ' for a Liberal who still believed in " peace, retrenchment and reform " '.[12] But Lloyd George's resolute (and not wholly characteristic) opposition to appeasement was vigorously commended by J. Chuter Ede (later Lord Chuter-Ede), a Unitarian M.P. who sat in the Labour interest for South Shields. ' Thank you very much for what you said at the City Temple about the Nonconformist attitude to the modern struggle for liberty and justice,' he wrote privately : ' One has been asking one's self for weeks what would Joseph Parker and John Clifford have said in these emergencies. . . . If totalitarianism is tolerable, nonconformity is indefensible. Our leaders do not seem to have realized that.'[13] Nothing could testify more conclusively to the dismemberment of political Nonconformity, and especially to the disparity between its spiritual and lay wings, than this complaint from a Labour member who worshipped in the same church as the Prime Minister whose policies he denounced.

Eleven months later, war was declared. Like other proponents of appeasement, the patriarchs of Nonconformity stood discredited by their misjudgment of men and events. But that was only an incidental factor in the waning of their authority. During the ensuing struggle for national survival, there was a further weakening of the church-going habit, a growing tendency towards disbelief among the young, and a general deflection of moral energies.[14] There were a few occasions when the self-appointed parliamentary spokesmen for Nonconformity managed to intervene with effect. In February 1941, for example, Magnay took issue with the government's order-in-council which permitted the opening of theatres and other recreational facilities, including racing, on Sundays. In a free vote in the Commons, the government was narrowly defeated, and the order was ' annulled '. Winston Churchill, who became Prime Minister the previous

May, was taken aback, having forgotten the disposition of the people among whom he had moved earlier in the century. He 'expressed surprise' when W. P. Crozier 'told him about the Puritan opposition' to Sunday entertainments 'in places like Manchester', where Churchill had once been elected to represent the North West division.[15]

'Puritan opposition', formerly a concomitant of the Nonconformist political tradition, was now virtually all that remained. As a rule, Free Church opinion was chiefly conspicuous by its absence, especially in those realms where it had formerly waxed strong. R. A. (later Lord) Butler, appointed to the Board of Education in the autumn of 1941, was given explicit instructions by the Prime Minister: 'It would be the greatest mistake to raise the 1902 controversy during the war, and I certainly cannot contemplate a new Education Bill.' Nonetheless Butler, with Chuter Ede as his 'loyal collaborator', proceeded according to his inclination. He promulgated an educational formula, 'not unlike . . . Birrell's Bill of 1906', while managing to avert the sectarian disputes which Churchill recalled so vividly from his days as Birrell's colleague. The outcome was, above all else, a tribute to Butler's consummate diplomatic skills; but it also reflected the decline, during the intervening years, of education as a sectarian issue and, more generally, of religion as the source and generator of political opinion. Butler encountered greater intractability on the part of Roman Catholic authorities than among Free Church stalwarts, who readily accepted the compromise, embodied in the 1944 Act, by which the provision of religious teaching was made compulsory, but (in schools maintained by public funds) non-denominational. Not that Butler's solution afforded universal satisfaction in Nonconformist circles. Sir Richard Winfrey, a veteran of the passive resistance agitation, was sufficiently aggrieved by the proposed arrangements to throw his support to Samuel Bennett, the Common Wealth and Independent Labour challenger, against the National Government nominee in a 1943 by-election at Peterborough. The venerable Winfrey reasoned that Bennett, being a Nonconformist as well as an insurgent, could be better expected to resist the Butler Bill than his Anglican adversary, Viscount Suirdale. One of his local critics tellingly reproved him: 'The question is not whether people will be Anglicans or Nonconformists, but whether they will be Christians at all.'[16]

Conclusion

At the same time that Butler was cautiously drafting his education proposals, D. W. Brogan was pungently setting forth his 'impressions and observations' on *The English People*. Surveying the wartime scene, he could find ample justification for his assertion that

> in the generation that has passed since the great Liberal landslide of 1906, one of the greatest changes in the English religious and social landscape has been the decline of Nonconformity. Partly that decline has been due to the general weakening of the hold of Christianity on the English people, partly it has been due to the comparative irrelevance of the peculiarly Nonconformist (as apart from Christian) view of the contemporary world and its problems.[17]

The foregoing chapters have been directed to a chronicle of the process, fitful but continuous, which Brogan so clearly discerned; it is hoped that they also provide an analysis of the institutional and personal factors that made for change.

On the face of things, the reaction and ultimate disappearance of political Nonconformity is intimately linked to the drop in church memberships. In the period from 1910 to 1966, the Methodist population of Britain declined from 1,168,415 to just over 700,000; Baptists went from 400,000 to 280,000; and Congregationalists in England and Wales fell from 456,613 to approximately 200,000. The smaller bodies – the Unitarians, the Quakers, the Salvation Army, and the Presbyterian Church of England – experienced a comparable contraction and were estimated in 1966 to total a quarter of a million members. While the drop in the birth rate is an important factor, it has also been noted that 'the age structure . . . of all Free Churches is heavily weighted towards the over forties by comparison with the population at large'. This generational distinction, which incidentally holds true neither for the Anglican nor Roman Catholic communities, was already evident in 1933, when J. B. Priestley interrupted his *English Journey* to attend Sunday morning worship at a chapel in Birmingham: 'It did not belong to the particular denomination that had claimed me', but nevertheless the 'service was almost exactly like the ones I remember from thirty years ago', the most perceptible difference being that the congregation and choir were markedly middle-aged, with not so many as 'half-a-dozen men under thirty-five' to be seen.[18]

Bryan Wilson, who has undertaken a sociological investigation of *Religion in Secular Society*, has concluded that 'The churches are still used extensively for those rituals associated with the rites of passage – birth, marriage and death – but otherwise fail to influence moral conduct.'[19] His speculative theory is given substance by the experience of political Nonconformity. So, too, is Brogan's educated impression. Still a numerically significant segment of the overall population of England and Wales, Free Churchmen, instead of wielding a diminished corporate influence, have come to wield virtually none at all. Religious preference has been superseded by class alignment as the dominant factor in the determination of party allegiance. Political antagonisms have ceased, to any meaningful extent, to reflect religious cleavage. Parliamentary careers are more likely to be sacrificed than advanced by formal sectarian alliances. As piety no longer motivates public behaviour, politics is no longer regarded as a channel for the pursuit of religious objectives. As individuals, Nonconformists might well retain both a belief in inherited dogma and a commitment to political activism; yet it has grown increasingly unlikely that one will seriously influence, let alone determine, the other.

We have also seen evidence to support Wilson's hypothesis that, at least among Protestants, there has been ' far less disposition to claim that the opinions of the clergy are expression of the will of God towards men and their concerns '.[20] Gradually, a distinction has been drawn between pulpit and platform, and between the issues suitable for each to address. In late Victorian and Edwardian times, Nonconformists were elected to Parliament as the avowed auxiliaries of their denominational authorities, and often with their indispensable support. Before 1914, these M.P.s had already eclipsed the giants of the pulpit, whom they eventually repudiated in deed if not always in word. Nonconformist agencies like the National Council of Evangelical Free Churches, willing to admit no discrepancy between their members' spiritual and secular interests, were doomed to impotence and frustration. Eminent divines like J. D. Jones and John Scott Lidgett, to name only two among many, invited embarrassment and even ridicule by presupposing the survival of traditional loyalties. They, no less than the party chieftains with whom they fraternised, were hamstrung by a reliance on decaying institutions and outdated frames of reference. Their self-righteousness militated against a realistic assessment of their involvements and rendered them unduly vulnerable to shifts in the public mood. Yet, in their complex relations with secular leaders, it is not always clear who led whom astray. Sometimes as much by virtue of their longevity as their indisputable moral stature, they fostered the impression, to which they themselves fell victim, that political Nonconformity was an eternal constellation in the firmament of parliamentary democracy. It was more analogous, however, to Halley's Comet, another phenomenon of the Edwardian age.

The product of a unique set of social circumstances and cultural attitudes, the Free Church political movement served as the vehicle for a particular generation of personalities, lay and spiritual, whose ambitions far outlasted their capacity to accomplish them. Even so, certain vague tendencies survive as its legacy. A study of voting patterns at Newcastle-under-Lyme during the 1959 general election has pointed to a Labour orientation among Nonconformist electors, as opposed to a Conservative one among Roman Catholics and, more definitely, Anglicans. But, again, class differences appear to have been the overriding factor.[21] ' There is a tendency for Nonconformists and Roman Catholics to be less Conservative than Anglicans ', Jean Blondel has written in his masterly survey of *Voters, Parties, and Leaders,* ' but this tendency seems to be subjected to large variations from area to area. The least that can be said is that, over the country as a whole, Nonconformist and Roman Catholic Conservatives are far from being exceptional.'[22] Proceeding a step further, David Butler and Donald Stokes have found least frequent incidence of Conservative support among those Nonconformist respondents – middle no less than working-class – in the oldest of their age-cohorts, specifically those whose conscious experience stretches back to before the first world war, when political Nonconformity was at its peak and the differences between themselves and Anglicans were most enormous. ' As new generations entered the electorate the parties arrayed against the Conservatives drew their support less from religious beliefs than from class interests.'[28]

Traditions of electoral leadership die hard, even when they have lost any consequential basis in social fact: generals have often continued to lead crusades after their troops have silently stolen away, and, for that matter, even after they themselves have forgotten the particular reasons that induced them to take up arms. On the other hand, social facts do not necessarily give issue to political movements, at least not in the first instance. Noncon-

P

formity, by the time it came to qualify as a positive political force, had already begun to deteriorate as a social organism and, more arguably perhaps, as a theological matrix. With the further passage of time, the futility of the enterprise became all the more apparent, but the messianic zeal of its participants left them no option but to persevere.

The intervention of Nonconformity in modern political affairs – measured in terms of organised, explicit pressure-group activity – was a relatively brief episode that had run its course before most of those responsible were aware that it had even begun. Basically, it is a dispiriting story with a premature climax and a long denouement, with too many skulking villains and too few unalloyed heroes. The quality of innocence, which had nurtured the movement, eventually proved its undoing. A spectacular victory at the polls, achieved in alliance with potential rivals who thereupon robbed them of its fruits, deprived Free Churchmen of the sense of communal alienation that had initially galvanised them into action. Their distinctive world-view soon crumbled under the impact of twentieth-century social pressures and international crises, for neither of which had they any collective response. In large measure, the utter impracticability of their designs and their own contradictory impulses helped to create the very situations which they had most dreaded. Instead of precipitating political change, as they had intended, they were overtaken by it.

But surely it would be tautological as well as uncharitable to fault men of God for their credulity. However misguided, inappropriate, or chimerical, their activities gave evidence of an idealism for which national life was none the worse. Their beliefs do not deserve to be condemned by their ultimate failure, nor their aspirations by their frequently maladroit tactics. Their experience provides a case study in electoral displacement, an index to the realignments that have occurred within and between parties, and an implicit commentary on the role of nostalgia as a lingering influence on political preferences. Gradually, organised Nonconformity has become – to borrow Arthur Schlesinger's felicitous phrase – 'a party of memory'. Less than sacred, that memory is all the more worthy of consideration by those who attempt to explain the process by which men have attuned their loyalties to the fearful complexities of modern times.

Appendix

Nonconformist Candidates and MPs in General Elections, 1900–1935

The following figures are based upon lists in the *Christian World*, as corroborated and amended by reports in the national press (principally the *Daily News*) and the various denominational weeklies:

1900 GENERAL ELECTION

	Liberal		Labour & Lib-Lab		Conservative & Unionist		Other		Total	
	Candidates	MPs	Candidates	MPs	Candidates	MPs	Candidates	MPs	Candidates	MPs
CONGREGATIONALIST	32	21	2	1	1	1	1	1	36	24
BAPTIST	7	4	1	—	—	—	—	—	8	4
PRESBYTERIAN*	29	21	—	—	21	15	—	—	50	36
WESLEYAN METHODIST**	31	10	3	3	6	6	1	1	41	20
ALL OTHER METHODISTS	10	7	1	1	2	1	—	—	13	9
QUAKER	10	5	—	—	1	1	—	—	11	6
UNITARIAN	8	6	—	—	4	4	—	—	12	10
TOTAL	127	74	7	5	35	28	2	2	171	109

* Including Scottish and Irish Presbyterians
** Identified by the *Methodist Recorder* as 'more or less connected with Wesleyan Methodism'

1906 GENERAL ELECTION

	Liberal		Labour & Lib-Lab		Conservative & Unionist		Other		Total	
	Candidates	MPs	Candidates	MPs	Candidates	MPs	Candidates	MPs	Candidates	MPs
CONGREGATIONALIST	81	63	9	9	—	—	2	1	92	73
BAPTIST	20	16	1	1	—	—	—	—	21	17
PRESBYTERIAN	5	3	—	—	1	1	—	—	6	4
WESLEYAN METHODIST	32	27	5	5	4	2	1	1	42	35
PRIMITIVE METHODIST	5	4	3	3	—	—	—	—	8	7
WELSH CALVINISTIC METHODIST	8	7	1	1	—	—	—	—	9	8
INDEP. & UNITED METHODIST	9	6	1	1	—	—	—	—	10	7
QUAKER	8	8	—	—	—	—	—	—	8	8
UNITARIAN	14	14	—	—	4	3	—	—	18	17
DENOMINATION UNSPECIFIED	9	9	—	—	—	—	—	—	9	9
TOTAL	191	157	20	20	9	6	3	2	223	185

JANUARY 1910 GENERAL ELECTION

	Liberal		Labour		Conservative & Unionist		Total	
	Candidates	MPs	Candidates	MPs	Candidates	MPs	Candidates	MPs
CONGREGATIONALIST	74	46	9	7	—	—	83	53
BAPTIST	16	13	2	2	—	—	18	15
PRESBYTERIAN	4	1	—	—	—	—	4	1
WESLEYAN METHODIST	30	21	4	3	5	4	39	28
PRIMITIVE METHODIST	2	2	7	5	—	—	9	7
WELSH CALVINISTIC METHODIST	7	7	1	1	—	—	8	8
INDEP. & UNITED METHODIST	4	1	2	2	—	—	6	3
QUAKER	11	6	—	—	—	—	11	6
UNITARIAN	12	7	—	—	5	3	17	10
TOTAL	160	104	25	20	10	7	195	131

DECEMBER 1910 GENERAL ELECTION

	Liberal		Labour		Conservative & Unionist		Total	
	Candidates	MPs	Candidates	MPs	Candidates	MPs	Candidates	MPs
CONGREGATIONALIST	67	40	7	7	—	—	74	47
BAPTIST	16	12	4	3	—	—	20	15
PRESBYTARIAN	3	3	—	—	1	1	4	4
WESLEYAN METHODIST	31	22	4	4	3	2	38	28
PRIMITIVE METHODIST	3	2	5	5	—	—	8	7
WELSH CALVINISTIC METHODIST	10	9	1	1	—	—	11	10
INDEP. & UNITED METHODIST	4	3	2	2	1	1	7	6
QUAKER	11	9	—	—	—	—	11	9
UNITARIAN	10	7	—	—	3	3	13	10
TOTAL	155	107	23	22	8	7	186	136

1918 GENERAL ELECTION

	Liberal Coalition		Ind. Liberal		Coalition Labour		Labour		Conservative & Unionist		Other		Total	
	Candidates	MPs	Candidates	MPs	Candidates	MPs	Candidates	MPs	Candidates	MPs	Candidates	MPs	Candidates	MPs
CONGREGATIONALIST	18	18	15	1	1	1	12	6	—	—	1	—	47	26
BAPTIST	9	6	11	3	—	—	10	3	—	—	—	—	30	12
PRESBYTERIAN	5	5	2	1	—	—	1	—	—	—	—	—	8	6
WESLEYAN METHODIST	16	13	25	1	—	—	12	2	6	5	—	—	59	21
PRIMITIVE METHODIST	—	—	—	—	—	—	6	6	—	—	—	—	6	6
WELSH CALVINISTIC METHODIST	6	5	3	1	—	—	3	1	—	—	—	—	12	7
INDEP. & UNITED METHODIST	4	4	4	—	1	1	2	2	—	—	—	—	11	7
QUAKER	1	1	2	—	—	—	1	—	—	—	—	—	4	1
UNITARIAN	—	—	3	—	—	—	—	—	2	2	—	—	5	2
TOTAL	59	52	65	7	2	2	47	20	8	7	1	—	182	88

1922 GENERAL ELECTION

	Liberal-Asquitbian		Liberal-Lloyd Georgite		Labour		Conservative		Ind.		Total	
	Candidates	MPs	Candidates	MPs	Candidates	MPs	Candidates	MPs	Candidates	MPs	Candidates	MPs
CONGREGATIONALIST	27	5	12	6	14	6	1	1	2	1	56	19
BAPTIST	11	3	10	5	18	7	—	—	—	—	39	15
PRESBYTERIAN	3	1	1	1	—	—	1	1	—	—	5	3
WESLEYAN METHODIST	17	1	8	2	22	8	6	6	1	1	54	18
PRIMITIVE METHODIST	4	2	3	—	10	5	—	—	1	—	18	7
WELSH CALVINISTIC METHODIST	16	2	5	4	6	2	—	—	1	—	18	8
INDEP. & UNITED METHODIST	4	—	2	2	3	2	2	2	1	—	12	4
QUAKER	4	—	1	—	8	2	—	—	—	—	13	2
UNITARIAN	2	—	1	—	—	—	2	2	—	—	5	2
FRINGE SECTS	1	—	—	—	1	—	—	—	—	—	2	—
TOTAL	79	14	43	18	82	32	12	12	6	2	222	78

1923 GENERAL ELECTION

	Liberal		Labour		Conservative		Ind.		Total	
	Candidates	MPs	Candidates	MPs	Candidates	MPs	Candidates	MPs	Candidates	MPs
CONGREGATIONALIST	41	23	14	9	3	2	1	—	59	34
BAPTIST	17	6	11	8	—	—	—	—	28	14
PRESBYTERIAN	4	1	2	2	2	2	—	—	8	5
WESLEYAN METHODIST	26	15	16	12	7	3	1	1	50	31
PRIMITIVE METHODIST	10	4	8	6	—	—	—	—	18	10
WELSH CALVINISTIC METHODIST	7	6	4	1	—	—	—	—	11	7
INDEP. & UNITED METHODIST	6	2	2	2	—	—	—	—	8	4
QUAKER	4	2	6	3	—	—	—	—	10	4
UNITARIAN	7	4	3	3	2	2	—	—	12	9
FRINGE SECTS	1	1	1	—	—	—	1	—	3	1
TOTAL	123	64	67	45	14	9	3	1	207	119

1924 GENERAL ELECTION

	Liberal		Labour		Conservative		Ind.*		Total	
	Candidates	MPs	Candidates	MPs	Candidates	MPs	Candidates	MPs	Candidates	MPs
CONGREGATIONALIST	46	8	13	8	2	1	1	1	62	18
BAPTIST	9	3	9	7	—	—	—	—	18	10
PRESBYTERIAN	3	—	6	6	1	1	1	—	11	7
WESLEYAN METHODIST	30	2	20	8	6	6	1	1	57	17
PRIMITIVE METHODIST	9	2	6	4	—	—	—	—	15	6
WELSH CALVINISTIC METHODIST	9	6	8	2	—	—	—	—	17	8
INDEP. & UNITED METHODIST	4	—	3	3	—	—	1	1	8	4
QUAKER	4	—	13	4	—	—	—	—	17	4
UNITARIAN	5	—	6	3	3	3	—	—	14	6
FRINGE SECTS	1	—	2	—	—	—	—	—	3	—
TOTAL	120	21	86	45	12	11	4	3	222	80

* Including Constitutionalist

1929 GENERAL ELECTION

	Liberal		Labour		Conservative		Ind.		Total	
	Candidates	MPs	Candidates	MPs	Candidates	MPs	Candidates	MPs	Candidates	MPs
CONGREGATIONALIST	48	7	16	12	—	—	—	—	64	19
BAPTIST	12	3	7	7	—	—	1	—	20	10
PRESBYTERIAN	6	1	4	3	—	—	—	—	10	4
WESLEYAN METHODIST	46	12	17	15	8	1	2	1	73	29
PRIMITIVE METHODIST	16	1	11	9	—	—	—	—	27	10
WELSH CALVINISTIC METHODIST	9	7	3	2	—	—	—	—	12	9
INDEP. & UNITED METHODIST	7	—	3	3	1	—	1	1	12	4
QUAKER	6	—	18	8	2	2	—	—	26	10
UNITARIAN	5	1	5	3	3	2	2	1	15	7
FRINGE SECTS	1	—	2	1	—	—	—	—	3	1
TOTAL	156	32	86	63	14	5	6	3	262	103

1935 GENERAL ELECTION

	Liberal		Liberal National		Labour		Conservative		Ind.		Total	
	Candidates	MPs	Candidates	MPs	Candidates	MPs	Candidates	MPs	Candidates	MPs	Candidates	MPs
CONGREGATIONALIST	7	—	4	3	12	7	—	—	1	—	24	10
BAPTIST	2	1	2	2	3	3	1	1	—	—	8	7
PRESBYTERIAN	—	—	1	1	—	—	—	—	—	—	1	1
METHODIST*	15	2	11	8	30	12	7	5	—	—	63	27
WELSH CALVINISTIC METHODIST	9	6	2	2	4	—	—	—	—	—	15	8
QUAKER	6	—	—	—	15	3	1	1	1	—	23	4
UNITARIAN	1	—	1	—	4	3	3	3	1	1	10	7
FRINGE SECTS	—	—	—	—	1	1	—	—	1	—	2	1
TOTAL	40	9	21	16	69	29	12	10	4	1	146	65

* after union in 1932

Bibliography

As any scholar will readily appreciate, a bibliography represents no more than the tip of the iceberg: it is a catalogue of those relatively few sources which an author has come to regard as particularly significant after surveying and sifting through masses of available literature. Often, too, the author is forced to expend considerable time and effort in pursuit of the unavailable, namely unpublished materials that cannot be traced or, if located, cannot be consulted. The general reader, while he may not be oblivious to these archival adventures, cannot be expected to take an especially keen interest in them. The specialist, on the other hand, may find them as instructive as the work itself, and therefore may appreciate some further explanation not only of the manuscript collections that are cited below, but also of those which conspicuously fail to appear.

When one detours from the broad avenues of 'high politics', documents become notoriously more difficult to obtain and usually exist – if at all – in lesser quantity. Disappointingly, the quest for private papers has frequently led into blind alleys or along byways that diverged from the purpose of the present inquiry. As much for reasons of temperament as by accident, a number of the individuals who figure prominently in the foregoing text did not collect or retain their correspondence. Others apparently did, but their collections were reportedly destroyed after the publication of memoirs (the Revs J. Guinness Rogers and J. C. Carlile) or hagiographical volumes of biography (Dr John Clifford, R. Wilson Black, and, almost certainly, the Revs Hugh Price Hughes and F. B. Meyer).

In several instances, the potential subject took action to thwart any future historian: Dr Sidney M. Berry, it is reported on good authority, 'had a kind of horror of any biography being written and deliberately destroyed what materials could have been used'. The Rev J. H. Shakespeare, who had no such horror, was betrayed by an over-zealous housemaid who, finding his assorted papers stacked atop the dining-room table, chucked them into the fire. The archives of London's City Temple are known to have perished in the Blitz, and the personal papers of more than one individual are said to have suffered the same fate. Some, like the papers of the Revs Thomas Phillips and Charles Brown, disappeared as they passed from the custody of one generation to that of another. Others have survived in a sadly depleted state: the son of the Rev J. Ivory Cripps inherited some manuscripts of sermons and addresses; the daughter of the Rev J. H. Rushbrook has saved magazines to which her father contributed; the son of Sir Robert Perks has kept a selection of letters from better known correspondents; the sons of the Rev C. Ensor Walters and J. H. Whitley M.P. possess scrapbooks of cuttings. In a number of cases, individuals replied that they or members of their families had discarded materials in the course of moving house, usually to smaller quarters: the Rev Malcolm Thomson, who served as private secretary to Lloyd George, described how he had 'consigned . . . quite a wealth of documentation to the dustbin or incinerator'. Other collections have been lost through their owners' ignorance or apprehension: jostled by my request, the first she had received, one widow proclaimed her intention to burn her husband's 'confidential papers' sooner than expose them to the prying eyes of posterity.

Finally, one must presume that a number of potentially rich sources no longer exist. The bulk of the Rev S. E. Keeble's notebooks seem to have vanished in the decade since they were last consulted. Exhaustive searches have failed to uncover the personal papers of Sir Joseph Compton-Rickett M.P., the Rev Silvester Horne M.P., or the Rev Thomas Law. Most perplexing is the disappearance of Dr John Scott Lidgett's papers, which were known to exist as late as 1953, when he bequeathed them to a Methodist sister who had attended him in his later years of infirmity and whom he designated to write his official life. She subsequently married and died without fulfilling her commission; both her husband and the papers have proved impossible to trace.

I am grateful to numerous librarians and fellow-researchers who have assisted me in my efforts, acquainting me with sources and occasionally corroborating my negative findings: Mr George Awdry of the Gladstone Library, the National Library Club; Mr David Bebbington; Dr Clyde Binfield; the Rev John C. Bowmer, archivist of the Methodist Archives and Research Centre; Dr C. P. Cook and his enterprising staff at the Historical Records Project; the Rev Rupert E. Davies; Dr Roy Douglas; the Rev A. Ian Dunlop; the Rev Michael S. Edwards; the Rev John Huxtable, minister-secretary of the Congregational Church in England and Wales; the Rev G. A. D. Mann, general secretary of the Free Church Federal Council; Dr Ross McKibbin; Dr Kenneth O. Morgan; Dr Geoffrey F. Nuttall; Mr W. E. Pigott, editor of the *Methodist Recorder*; the Rev G. W. Rusling, head of the department of ministry, the Baptist Union; Professor Allan Silver; Mr A. J. P. Taylor and the staff at the Beaverbrook Library; and Professor Hugh Tinker. Not least, I wish to thank the Rev Dr Ernest A. Payne, C.H., for his learned counsel and for the admirable example of his own scholarship.

The descendants of various ministerial and lay leaders replied to my inquiries, often at length, with helpful information and personal recollections. They include Mr A. J. Cripps, Mrs Ruth Gordon, Sir Geoffrey Haworth, Mr Thomas Magnay, Mrs Phyllis Newman, Mrs S. T. M. Newman, Mr Clarence E. Norwood, Mr Geoffrey S. Rowland, Dr John Rowland, the Rev Professor Peter Saunders, Mr Gerald Spicer, and Mr O. J. Whitley. Sir Richard Acland responded with a detailed account of his father's collaboration with Lloyd George – and his own – during the 1935 Council of Action campaign.

Other individuals, who apologised that they could offer no papers to examine, granted interviews of inestimably greater value than they were perhaps able to perceive. Among them were Dame Margery Corbett Ashby, Sir Cyril Black, Sir Dingle Foot, Sir Arnold Lunn, Dr A. L. Rowse, Sir Geoffrey Shakespeare, the Rev the Lord Soper, and the Rev Malcolm Thomson. Mr David Newton kindly allowed me to read extracts from his draft manuscript on Sir Richard Winfrey, and, with Miss Barbara Clapham, arranged for me to consult unpublished materials in the archives of the Sir Halley Stewart Trust. Canon David L. Edwards of Westminster Abbey offered an afternoon of lively conversation that afforded many new perspectives.

Lastly, it is my pleasant duty to record my debt of gratitude to those who permitted me access to documents in their keeping, as well as generous hospitality during the course of my research: Mr Michael Foot M.P. and Mrs Foot, who resourcefully helped me to unearth further materials in storage at Callington in Cornwall; Mrs I. V. Horton; Major and Mrs Grange Kirkcaldy; Sir Malcolm Perks; Mr Lancelot Spicer; and the Baroness White.

MANUSCRIPT SOURCES

H. H. Asquith (Earl of Oxford and Asquith) Papers, Bodleian Library, Oxford.

A. J. Balfour (Earl of Balfour) Papers, British Museum.

Viscount Bryce Papers, Bodleian Library, Oxford.

Sir Henry Campbell-Bannerman Papers, British Museum.

Cromwell Association, records and cuttings, courtesy of Miss Hilary Platt, honorary secretary.

Isaac Foot Papers, courtesy of Mr Michael Foot M.P. and Lord Foot.

D. R. Daniel Papers, National Library of Wales.

Federal Council of Free Churches, minutes and records (1917–1940), Free Church Federal Council archives, London.

H. A. L. Fisher Papers, Bodleian Library, Oxford.

General Body of Protestant Dissenting Ministers of the Three Denominations, minutes, Dr Williams's Library, London (by permission of the Rev H. A. Jacquet).

Viscount Gladstone Papers, British Museum.

W. E. Gladstone Papers, British Museum.

Arthur Henderson Papers, Labour Party archives, Transport House, London.

R. B. Haldane (Viscount Haldane) Papers, National Library of Scotland.

Rev Robert Forman Horton Papers, courtesy of Mrs I. V. Horton.

Rev Hugh Price Hughes material, Methodist Archives and Research Centre, London.

Rev H. M. Hughes Papers, National Library of Wales.

Hayden Jones Papers, National Library of Wales.

Rev J. D. Jones Papers, National Library of Wales.

Thomas Jones Papers, copies courtesy of the Baroness White.

Labour Party archives, Transport House, London.

Sir Herbert Lewis Papers, National Library of Wales (by permission of Mrs K. Idwal Jones).

Liberation Society, minutes and records, Greater London Record Office, County Hall, London.

David Lloyd George (Earl Lloyd-George of Dwyfor) Papers, National Library of Wales and the Beaverbrook Library, London.

Marquess of Lothian (Philip Kerr) Papers, Scottish Record Office, Edinburgh.

Sir Donald Maclean Papers, Bodleian Library, Oxford.

National Council of Evangelical Free Churches, minutes and records (1896–1940), Free Church Federal Council archives, London.

National Education Association, records, Greater London Record Office, County Hall, London.

Sir William Robertson Nicoll Papers, courtesy of Mrs Midred Kirkcaldy.

Sir Robert Perks Papers, courtesy of Sir Malcolm Perks.

Eleanor Rathbone Papers, the Library, the University of Liverpool.

John Bryn Roberts Papers, National Library of Wales.

Earl of Rosebery Papers, National Library of Scotland.

Walter Runciman (1st Viscount Runciman of Doxford) Papers, the University Library, Newcastle upon Tyne.

Sir Albert Spicer Papers, courtesy of Mr Lancelot Spicer.

Sir Halley Stewart material, Sir Halley Stewart Trust, London.

J. St Loe Strachey Papers, Beaverbrook Library, London.

Rev C. Ensor Walters Papers, Methodist Archives and Research Centre, London (by permission of Mr Peter Ensor Walters).

Sir Angus Watson Papers, courtesy of Mrs Jan Burt and Mr Graham Watson.

H. J. Wilson Papers, City Library, Sheffield.
Sir Richard Winfrey material, courtesy of Mr David Newton.

SERIAL PUBLICATIONS

A virtually untapped source for the social and political history of the period, the religious press has been consulted not only for information, but also as an index to opinion. Especially close scrutiny was given to the following:

Baptist Times
British Weekly
Christian World
Church Times
City Temple Tidings
Crusader
Examiner (later the *British Congregationalist*)
Free Church Chronicle
London (Whitefield's) Signal
Methodist Recorder
Methodist Times
Methodist Weekly
Nonconformist
Primitive Methodist (later the *Primitive Methodist Leader*)
Review of the Churches

A wide range of other newspapers and periodicals yielded further material, the most important being:

Contemporary Review
Daily Chronicle
Daily News
Goodwill
Manchester Guardian
Nation
New Statesman
News Chronicle
Nineteenth Century and After
Peacemaker
Speaker
The Times
Westminster Gazette

Reference was also made to a number of provincial newspapers, which are identified in the appropriate citations, to the annual editions of the *Free Church Year Book*, and to the yearbooks of the respective denominations.

BOOKS AND ARTICLES
There is a good deal to be gleaned from memoirs and biographies which exist in staggering quantity and usually depressing quality. The reader is directed to footnote references for specific citations. The following is a select list of secondary works that afford general background and often new interpretations:

Butler, David and Donald Stokes, *Political Change in Britain* (New York, 1971).

Chadwick, Owen, *The Victorian Church*, II (Oxford, 1970).

Clarke, P. F., 'Electoral Sociology of Modern Britain', *History*, lvii (1972), 31–55.

——, *Lancashire and the New Liberalism* (Cambridge, 1971).

Currie, Robert, *Methodism Divided* (London, 1968).

Edwards, Maldwyn, *Methodism and England, 1850–1932* (London 1943).

Glaser, J. F., 'English Nonconformity and the Decline of Liberalism', *American Historical Review*, lxiii (1957–58), 352–63.

Grant, J. W., *Free Churchmanship in England, 1870–1940* (London, 1959).

Halévy, Elie, *Imperialism and the Rise of Labour, 1895–1905* (New York, 1961).

——, *The Rule of Democracy, 1905–1914* (New York, 1961).

Harrison, Paul M., *Authority and Power in the Free Church Tradition* (Princeton, 1959).

Herrick, F. H., 'The Origins of the National Liberal Federation', *Journal of Modern History*, xvii (1945), 116–29.

Holt, R. V., *The Unitarian Contribution to Social Progress in England* (London, 1938).

Inglis, K. S., *Churches and the Working Classes in Victorian England* (London, 1963).

——, 'English Nonconformity and Social Reform, 1880–1900', *Past and Present*, xiii (1958), 73–88.

Jones, R. T., *Congregationalism in England, 1662–1962* (London, 1962).

Jordan, E. K. H., *Free Church Unity: a History of the Free Church Council Movement, 1896–1941* (London, 1956).

Kent, John, 'Hugh Price Hughes and the Nonconformist Conscience', in G. V. Bennett and J. D. Walsh, eds., *Essays in Modern English Church History in Memory of Norman Sykes* (London, 1966).

Koss, Stephen, 'Wesleyanism and Empire', *Historical Journal*, xviii (1975).

Manning, Bernard Lord, *The Protestant Dissenting Deputies* (Cambridge, 1952).

Martin, David, *A Sociology of English Religion* (London, 1967).

Morgan, Kenneth O., 'Cardiganshire Politics: The Liberal Ascendancy, 1885–1923', *Ceredigion*, v (1968), 311–46.

——, 'The New Liberalism and the Challenge of Labour: The Welsh Experience, 1885–1929', in Kenneth D. Brown, ed., *Essays in Anti-Labour History* (London, 1974).

——, *Wales in British Politics, 1868–1922* (Cardiff, 1963).

Payne, Ernest A., *The Baptist Union: a Short History* (London, 1959).

——, *The Free Church Tradition in the Life of England* (London, 1944).

Pelling, Henry, *Social Geography of British Elections, 1885–1910* (London, 1967).

Read, Donald, *The English Provinces, c. 1760–1960: a study in influence* (London, 1964).

Russell, A. K., *Liberal Landslide: the General Election of 1906* (Hamden, Conn., 1973).

Shannon, R. T., *Gladstone and the Bulgarian Agitation, 1876* (London, 1963).

Sykes, John, *The Quakers* (London, 1958).

Thompson, Paul, *Socialists, Liberals and Labour: the Struggle for London, 1885–1914* (London, 1967).

Tillyard, Frank, 'The Distribution of the Free Churches in England', *Sociological Review* (Jan. 1935).

Vincent, John, *The Formation of the Liberal Party 1857–1868* (London, 1966).

Underwood, A. C., *History of the English Baptists* (London, 1947).

Wearmouth, R. F., *Methodism and the Struggle of the Working Classes, 1850–1900* (London, 1954).

——, *Social and Political Influence of Methodism in the Twentieth Century* (London, 1957).

Williams, C. R., 'The Welsh Religious Revival, 1904–5', *British Journal of Sociology*, iii (1952), 242–59.

Wilson, Bryan, *Religion in Secular Society* (London, 1966).

Wilson, Trevor, *The Downfall of the Liberal Party, 1914–1945* (London, 1966).

References

Introduction (pages 7–13).

1 *Parliamentary Debates* (*Commons*), 5th ser., DXXXIX, cols 629 ff. The Rev Ian Paisley, a Protestant Unionist MP and a minister in the Free Presbyterian Church of Ulster, raised a characteristic voice of protest.
2 *The Times*, 2 July 1974.
3 J. H. Hexter, 'Storm Over the Gentry' in *Reappraisals in History* (New York, Harper Torchbook ed., 1963), p. 148.
4 It was as such that Sir Albert Spicer, the Congregationalist leader and Liberal MP (1903–18), made his contribution, posing obvious problems for his biographer [Lancelot Spicer], *Albert Spicer 1847–1934, A Man of His Time* (London, 1938), p. 11.

1 The Victorian Prelude (pages 15–37).

1 Birrell, *Things Past Redress* (London, 1937) p. 38.
2 Quoted in J. B. Conacher, *The Aberdeen Coalition* (Cambridge, 1968), p. 494.
3 *The Free Church Year Book* for 1900 (London, 1900) contains a wealth of statistical data, much of it corrected from the previous year's survey, but still admittedly incomplete or otherwise unreliable. (*E.g.,* 'church accommodation' was tabulated at 7,993,708, but 'a large proportion of these places are unavailable'.) The number of communicants for each of the larger denominations was given as follows:

Baptists	333,634
Congregationalists	419,049
Presbyterians	73,249
Wesleyans	548,924
Primitive Methodists	184,523
Calvinistic Methodists	156,259
United Methodist Free Churches	79,951

Seven thousand communicants were added to the Baptist total to compensate for the failure of forty-six churches to submit returns; the Congregationalist total was increased by eight per cent for the same reason. There is a useful discussion of previous Nonconformist censuses in Owen Chadwick, *The Victorian Church*, II (New York, 1970), ch. V.

4 Arnold Lunn, *Come What May* (London, 1940), p. 117. Lunn, who began as a missionary, was a Wesleyan ecumenicist and a propagandist for internationalism, which his travel agency did much to foster.

5 Brian Harrison, *Drink and the Victorians* (London, 1971), p. 291.

6 Dorothea Price Hughes, *The Life of Hugh Price Hughes* (London, 1904), p. 119.

7 Entry for 22 Sept. 1882, *The Diary of Sir Edward Walter Hamilton* (ed. Dudley W. R. Bahlman; Oxford, 1972), I, 343.

8 Morley to A. J. Balfour, 10 Oct. 1915, Balfour Papers (British Museum).

9 G. Kitson Clark, *The Making of Victorian England* (London, 1962), p. 203.

10 *Greenock Telegraph* (n.d.), quoted in Mrs D. Gunnell, 'Sir Halley Stewart, 1838–1937', II, 476 (unpublished draft courtesy of the Sir Halley Stewart Trust, London).

11 Forster to Tait, 14 July 1874, quoted in P. T. Marsh, *The Victorian Church in Decline* (London, 1969), p. 111; G. F. A. Best, 'Popular Protestantism in Victorian Britain,' in R. Robson, ed., *Ideas and Institutions of Victorian Britain* (London, 1967), p. 138.

12 *History of Free Thought in the Nineteenth Century* (London, 1929), p. 391.

13 Smith to Tait, 15 June 1874, quoted in Marsh, p. 58.

14 J. W. Grant, *Free Churchmanship in England 1870–1940* (London, 1955), pp. 69–70.

15 John Sykes, *The Quakers* (London, 1958), p. 57.

16 Memorandum of a dinner at the Devonshire Club, 2 Nov. 1910, Nicoll Papers (courtesy of Mrs Mildred Kirkcaldy); Sir James Marchant, *Dr John Clifford, C.H.: Life, Letters and Reminiscences* (London, 1924), p. xii.

17 Bernard Lord Manning, *The Protestant Dissenting Deputies* (London, 1952), pp. 417 ff.

18 Michael Hurst, 'Liberal versus Liberal, 1874', in the *Historical Journal*, xv (1972), 680.

19 Lloyd George to his wife, 1 Jan. 1894, in *Lloyd George: Family Letters, 1885–1936* (ed. K. O. Morgan; Oxford and Cardiff, 1973), p. 66.

20 H. C. Colman, *Jeremiah James Colman, A Memoir* (London, 1905), p. 325.

21 E. K. H. Jordan, *Free Church Unity, A History of the Free Church Council Movement, 1896–1941* (London, 1956), pp. 36–38; A. W. W.

Dale, *The Life of R. W. Dale of Birmingham* (London, 1899), pp. 647 ff; A. G. Gardiner, *Life of George Cadbury* (London, 1923), pp. 174–76.

22 H. S. Lunn, *Chapters from My Life* (London, 1918), pp. 52–53.

23 Letter from Rome, Oct. 1894, quoted in D. P. Hughes, p. 473n.

24 Constitution of the National Council of Evangelical Free Churches; also President's Report for 1931–32, Free Church Council archives, London.

25 Dr Robert Forman Horton to Rosebery, 16 Dec. 1897, Rosebery Papers, Box 75 (National Library of Scotland, Edinburgh); Rosebery to Horton, 26 Dec. 1897, Horton Papers (courtesy of Mrs I. V. Horton).

26 Perks to Rosebery, 1 Feb. 1898, Rosebery Papers, Vol. 10,050, fol. 19.

27 Rosebery to A. G. Hunter, canon of Christ Church, Epsom, 25 Feb. 1901 (copy), Rosebery Papers, Box 76; Lloyd George, speech at the City Temple, 21 June 1906, quoted in the *Daily News*, 22 June 1906.

28 Perks to Rosebery, 8 Oct. 1896, Rosebery Papers, Vol. 10,050, fol. 6.

29 Perks to Rosebery, 5 Nov. 1896, Rosebery Papers, Vol. 10,050, fols. 8–9.

30 D. P. Hughes, pp. 112, 556–57, and 562.

31 Robert Currie, *Methodism Divided* (London, 1968), p. 179.

32 *Methodist Times*, 3 Feb. 1898; also C. S. Horne, *Popular History of the Free Churches* (London, 1927?), p. 425.

33 *Methodist Times*, 20 Jan. 1898.

34 Letter to the editor of the *Manchester Guardian*, 25 Oct. 1901; letter to the editor of the *Methodist Weekly*, 5 Dec. 1901.

35 Entry for 3 Oct. 1899, quoted in Hirst, *In the Golden Days* (London, 1947), p. 191; Hocking, *My Book of Memory* (London, 1923), p. 180.

36 *The Times*, 12 and 17 Oct. 1900. For a more complete discussion of Wesleyan Imperialism and its electoral consequences, see S. Koss, 'Wesleyanism and Empire', in the *Historical Journal*, xviii (1975).

37 Perks to Rosebery, 2 Dec. 1899, Rosebery Papers, Vol. 10,050, fols. 42–45; also 'Lord Rosebery's Interest in Nonconformity', in the *Christian World*, 30 May 1929.

38 Perks to Rosebery, 20 May 1899, Rosebery Papers, Vol. 10,050, fols. 33–36.

39 Campbell to Perks, 10 July 1902, Perks Papers (courtesy of Sir Malcolm Perks); on the 16th, Perks informed Rosebery of Campbell's acceptance. Rosebery Papers, Vol. 10,050, fol. 278.

40 Lloyd George made his provocative assertion in a pair of leading articles in the *Daily News*, published without a by-line, but privately

acknowledged as his handiwork. Lloyd George to his wife, 18 and
23 Aug. 1898, in *Lloyd George: Family Letters, 1885–1936*, pp.
114–15.

41   Compton-Rickett to Campbell-Bannerman, 3 March 1902, Camp-
bell-Bannerman Papers, British Museum Add. MSS. 41,237, fols. 18–21;
Compton-Rickett to Rosebery, 11 March 1902 (copy) and Rosebery
to Compton-Rickett, 14 March 1902 (copy), Viscount Gladstone
Papers, British Museum Add. MSS. 46,059, fols. 149–51; W. B. Selbie,
The Life of Charles Silvester Horne (London, 1920), pp. 127–29;
J. D. Jones, *Three Score Years and Ten* (London, 1940), p. 226.
Mackennal had declared his position in a letter read to a meeting of
antiwar Congregationalists at Manchester on 17 Oct. 1901. *Manchester
Guardian*, 18 Oct. 1901.

42   Maclaren to Nicoll, 31 Jan. 1902, Nicoll Papers.

2 Revival and Revivalism (pages 38–54).

1   Nicoll to Perks, 14 Oct. 1902, enclosed in Perks to Rosebery, 14
Oct. 1902, Rosebery Papers, Box 40.

2   *England 1870–1914* (Oxford, 1941), p. 355.

3   Quoted in Michael Foot, *Aneurin Bevan*, II (New York, 1974),
127.

4   Minutes of the annual meeting of the General Body of the Three
Denominations, Memorial Hall, London, 28 Mar. 1901 and 30 Mar.
1905 (Dr Williams's Library, London); minutes of the Organising Committee, 7 Oct. 1904, Free Church Council archives; Morley to Perks,
27 Mar. 1905, Perks Papers.

5   Quoted in Arthur Walters, *Hugh Price Hughes, Pioneer and Reformer* (London, 1907?), p. 92.

6   Minutes of the General Council, 5 Feb. and 11 June 1900, 7 Oct.
1901, Free Church Council archives; *Daily News*, 3 Oct. 1900; *The
Times*, 28 Jan. and 2 Feb. 1901.

7   Minutes of the General Council, 28 Mar. 1905, Free Church Council archives; also Jordan, *Free Church Unity*, pp. 104–5.

8   *Daily Chronicle*, 13 Dec. 1904; C. R. Williams, 'The Welsh Religious Revival, 1904–5', in the *British Journal of Sociology*, iii (1952),
242–59; K. O. Morgan, *Wales in British Politics, 1868–1922* (Cardiff,
1963), pp. 217–18.

9   *Examiner*, 5 Jan. 1905; Shakespeare, letter to the editor of the
Christian World, 9 Feb. 1905; *Free Church Year Book, 1906*, pp.
168 ff.

10   *Examiner*, 16 Feb. 1905; W. T. Stead, *The Revival of 1905* (London, 1905), p. 77; *British Weekly*, 30 Nov. 1905.

11   *Christian World*, 5 Jan. 1905.

12   E. A. Payne, *The Baptists of Berkshire* (London, 1951), p. 124.

13 Presidential address, ninth annual meeting of the National Council, 1904, quoted in Stead, p. 12.

14 Lewis, 'The Revival in Wales', *British Weekly* (supplement), 7 Dec. 1905.

15 Perks to Rosebery, 3 and 20 May, 24 July 1902, Rosebery Papers, Vol. 10,050, fols. 249, 256–57, and 282.

16 Campbell-Bannerman to Herbert Gladstone, [4 May 1902] Viscount Gladstone Papers, Add. MSS. 45,988, fol. 14.

17 Lloyd George to his wife, [4] and 5 May 1902, Lloyd George Papers (National Library of Wales, Aberystwyth), 20425c. Lloyd George did not prepare in vain; his was perhaps the most bitter attack on the 'clerical yoke'. *Parliamentary Debates* (Commons), 4th ser., cvii, cols. 1098 ff.

18 Lloyd George to Nicoll, 19 July 1902, Nicoll Papers.

19 Denny to Nicoll, 29 July 1902, *Letters of Principal James Denny to W. Robertson Nicoll, 1893–1917* (London, 1920?), p. 27.

20 Foot to his fiancée, July 1903, Foot Papers; diary entry for 10 May 1903; D. R. Daniel Papers (National Library of Wales, Aberystwyth); memorandum of a conversation with Lloyd George, 12 Oct. 1911 (typescript), Nicoll Papers.

21 Maldwyn Edwards, *Methodism and England, 1850–1932* (London, 1943), p. 124.

22 Perks to Campbell-Bannerman, 1 Jan. 1903, Campbell-Bannerman Papers, Add. MSS. 41,237, fols. 70–71.

23 Lloyd George to Nicoll, 4 Nov. 1902, Nicoll Papers.

24 Letter postmarked 8 Oct. 1902, Foot Papers.

25 Quoted in the *Crusader*, 15 May 1903.

3 *Nonconformity Redivivus (pages 55–75).*

1 Sir William Harcourt to Campbell-Bannerman, 18 Oct. 1900, Campbell-Bannerman Papers, Add. MSS. 41,219, fols. 144–45.

2 Perks to Rosebery, 30 July 1902, Rosebery Papers, Vol. 10,050, fol. 286; W. B. Selbie, *The Life of Charles Silvester Horne* (London, 1920), pp. 130–31. Henry Pelling, who has dismissed the suggestion that the Bury result owed anything to Free Church grievances, has conceded that the North Leeds by-election was a 'Nonconformist explosion'. *Social Geography of British Elections, 1885–1910* (London, 1967), pp. 255, 293.

3 *The Times*, 23 Aug. 1902.

4 Quoted in Julian Amery, *Life of Joseph Chamberlain*, IV (London, 1951), 495.

5 Perks to Rosebery, 24 Dec. 1902, Rosebery Papers, Vol. 10,051, fol. 46; minutes of a joint meeting of the legal and organising committees, 15 Dec. 1902, Free Church Council archives.

6 Campbell-Bannerman to Bryce, 23 Sept. 1902, Bryce Papers (Bodleian Library, Oxford).

7 Balfour to Devonshire, 4 June 1903, quoted in Bernard Holland, *The Life of Spencer Compton, 8th Duke of Devonshire* (London, 1911), II, 308.

8 Bryce to Clifford, 2 Oct. 1902, quoted in Marchant, *Clifford*, pp. 123–24.

9 Minutes of the education committee, 7 Apr. 1903, Free Church Council archives; *Primitive Methodist*, 13 Aug. 1903.

10 Minutes of the annual meeting of the general body, Protestant Dissenting Deputies, 28 Mar. 1904, Dr Williams's Library.

11 Amery to Milner, 26 Feb. 1904, quoted in A. M. Gollin, *Proconsul in Politics* (New York, 1964), p. 65.

12 Porritt, *The Best I Remember* (London, 1922), pp. 51–52.

13 Diary entry for 17 June 1903, Viscount Gladstone Papers, Add. MSS. 46,484, fol. 44.

14 Ibid., 16 July 1903, fol. 49.

15 Maclean to his fiancée, [July] 1905, Maclean Papers (Bodleian Library).

16 Cf. Jordan, *Free Church Unity*, p. 104.

17 Perks to Rosebery, 23 Sept. 1903, Rosebery Papers, Vol. 10,051, fols. 134–35.

18 Diary entry for 29 Sept. 1903, Viscount Gladstone Papers, Add. MSS. 46,484, fol. 53.

19 *Parliamentary Reminiscences and Reflections* (London, 1922), p. 317.

20 Campbell-Bannerman to Vaughan Nash, 26 Sept. 1903 (copy), Campbell-Bannerman Papers, Add. MSS. 41,237, fols. 168–70.

21 Perks to Rosebery, 21 Dec. 1903, 1 Apr. and 8 July 1904, Rosebery Papers, Vol. 10,051, fols. 171–72, 205–8.

22 Lloyd George to his wife, 23 Dec. 1903, Lloyd George Papers, NLW 20426c; Perks to Rosebery, 23 Dec. 1903, Rosebery Papers, Vol. 10,051, fol. 173; Perks to Asquith, 23 Dec. 1903, Asquith Papers (Bodleian Library), X, fol. 118.

23 Gladstone to Asquith, 24 Dec. 1903, Asquith Papers, X, fol. 120; Asquith to Gladstone, 27 Dec. 1903, Viscount Gladstone Papers, Add. MSS. 45,989, fol. 98; Bryce to Campbell-Bannerman, 16 Jan. 1904, Campbell-Bannerman Papers, Add. MSS. 41,211, fols. 269–70; diary entry for 13 Jan. 1904, Viscount Gladstone Papers, Add. MSS. 46,484, fol. 61; Gladstone to Campbell-Bannerman, 18 Jan. 1904, Campbell-Bannerman Papers, Add. MSS. 41,217, fol. 82; Clifford to Bryce, 2 Feb. 1904, Bryce Papers.

24 The 'author' is identified only as 'the Special Commissioner of the National Council', which was one of Law's titles.

25   Diary entry for 14 Mar. 1904, Viscount Gladstone Papers, Add. MSS. 46,485, fol. 3; also Jesse Herbert to Gladstone, 29 Oct. 1903, Viscount Gladstone Papers, Add. MSS. 46,026, fols. 11–12; Selbie, *Horne,* pp. 185–86.

26   *Crusader,* 23 June and 7 July 1904.

27   Herbert to Gladstone, 2 Feb. 1905, Viscount Gladstone Papers, Add. MSS. 46,026, fol. 103; *Christian World,* 2 Feb., 13 Apr., 1, 8, and 15 June, 13 and 20 July 1905; minutes of the general committee, 5 June 1905, Free Church Council archives.

28   Lloyd George to Nicoll, 15 Sept. 1904, Nicoll Papers; minutes of the finance and education sub-committee, 4 Feb. 1904, and minutes of the election campaign committee, 23 Sept. 1904, 20 Jan. 1905, and 8 June 1906, Free Church Council archives.

29   Diary entry for 16 Feb. 1905, Viscount Gladstone Papers, Add. MSS. 46,485, fol. 23; Lionel Holland to Lloyd George, 19 Feb. 1905, Lloyd George Papers, NLW 20462c.

30   Bryce to Gladstone, 27 Dec. 1904, Viscount Gladstone Papers, Add. MSS. 46,019, fol. 95.

31   Ll[ewellyn] Hugh-Jones to John Bryn Roberts, MP, 19 Oct. 1904, Bryn Roberts Papers (National Library of Wales), 355.

32   Diary notes, 3 Apr, 1904 (copy), Herbert Lewis Papers (National Library of Wales). Lewis, then MP for Flint District, was himself a Calvinistic Methodist.

33   Perks to Rosebery, 1 Apr. 1904, Rosebery Papers, Vol. 10,051, fols. 207–8.

34   Lloyd George to Lewis, 13 Dec. 1904 ('private and confidential'), Herbert Lewis Papers.

35   Porritt, *The Best I Remember,* pp. 96–97; *Christian World,* 2 and 9 Mar. 1905.

36   Minutes of the parliamentary and electoral committee, 5 July 1904, Liberation Society Records, G. L. C. Record Office A/LIB/14.

37   Perks to Rosebery, 22 Sept. 1905, Rosebery Papers, Vol. 10,052, fol. 83.

38   Sir Alexander Acland Hood to J. S. Sandars, 23 Sept. [1905], Balfour Papers, Add. MSS. 49, 771.

39   Minutes of the general council, 24 Sept. 1905, Free Church Council archives; minutes of the executive committee, 17 Apr. 1905, Liberation Society Records A/LIB/9.

40   *Daily News,* 12 Oct. 1905; Arthur Porritt, *John Henry Jowett* (London, 1924), p. 116; *Examiner,* 19 Oct. 1905; *London (Whitefields) Signal,* Nov. 1905; *Crusader,* 23 Nov. 1905.

41   *Crusader,* 26 Oct. 1905; *Daily News,* 16 Oct. 1905.

42   Gladstone to Campbell-Bannerman, 25 Nov. 1905 ('secret'), Campbell-Bannerman Papers, Add. MSS. 41,217, fols. 279–80; Gladstone

to Hudson, 27 Nov. 1905, Viscount Gladstone Papers, Add. MSS 46,021, fol. 89.

43 Perks to Rosebery, 4 Dec. 1905, Rosebery Papers, Vol. 10,052, fol. 110.

44 Minutes of the executive committee, 18 Dec. 1905, Liberation Society Records A/LIB/9.

45 Perks to Campbell-Bannerman, 11 Dec. 1905, Campbell-Bannerman Papers, Add. MSS. 41,238, fol. 170; *British Weekly*, 4 Jan. 1906.

46 Grey to Perks, 18 Dec. 1905, Perks Papers.

47 Carlile, *My Life's Little Day*, pp. 114-15; also Carlile, 'A Confusion of Issues', *Baptist Times*, 4 July 1935.

48 A. K. Russell, 'The General Election of 1906', Oxford D. Phil. thesis, 1962, p. 387.

49 'Patriotism and Christianity', *Contemporary Review*, lxxxvii (1905), 193-94.

50 *Free Church Year Book, 1906*, pp. 187, 196; Jones, *Three Score Years and Ten* (London, 1940), pp. 227–30; Selbie, *Horne*, pp. 194–95; *Examiner*, 25 Jan. 1906; *Parliamentary Debates* (Commons), 4th ser., cliii, col. 1023 (12 Mar. 1906).

51 *Parliamentary Debates (Commons)*, 4th ser., clvi, col. 1215 (8 May 1906); Perks to Rosebery, 25 Jan. 1906, Rosebery Papers, Vol. 10,052, fol. 126; *British Weekly*, 25 Jan. 1906; Sir Richard Winfrey, *Leaves from My Life* (King's Lynn, 1936), p. 151; Philip, Viscount Snowden, *An Autobiography* (London, 1934), I, 309–10.

52 Dilke to Chamberlain, 30 Nov. 1885, quoted in A. B. Cooke and John Vincent, *The Governing Passion* (Brighton, 1974), p. 13.

53 Minutes of the education committee, 7 Apr. 1903, Free Church Council archives.

54 Quoted in the *National Review*, Feb. 1906.

55 *Daily News*, 25 Nov. 1905; London (*Whitefield's*) *Signal*, Jan. 1906; Horne to his wife, 14 Jan. 1906, quoted in Selbie, pp. 196–97.

56 Paul Thompson, *Socialists, Liberals and Labour: the Struggle for London, 1885–1914* (London, 1967), p. 168.

57 London (*Whitefield's*) *Signal*, Nov. 1905; *British Weekly*, 25 Jan. 1906.

58 Porritt, *The Best I Remember*, p. 52.

59 Gladstone put each English and Welsh constituency into one of six categories: 'certain win', 'probable win', 'possible win', 'off chance', 'probable loss', or 'certain loss'. The present calculations are based on his list of 21 Nov. 1903 (Viscount Gladstone Papers, Add. MSS. 46,106, fols. 43–62), which tends to be more complete than subsequent lists and gives a better picture of the situation that prevailed at the time that most candidates were adopted.

60 Quoted in *The Times*, 17 June 1931.

4 Pilgrims' Progress (pages 76–99).

1   Quoted in S. D. Waley, *Edwin Montagu* (Bombay, 1964), p. 30.
2   Perks, *Sir Robert William Perks, Baronet* (London, 1936), pp. 120–23.
3   Perks to Rosebery, 18 Feb. and 23 Mar. 1906, Rosebery Papers, Vol. 10,050, fols. 128, 136.
4   Minutes of the general committee, 5 Feb. 1906, Free Church Council archives; minutes of the executive committee, 5 Feb. 1906, Liberation Society records A/LIB/9; Perks to Rosebery, 7 Mar. 1906, Rosebery Papers, Vol. 10,052, fol. 134.
5   Arthur Porritt, *John Henry Jowett* (London, 1924), pp. 116-17; J. Scott Lidgett, *My Guided Life* (London, 1936), pp. 191–93.
6   Lewis to Lloyd George, 9 Apr. 1906, Lewis Papers.
7   Hirst Hollowell to Birrell, 22 Apr. 1906, quoted in W. Evans and W. Claridge Jones, *J. Hirst Hollowell and the Movement for Civic Control in Education* (Manchester, 1911), pp. 121-22.
8   Minutes of special meeting, 30 Apr. 1906, Dr Williams's Library.
9   Denny to Nicoll, 6 June 1906, quoted in *Letters of Principal James Denny*, pp. 66-67.
10 'Education address' (undated, probably post-1918), J. D. Jones Papers (National Library of Wales).
11 *British Congregationalist*, 30 Aug. 1906; minutes of the committee of the general body of the Three Denominations, 5 Dec. 1906, Dr Williams's Library.
12 Perks to Rosebery, 24 Nov. 1906, Rosebery Papers, Vol. 10,052, fols. 222-23.
13 Memorandum entitled 'L.G. & Education Bill', 29 Dec. 1906, Lewis Papers.
14 Perks to Rosebery, 20 Dec. 1906, Rosebery Papers, Vol. 10,052, fol. 246.
15 Perks to Rosebery, 2 and 7 Feb. 1907, Rosebery Papers, Vol. 10,053, fols. 19, 21.
16 Perks to Rosebery, 13 Feb. 1907, Rosebery Papers, Vol. 10,053, fol. 26.
17 Perks to Rosebery, 1 Mar. 1907, Rosebery Papers, Vol. 10,053, fols. 30–31.
18 *Baptist Times*, 8 Mar. 1907.
19 Diary Notes, 16 July 1907, Lewis Papers.
20 *British Weekly*, 13 June 1907; Campbell to MacDonald, 22 June 1907, Labour Party archives LP GC 16/177 (Transport House, London): *Primitive Methodist Leader*, 11 and 25 July and 8 Aug. 1907; *Baptist Times*, 26 July 1907; Pelling, *Popular Politics and Society*, pp. 133–46.
21 *South Wales Daily News*, 8 Feb. 1906; *Baptist Times*, 14 June 1907.
22 Morgan, *Wales in British Politics*, pp. 243 ff.

23 *British Weekly*, 8 Nov. 1906, 25 Apr. 1907.
24 Lloyd George to Hughes, 18 June 1907, Hughes Papers (National Library of Wales).
25 Memorandum on 'L.G., Robertson Nicoll & Disestablishment', 7 Aug. 1907, Lewis Papers.
26 Hughes to Lloyd George, 3 Oct. 1907 (copy), Nicoll Papers.
27 Lloyd George to Hughes, 5 Oct. 1907, Hughes Papers.
28 Lloyd George to Nicoll, 6 Oct. 1907, Nicoll Papers.
29 Lloyd George to Lewis, 25 Jan. 1908 (copy), Lewis Papers.
30 *Baptist Times*, 30 Aug. 1907.
31 Memorandum on 'L.G. on the Education Bill and Liberal Policy', 29 Dec. 1907, Lewis Papers.
32 Perks to Rosebery, 21 Feb. 1908, Rosebery Papers, Vol. 10,053, fol. 68.
33 McKenna to Nicoll, 27 Feb. 1908, quoted in T. H. Darlow, *William Robertson Nicoll* (London, 1925), p. 196.
34 Quoted in Evans and Jones, *Hollowell*, pp. 137–38.
35 Minutes of the annual meeting of the general body of the Three Denominations, 30 Mar. 1908, Dr Williams's Library.
36 Minutes of the executive committee, 6 Apr. 1908, Liberation Society records A/LIB/10.
37 Minutes of the education committee, 26 Oct. 1908, Free Church Council archives.
38 Wilson to his 'relatives', 11 Nov. 1908, Wilson Papers (Sheffield City Library).
39 Evans and Jones, *Hollowell*, pp. 145–51.
40 Lloyd George to Nicoll, 21 Dec. 1908, Nicoll Papers.

5 Decline and Disenchantment (pages 100–124).

1 Speech to the Baptist Union Sustentation Fund, Westminster Chapel, 28 Oct. 1913, *North Wales Observer*, 31 Oct. 1913.
2 *British Congregationalist*, 4 Oct. 1906.
3 *Nonconformity and Politics* (London, 1909), *passim*.
4 Lloyd George to Nicoll, 9 Sept. 1909, Nicoll Papers.
5 Minutes of the organising committee, 29 Sept. and 7 Oct. 1909, Free Church Council archives.
6 Minutes of the organising committee, 26 Nov. 1909, Free Church Council archives; executive committee minutes, 30 Nov. 1909, Liberation Society records A/LIB/10.
7 *Baptist Times*, 7 and 14 Jan. 1910; *Christian World*, 6, 13 and 20 Jan. 1910.
8 *Christian World*, 16 Dec. 1909, 13 Jan. 1910; *Methodist Recorder*, 20 Jan. 1910; *British Congregationalist*, 27 Jan. 1910; Porritt, *The Best I Remember*, pp. 53–54.

9   Neal Blewett, *The Peers, the Parties and the People: the British General Elections of 1910* (London, 1972), p. 343.

10   Albert Peel, *Three Hundred Years, 1631–1931* (London, 1931), p. 366.

11   Blewett, pp. 229, 233.

12   The preceding paragraphs are based on leaders and reports in the *British Weekly*, 20 and 27 Jan., 3 Feb. 1910; the *Christian World*, 2 and 30 Dec. 1909, 6, 13, 20 and 27 Jan., and 3 Feb. 1910; *Baptist Times*, 14 and 28 Jan., 4 and 11 Feb. 1910; *Methodist Recorder*, 3 Feb. 1910; *British Congregationalist*, 20 and 27 Jan., 3 and 10 Feb. 1910; *Primitive Methodist Leader*, 27 Jan. 1910; and the *Free Church Year Book, 1910.*

13   Clarke, 'Electoral Sociology of Modern Britain', *History*, lvii (1972), 51.

14   Blewett, pp. 405–6.

15   *Daily News*, 17 Jan. 1910.

16   *British Weekly*, 6 Jan. and 3 Feb. 1910.

17   *British Weekly*, 24 Feb. 1910.

18   *Daily News*, 4, 5 and 6 Apr. 1910.

19   *Daily News*, 7 Apr. 1910; *British Weekly*, 7 Apr. 1910; *Methodist Recorder*, 14 Apr. 1910.

20   *Baptist Times*, 11, 18 and 25 March, 29 July 1910; *British Weekly*, 31 July 1910.

21   *Christian World*, 2 June 1910, 23 July 1914; K. O. Morgan, 'The New Liberalism and the Challenge of Labour: The Welsh Experience, 1885–1929', and K. D. Brown, 'The Anti-Socialist Union, 1908–49', in K. D. Brown, ed., *Essays in Anti-Labour History* (London, 1974), pp. 164–68, 243–44.

22   *Daily News*, 7 Oct. 1910.

23   *Daily News*, 10 and 15 Oct. 1910; *Sheffield Telegraph*, 14 Oct. 1910; *Primitive Methodist Leader*, 3 Nov. 1910.

24   *Baptist Times*, 18 Nov. 1910; *Christian World*, 1 Dec. 1910; *British Weekly*, 1 Dec. 1910.

25   Executive committee minutes, Liberation Society records A/LIB/10.

26   Memorandum (typescript), 16 Mar. 1911, Nicoll Papers.

27   Minutes of the management committee, 25 Jan. 1912, Liberation Society records A/LIB/11.

28   Marchant, *Clifford*, p. 134.

29   Minutes of the general committee, 13 June 1913, Free Church Council archives.

30   Horton to A. V. Dicey, 22 July 1911, enclosed in Dicey to Bryce, 23 July 1911, Bryce Papers, Vol. III, fols. 98–99.

31   Memorandum (typescript), 9 July 1913, Nicoll Papers.

32   Marchant, *Clifford*, p. 135; *Primitive Methodist Leader*, 1 Jan. 1914; *British Congregationalist*, 1 Jan. 1914; *Baptist Times*, 13 Feb. 1914.

33 *Baptist Times*, 2 Jan. 1914.
34 Nicoll to Lloyd George, 14 Mar. 1914, Lloyd George Papers, C/11/1/9.
35 Minutes of the general committee, 12 June 1914, Free Church Council archives.

6 The Impact of War (pages 125–144).

1 Royle, *Opened Doors* (London, 1949), p. 37; significantly Royle's son sat in Parliament from 1945 to 1954 on the Labour benches.
2 Unidentified cutting [Oct (?) 1914], Ensor Walters Papers.
3 *Christian World*, 8 Jan. 1914; minutes of the annual meeting, general body of the Three denominations, 2 Apr. 1914; *Peacemaker*, June 1914.
4 *Baptist Times*, 11 Sept. 1914.
5 *Primitive Methodist Leader*, 6 and 13 Aug. 1914; *British Weekly*, 14 Mar. 1918.
6 MacDonald to Nicoll, 4 Aug. 1914, Nicoll Papers.
7 Riddell to Nicoll, 13 Aug. 1914, Nicoll Papers.
8 Riddell, *Intimate Diary of the Peace Conference and After* (London, 1933), p. 406.
9 Cadbury to Gardiner, 27 Nov. 1914, quoted in Gardiner, *Cadbury*, p. 274.
10 Minutes of the general committee, 5 Aug. 1914, Free Church Council archives.
11 *Christian World*, 13 and 20 Aug. 1914; *Baptist Times*, 7 Aug. 1914.
12 Payne, *The Baptist Union* (London, 1959), pp. 179–80; also *Goodwill*, Jan. 1915.
13 *Daily News*, 10 Nov. 1914; *Manchester Guardian*, 11 Nov. 1914; *Baptist Times*, 13 Nov. 1914; Nicoll to Strachey, 11 Nov. 1914, Strachey Papers (Beaverbrook Library, London), S/11/2/4.
14 Riddell, *War Diary* (London, 1933), p. 44.
15 Nicoll to Riddell, 30 Aug. 1914, quoted in Darlow, *Nicoll*, p. 240.
16 Jones to Nicoll, 21 and 25 Oct. 1915, Nicoll Papers; extracts from this correspondence are reproduced in Jones, *Three Score Years and Ten* (pp. 235–36), where Jones concedes that, 'Looking back, I dare say Nicoll was right in his judgment.'
17 Riddell to Nicoll, 21 Aug. 1915, Nicoll Papers.
18 F. W. Hirst to C. P. Scott, 28 May 1915, quoted in Trevor Wilson, ed., *The Political Diaries of C. P. Scott* (London, 1970), p. 126.
19 *Daily News*, 4 Jan. 1916.
20 *Daily News*, 12 and 13 Jan. 1916; Simon to Horton, 17 Jan. 1916, Horton Papers.
21 E. Vipont [Foulds], *Arnold Rowntree: A Life* (London, 1955), pp. 68–69.
22 M. Edwards, *Methodism and England*, pp. 196–97.

23   A. E. Garvie, *Memories and Meanings of My Life* (London, 1938), p. 169; *Parliamentary Debates (Commons)*, 5th ser., XCIX, cols. 1214 ff. (21 Nov. 1917); *British Weekly*, 27 Jan. 1916; Thomson, *Lloyd George* (London, 1948), pp. 235 ff.

24   Morgan, *Wales in British Politics*, pp. 278 ff.

25   Memorandum of 7 Feb. 1917 (copy), Spicer Papers.

26   *Alliance News*, 28 Jan. 1898, quoted in Harrison, *Drink and the Victorians*, p. 287.

27   Lady Robertson Nicoll's memorandum of 17 Apr. 1917, Nicoll Papers.

28   Edwards to Nicoll, 21 Apr. 1917, Nicoll Papers.

29   Mee to Nicoll, 2 July 1917, Nicoll Papers; Sir John Hammerton, *Child of Wonder: an Intimate Biography of Arthur Mee* (London, 1946), pp. 161–62; Strachey to Lloyd George, 12 Jan. 1917, Strachey Papers, S/9/13/7.

30   Lloyd George, *War Memoirs* (London, 1934?), I, 791–92.

31   Nicoll to Dr James Moffat, 31 Mar. 1917, quoted in Darlow, *Nicoll*, pp. 260–62.

32   Reprinted in *Goodwill*, 23 June 1917.

33   *British Weekly*, 28 Dec. 1916; Nicoll, who approved of the step, expressed confidence that 'Mr Lloyd George will know how to appreciate this wise suggestion.'

34   Minutes of the organising committee, 20 Sept. 1917, Free Church Council archives.

35   Report of the executive committee, 30 Apr. 1917, Liberation Society records A/LIB/23.

36   Clifford to John Colbrook [1916], quoted in Marchant, *Clifford*, p. 224.

37   *British Weekly*, 16 Mar. 1916.

38   Clifford to Nicoll [1917], Nicoll Papers.

39   Federal Council, *Report* (1927), Free Church Council archives.

40   Clifford's diary entry, 26 Oct. 1917, quoted in Marchant, *Clifford*, pp. 230–31.

41   *British Weekly*, 3 and 10 Jan. 1918; *Baptist Times*, 4 Jan. 1918.

42   Asquith to Horton, 11 Oct. 1917, Horton Papers.

43   As indeed Lloyd George did, when he wrote to thank Horton for defending him in the Marconi affair. Lloyd George to Horton, 23 June 1913, Horton Papers.

44   *Methodist Times*, 3, 10 and 31 Jan. 1918.

45   The present account is based on articles in the *Christian World*, 28 Feb. and 14 Mar. 1918; *Westminster Gazette*, 12 and 13 Mar. 1918; *British Weekly*, 7 and 14 Mar. 1918; and *Methodist Times*, 14 and 21 Mar. 1918.

46   Mee to Nicoll, 26 Mar. 1918, Nicoll Papers.

47   Minutes of the management committee, 23 Oct. 1918, Liberation

Society records A/LIB/11; minutes of the organising committee, 19 Sept. 1918, Free Church Council archives; *Methodist Times*, 5 Dec. 1918.

48 *The Downfall of the Liberal Party* (London, 1966), p. 27.

7 Peace Restored *(pages 145–165)*.

1 Memorandum of a lunch with Lloyd George at the Savoy, 12 Oct. 1911, Nicoll Papers.

2 *Baptist Times*, 15 and 22 Nov. 1918; *Methodist Times*, 21 and 28 Nov. 1918.

3 *The Times*, 18 Nov. 1918; *Baptist Times*, 22 Nov. 1918; *British Weekly*, 28 Nov. 1918; *Christian World*, 28 Nov. and 5 Dec. 1918; A. C. Underwood, *A History of the English Baptists* (London, 1947), p. 229.

4 Ensor Walters, 'Labour: Its History, Conditions, and Prospects', in S. E. Keeble, ed., *The Citizen of Tomorrow* (London, 1906?); various cuttings, Ensor Walters Papers; copy of a letter to Clifford, 14 Nov. 1907, Labour Party archives LP GC 21/76; G. N. Barnes *et al, Religion in the Labour Movement* (London, 1919).

5 Henry Pelling, *The Origins of the Labour Party* (London, 1954), p. 151.

6 M. A. Hamilton, *Arthur Henderson* (London, 1938), pp. 32–33. For a catalogue of early Labour leaders and their Methodist connections, see R. F. Wearmouth, *The Social and Religious Influences of Methodism in the Twentieth Century* (London, 1957), pp. 80–184 *passim.*

7 Quoted in Michael Foot, *Aneurin Bevan*, I (London, 1962), 88.

8 *Primitive Methodist Leader*, 5 Feb. 1914.

9 *British Weekly*, 18 Apr. 1918.

10 MacDonald to Law, 20 June 1905 (copy), Labour Party archives 24/119; also minutes of the general committee, 12 July 1905, Free Church Council archives.

11 *Leicester Mail*, 9 Dec. 1918; Garvie, *Memories and Meanings*, p. 171; *Westminster Gazette*, 13 Dec. 1918; *Christian World*, 12 and 19 Dec. 1918.

12 The following account is based on reports in the *Methodist Times*, 19 Dec. 1918; *Christian World*, 12 Dec. 1918; *British Weekly*, 5 and 19 Dec. 1918; *Baptist Times*, 20 Dec. 1918.

13 The identity of the 'Baptist MP' cannot be ascertained from either candidate lists or the *Baptist Times*, which has kept 'no record of his name presumably because this was a confidential arrangement' Letter to the author, 15 May 1974.

14 Jones to Nicoll, 6 Dec. 1918, Nicoll Papers.

15 *Methodist Times*, 19 Dec. 1918, 2 and 9 Jan. and 13 Feb. 1919;

Baptist Times, 27 Dec. 1918; Edwards, *Methodism and England,* p. 186.

16   Minutes of the executive committee, 16 Jan. 1919; minutes of the management committee, 23 Feb. and 10 June 1920, Liberation Society records A/LIB/11.

17   Quoted in Michael Kinnear, *The Fall of Lloyd George* (London, 1973), p. 185.

18   Minutes of the management committee, 23 Feb. 1920, Liberation Society records A/LIB/11.

19   I am grateful to Dr Ross McKibbin, who is preparing a new biography of Henderson, for this information.

20   Asquith to Horton, 28 Feb. 1920, Horton Papers.

21   Memorandum (typescript) of a luncheon at 10 Downing Street, Tues., Dec. 1919, Nicoll Papers.

22   *British Weekly,* 25 May and 1 June 1920.

23   Lewis to Lloyd George [May 1920] (copy), Lewis Papers; diary note, 22 Oct. 1920 (copy), Lewis Papers.

24   Rees, *A Chapter of Accidents* (London, 1971), pp. 15–18; K. O. Morgan, ' Cardiganshire Politics : The Liberal Ascendancy, 1885–1923 ', *Ceredigion,* v (1968), 332–36; Kinnear, *The Fall of Lloyd George,* pp. 190–92.

25   Minutes of the organising committee, 16 June 1921, Free Church Council archives.

26   British Weekly, 26 Jan. 1922.

27   Minutes of the executive committee, 21 Mar. 1922, Liberation Society records A/LIB/11.

28   *British Weekly,* 18 May 1922.

29   F. Bealey, J. Blondel and W. McCann, *Constituency Politics, a Study of Newcastle-under-Lyme* (London, 1965), p. 126.

30   *British Weekly,* 26 Jan. and 2 Nov. 1922; *Methodist Times,* 26 Oct. and 23 Nov. 1922.

31   Kinnear, *The Fall of Lloyd George,* p. 86.

32   Quoted in Sir Harold Nicolson, *King George the Fifth* (London, 1952), p. 371.

33   *British Weekly,* 26 Oct. and 2 Nov. 1922.

34   Quoted in Henry Pelling, *Winston Churchill* (London, 1974), p. 112.

8 *Beyond Liberalism (pages 166–186).*

1   Lloyd George to Lady Nicoll, 7 May 1923 (telegram), Nicoll Papers.

2   Rosebery to Perks, 31 May 1924, Perks Papers. Rosebery disagreed: ' I think Winston Churchill is fully as capable.'

3   *British Weekly,* 10 and 17 Jan. 1924.

4   Brockway, *Inside the Left* (London, 1942), pp. 145 ff.

5 *Methodist Times*, 6 and 13 Mar. 1924; *Christian World*, 6 and 13 Mar. 1924.

6 *British Weekly*, 16 Oct. 1924; *Christian World*, 23 Oct. 1924; *Methodist Times*, 16, 23 and 30 Oct. 1924.

7 Memorandum by Viscount Gladstone, July 1925, Maclean Papers.

8 Lloyd George to J. D. Jones, 12 Nov. 1924, Hayden Jones Papers.

9 Memorandum by Asquith, 6 Oct. 1926, J. A. Spender Papers, quoted in Wilson, *Downfall of the Liberal Party*, p. 329.

10 *British Weekly*, 6, 13 and 20 Nov. and 11 Dec. 1924; Cowling, *The Impact of Labour* (Cambridge, 1971), pp. 408, 421.

11 Wearmouth, *The Social and Political Influence of Methodism*, pp. 46 ff; Currie, *Methodism Divided*, p. 85; D. Butler and J. Freeman, *British Political Facts, 1900–1968* (London, 1969), pp. 296–301.

12 The Right Rev the Lord Bishop of Durham, 'Disestablishment by Consent', *Nineteenth Century and After*, cv (Jan. 1929), 44–58; Birrell, 'Disestablishment by Consent', *Nation*, 9 Feb. 1929; *The Review of the Churches*, vi (Apr. 1929), 143.

13 *Christian World*, 14 Feb. 1929.

14 *Church Times*, 17 and 24 May, 1929.

15 Minutes of the 34th annual assembly, 13 Mar. 1929, *Free Church Year Book, 1929*; also *Free Church Chronicle*, various issues.

16 *Christian World*, 13 June 1929; *British Weekly*, 7 Jan. 1932; MacDonald to Horton, 17 Feb. 1930, and Lloyd George to Horton, 20 Feb. 1930, Horton Papers.

17 Cyril Asquith to Gilbert Murray, 1 Oct. 1931, Murray Papers, quoted in Wilson, *Downfall of the Liberal Party*, p. 369.

18 *Christian World*, 28 Jan., 4 and 25 Feb. 1932; *Baptist Times*, 10 Jan. 1935.

19 *Free Church Chronicle*, Oct. 1931; Hughes, 'The Work of the Year', *Report for 1932–33, National Council of Evangelical Free Churches*.

9 The Last Rally (pages 187–215).

1 For a more detailed discussion of this episode, see my article, 'Lloyd George and Nonconformity: the last rally', in the *English Historical Review*, lxxxix (1974), 77–108.

2 This impression was confirmed by interviews with, among others, the Rev Malcolm Thomson (Lloyd George's biographer and private secretary), Sir Cyril Black (son of R. Wilson Black), and Mr Graham Watson (son of Angus Watson).

3 Cf. E. K. H. Jordan, *Free Church Unity*, pp. 160–62; for an account of this speech, see *The Times*, 14 Mar. 1933.

4 *Baptist Times*, 3 Jan. 1935; Scott Lidgett, 'The Christian Religion and the Exercise of Force', *Contemporary Review*, cxlvi (1934), 573–79; E. A. Payne, *The Baptist Union* (London, 1959), p. 207.

5   Entry for 28 Mar. 1934, Frances Stevenson, *Lloyd George: a Diary;*
    p. 264; *Methodist Recorder*, 15 Nov. 1934: memorandum by A. J.
    Sylvester, 4 Dec. [1934], Lloyd George Papers G/20/2/96.
6   Jones to Flexner, 16 Dec. 1934, Jones, *A Diary with Letters* (London,
    1954), pp. 139–40.
7   Lothian acknowledged receipt of his copy on 20 Dec., after discussing
    the situation with Lloyd George the previous evening. Lothian to Lloyd
    George, 20 Dec. 1934 (copy), Lothian Papers GD 40/17/283, fols.
    357–61 (Scottish Record Office).
8   *The Times*, 18 Jan. 1935; *Baptist Times*, 3 and 17 Jan. 1935; *Metho-
    dist Recorder*, 24 Jan. and 14 Feb. 1935.
9   Jones to Flexner, 22 Feb. 1935, Jones, *Diary with Letters*, pp. 141–44.
10 *The Times*, 27 Mar. 1935; Colin Cross, *Philip Snowden* (London,
    1966), pp. 336–37; Arthur Marwick, *Clifford Allen, the Open Con-
    spirator* (London, 1964), pp. 130 ff; Macmillan, *Winds of Change* (Lon-
    don, 1966), pp. 376–77; Lothian Papers GD 40/17/112, fols. 97–99,
    and GD 40/17/307, fol. 171.
11 Quoted in Jordan, *Free Church Unity*, p. 183; also *Free Church
    Chronicle*, May and June 1935.
12 Garvin to Lord Astor, n.d., enclosed in Lady Astor to Jones, 2 May
    1935, Jones Papers (copy courtesy of Baroness White); Jones's memor-
    andum to Baldwin, 16 May 1935, Jones, *Diary with Letters*, pp. 145–47.
13 Lothian to Lloyd George, 16 May 1935, Lloyd George Papers
    G/141/28/12; entries for 18 May and 1 July 1935, Stevenson, p.
    310.
14 Lloyd George to H. A. L. Fisher, 6 June 1935, Fisher Papers, Box
    1 (Bodleian Library).
15 Reading to Samuel, 13 June 1935, Samuel Papers A/155/IX/24
    (House of Lords Record Office).
16 *Manchester Guardian*, 14 June 1935; *The Times*, 18 and 19 June
    1935; *British Weekly*, 20 June 1935; *Richmond Hill Magazine*, quoted
    in Arthur Porritt, *J. D. Jones of Bournemouth*, p. 129.
17 Jones, *Lloyd George* (London, 1951), p. 243.
18 Rowland (who was knighted in 1938) had been Lloyd George's
    private secretary at the Board of Trade and Exchequer, 1905–12.
    Rowland to Miss Stevenson, 18 June 1935, Lloyd George Papers
    G/141/41/6.
19 *News Chronicle*, 14 June 1935; Thomson, p. 422.
20 *The Times*, 24 and 26 June 1935; also the *Baptist Times*, 27 June
    1935. Of the 21 signatories, one – J. A. Leckie, the lone Liberal –
    denied that he had given permission for his name to be used.
21 *Western Daily Press and Bristol Mirror*, 17 July 1935; *British
    Weekly*, 25 July 1935; *Methodist Recorder*, 20 June and 4 July 1935;
    The Times, 17 June and 1 July 1935; Lloyd George Papers G/142.
22 *News Chronicle*, 27 June 1935; *Baptist Times*, 27 June, 4 July and

26 Sept. 1935; Carlile, *My Life's Little Day*, pp. 113–14, 178.

23 Entry for 1 July 1935, Stevenson, pp. 310–11. Miss Stevenson wrote not on the eve of the convention, as she suggested, but on the eve of Lloyd George's appearance on the second day.

24 *News Chronicle*, 27 June 1935; *British Weekly*, 4 July 1935; *Baptist Times*, 11 July 1935; Chamberlain's speech at Hinton Admiral, New Forest, 29 June 1935, *The Times*, 1 July 1935; *Methodist Recorder*, 4 July 1935.

25 *Baptist Times*, 18 July 1935; Scott Lidgett, 'The National Free Church Council and the Council of Action', *Free Church Chronicle*, Sept. 1935; Henry Townsend, *Robert Wilson Black* (London, 1954), pp. 19, 154–57.

26 Draft copy dated 22 July 1935, Lloyd George Papers G/142/3; the full text appears in Townsend, pp. 157–60. Hughes likewise defended himself in the *Baptist Times* (29 Aug. 1935) after he returned from a visit to Canada.

27 Jones to Lady Grigg, 28 July 1935 (after Jones had spent a weekend at Churt), Jones Papers (copy courtesy of Baroness White).

28 Stevenson, pp. 313–14.

29 Interview of 19 July 1935, W. P. Crozier, *Off the Record* (London, 1973), p. 49.

30 Entry of 28 Aug. 1935, Stevenson, p. 316.

31 Lady Layton and Will Arnold-Forster to Lloyd George, 15 Aug. 1935 (copy), Lothian Papers GD 40/17/113, fols. 118–21 (Arnold-Forster had evidently replaced Sir Walter Layton on the sub-committee); Betty Z. Arne, assistant secretary to the Council of Action, to Lothian, 9 Sept. 1935 (copy), Lothian Papers GD 40/17/113, fol. 149; interview with Dame Margery Corbett Ashby, 25 Sept. 1972; Acland to Lloyd George, 9 Sept. 1935 (copy), Lloyd George Papers G/141/1/1; *News Chronicle*, 20 Sept. 1935; *Western Daily Press and Bristol Mirror*, 26 Sept. 1935.

32 *Western Morning News and Daily Gazette* (Plymouth), 13 Sept. 1935; *The Times*, 16 Sept. 1935; *Christian World*, 19 and 26 Sept. 1935.

33 Memorandum to Lloyd George 'dictated by 'phone from Mr Sylvester', 21 Sept. 1935, Lloyd George Papers G/141/3/3; *Western Daily Press and Bristol Mirror*, 26 Sept. 1935; *News Chronicle*, 20 Sept. 1935.

34 *Manchester Guardian*, 27 and 30 Sept. 1935; *Christian World*, 3 Oct. 1935.

35 Jones to Lady Grigg, 18 Sept. and 12 Oct. 1935, Jones Papers (copy courtesy of Baroness White).

36 *News Chronicle*, 18 Oct. 1935; *The Times*, 18 Oct. 1935; *Free Church Chronicle*, Oct. 1935.

37 Entry for 23 Oct. 1935, Stevenson, p. 319; *News Chronicle*, 26

Oct. 1935; *The Times,* 30 Oct. 1935; see also Snowden, *The General Election* (London, Liberal Publication Dept. 1935).

38   *British Weekly,* 31 Oct. 1935; *The Times,* 14 Nov. 1935; *Western Daily Press and Bristol Mirror,* 24 Oct. 1935.

39   *Manchester Guardian,* 2 and 6 Nov. 1935; *The Times,* 20 Nov. 1935

40   *Western Morning News and Daily Gazette* (Plymouth), 1 Nov. 1935; *Western Daily Press and Bristol Mirror,* 25 Oct. 1935; interview with Sir Geoffrey Shakespeare, 17 Oct. 1972; Mrs Catlin to Lothian, 29 and 30 Oct. 1935, Lothian Papers GD 40/17/307, fols. 107 ff.

41   *News Chronicle,* 1, 6, and 9 Nov. 1935; *North Mail and Newcastle Chronicle,* 6 Nov. 1935; *Newcastle Journal,* 9 Nov. 1935; *Western Morning News and Daily Gazette* (Plymouth), 13 Nov. 1935; Gilbert Murray Papers (Bodleian Library); Macmillan, *Winds of Change,* pp. 427–28.

42   *Free Church Chronicle,* Nov. 1935.

43   Scott Lidgett to Lloyd George, 11 Nov. 1935, Lloyd George Papers G/141/27/1. This letter is marked ' not acknowledged '.

44   Speech by Simon at Devizes, 8 Nov. 1935; *The Times,* 9 Nov. 1935; Scott Lidgett, letter to *The Times,* 11 Nov. 1935; *News Chronicle,* 11 Nov. 1935; *Manchester Guardian,* 13 Nov. 1935.

45   Sir Richard Acland to the author, 31, Oct. 1972.

46   Jones to Flexner, 17 Nov. 1935, Jones, *Diary with Letters,* p. 157; Jones to Lady Grigg, 16 Nov. 1935, Jones Papers (copy courtesy of Baroness White).

47   Lothian to Lloyd George, 25 Nov. 1935 (copy), Lothian Papers GD 40/17/310, fols. 440–45; the greater part of this letter is re-produced in J. R. M. Butler, *Lord Lothian* (London, 1960), pp. 171–2.

10 Lazarus Unraised (pages 216–226).

1   J. A. and Olive Banks, *Feminism and Family Planning in Victorian England* (New York, 1964), p. x.

2   *Free Church Chronicle,* Dec. 1935 and Jan. 1936; *Report 1935–36.*

3   Lothian to Lloyd George, 25 Nov. 1935 (copy), Lothian Papers GD 40/17/310, fol. 445.

4   Circular letters of 20 Mar. and 30 Sept. 1936, and 4 Feb. 1937, Lloyd George Papers, Box G 142/1–3. Eleanor Rathbone to Lloyd George, 15 Sept. 1939 (copy), and V. H. Finney to Eleanor Rathbone, 25 Sept. 1939, Rathbone Papers (University of Liverpool Library).

5   *City Temple Tidings,* May 1936.

6   *Parliamentary Debates (Commons),* 5th ser., CCCXVII, cols. 1708–11.

7   Thomas Magnay to the author, 9 July 1973; Magnay, *English Institutions and Public Opinion* (London, 1939), pp. 58, 64.

8 *Western Morning News*, 25 Nov. 1935; *Cornishman and Cornish Telegraph*, 28 Nov. 1935.

9 Lady Violet Bonham Carter to Foot, 21 June 1937, Foot Papers.

10 Lothian to Lloyd George, 18 May 1936 (copy), Lothian Papers GD 40/17/321, fol. 435.

11 Memorandum of 22 Oct. 1938, Lloyd George Papers G/29/1/19.

12 *The Times*, 27 and 31 Oct. 1938; Arnold Lunn, *Come What May*, p. 130.

13 Chuter Ede to Lloyd George, 29 Oct. 1938, Lloyd George Papers G/6/9/1.

14 Mass Observation, *Puzzled People* (London, 1947), *passim*.

15 A. P. Herbert, *Independent Member* (London, 1950), pp. 176–80; interview with Churchill, 20 Mar. 1941, Crozier, *Off the Record*, p. 213.

16 Lord Butler, *The Art of the Possible* (London, 1971), pp. 94 ff; F. A. Iremonger, *William Temple* (London, 1948), pp. 475–76; draft manuscript, Winfrey Papers (courtesy of Mr David Newton and the Sir Halley Stewart Trust).

17 (London, 1943), p. 121.

18 David Martin, *A Sociology of English Religion* (London, 1967), pp. 39–40 (Martin's figures are drawn from Christopher Driver, 'The Nonconformist Conscience', in *New Society*, 27 June 1963); Priestley, *English Journey* (London, 1934), pp. 106–7.

19 Wilson, *Religion in Secular Society* (London, 1966), p. 178.

20 *Ibid.*, p. 56.

21 F. Bealey, J. Blondel, and W. P. McCann, *Constituency Politics*, pp. 173–74.

22 (London, 1967 ed.), pp. 60–61.

23 David Butler and Donald Stokes, *Political Change in Britain* (New York, 1971), pp. 101–6.

Index